ROMAN OXFORDSHIRE

Martin Henig and Paul Booth

with Tim Allen

SUTTON PUBLISHING

First published in the United Kingdom in 2000 by
Sutton Publishing Limited · Phoenix Mill
Thrupp · Stroud · Gloucestershire · GL5 2BU

British Library Cataloguing in Publication Data
A catalogue record for this book is available from the British Library

ISBN 0-7509-1959-9

Picture credits

Thanks are owed to the following for provision of and/or permission to reproduce illustrations. Ashmolean Museum, Figs 1.2, 1.3, 1.10, 2.4, 4.11, 4.14, 5.2, 5.3, 5.5, 5.6, 5.14, 5.16, 5.20a, 5.22, 5.23; British Museum, Fig. 6.12; English Heritage (Ancient Monuments Laboratory), Figs 5.13, 6.8; Institute of Archaeology, Oxford and R. Wilkins, Figs 5.9, 5.10, 5.17b, 5.21, 5.28; Oxford Architectural and Historical Society, Figs 4.5, 4.9, 7.5, 7.6; Oxfordshire Museums, Figs 5.7, 5.11, 5.15, 5.20b, 5.24, 5.25, 5.27, 7.8; RCHME, Figs 1.5, 3.1, 3.2, 3.5, 4.7, 4.11, 4.16, 4.17; Wallingford Historical and Archaeological Society, Fig. 5.18; Barry Eames, Figs 3.7, 3.8; Dr Anthony Hands, Figs 5.1, 5.17a; Julian Munby, Figs 5.8, 5.26; Haverfield Bequest, Fig. 5.4. Other uncredited illustrations are the work of the authors or in the copyright of the Oxford Archaeological Unit.

Typeset in 10/12pt Bembo Mono.
Typesetting and origination by
Sutton Publishing Limited.
Printed in Great Britain by
Bookcraft, Midsomer Norton, Somerset.

CONTENTS

ACKNOWLEDGEMENTS

Martin Henig wishes to acknowledge the help of many people who have encouraged him to explore Roman archaeology locally, especially Julian Munby, who has shared his discoveries over more than three decades and, indeed, made several valuable suggestions concerning the final chapter of this book, and the equally erudite Grahame Soffe. He has been much assisted by David Sturdy, David Brown, David Hinton, Michael Vickers and Arthur MacGregor, all of whom at different times have curated the Romano-British collections at the Ashmolean Museum. Carol Anderson, Dan Chadwick, John Rhodes, John Steane and particularly Lauren Gilmour have likewise revealed the riches of the county's own collection. Warm thanks are also due to David Howlett of the Medieval Latin Dictionary, Oxford, Cathy Capel-Davies and Colin Clarke of the Wallingford Historical and Archaeological Society, Roger Ainslie of the Abingdon Archaeological Society and many members of the Oxford University Archaeological Society, most especially Eberhard Sauer who continues to make very important discoveries in Roman Oxfordshire. Photographs have been freely provided by Joan Brasnett of Oxfordshire Museums and by Robert Wilkins, Chief Photographer at the Institute of Archaeology, Oxford, and himself a keen student of local archaeology.

Paul Booth would like to thank Chris Cheetham, Colin Clarke, Barry Eames, Anthony Hands, Roger Kendal, Gary Lock, Eberhard Sauer, Edward Shawyer and Margaret Ware for freely making available new and old information on Roman Oxfordshire, and Alison Roberts and Arthur MacGregor at the Ashmolean Museum for their unfailing kindness in tracing material in their collections. The specialist help of Fiona Roe on stone objects and Mark Robinson on environmental matters has been invaluable and is gratefully acknowledged. Many colleagues at the Oxford Archaeological Unit have contributed in numerous ways, in particular Tim Allen, Alistair Barclay, Anne Marie Cromarty, Angela Boyle, Gill Hey and Ian Scott, all of whom have tolerated questions and sustained discussions with a good grace. Mel Costello and Sarah Lucas are particularly thanked for their work on the line-drawings. The overall contribution of the Oxford Archaeological Unit is very considerable, and the support of the organisation and its past and present directors, David Miles and David Jennings, is also gratefully acknowledged. Particular thanks are owed to George Lambrick and Richard Hingley, both for their contributions to the study of Roman Oxfordshire, the debt to which is clear in the pages below, and for discussions on many of the sites referred to here. Tim Allen, Helena Hamerow, Richard Hingley and Mark Robinson all kindly commented on sections of draft text, improving it considerably. Finally, it is a pleasure to acknowledge the contribution of the Oxfordshire Sites and Monuments Record and the help offered by Susan Lisk, the SMR Officer, in many ways.

Tim Allen acknowledges the assistance given in relation to illustrations by Barry Eames, Sarah Lucas and Lesley Collett.

The authors are grateful to Peter Salway for kindly providing the preface.

LIST OF
ILLUSTRATIONS

PREFACE

BY

PETER SALWAY

There comes a time in research when the accumulation of data that had seemed too sparse to allow any generalisations suddenly reaches a point at which a coherent picture begins to emerge. This has happened with Roman Oxfordshire. Until now an account of the Roman period in the county had difficulty in progressing beyond the condition of a gazetteer, with individual sites of considerable interest but affording no overall view of its archaeology, and certainly no chronological narrative other than that of Roman Britain as a whole to which it could contribute relatively little of its own. Much work has, however, unobtrusively been in progress, both in the field and in the study, and it is now time to produce the kind of synthesis for which both the specialist and the interested general reader have been waiting. This was the purpose of the present book from the outset – and it will be clear to the reader that the process of writing has itself brought new insights. It is as if paintings by a particular artist that normally reside in many different museums have been brought together in a single exhibition and – just because they are juxtaposed – suddenly illuminate the painter and his world in all sorts of unexpected ways.

Britain was effectively part of the Roman world for at least 500 years, and within that period directly under Roman rule for three and a half centuries. That compares with, for example, barely two centuries of British India. It has always been inconceivable that this would not be powerfully reflected in the microcosm of Oxfordshire, for long recognised as within the wealthiest part of Roman Britain but without any clear identity of its own. This lack of identity has led to the Roman period being treated summarily in many general studies of the county, and (except on certain specialist aspects such as the Oxfordshire pottery industry) rating only passing reference in the wider literature of Roman Britain. It was recognised, for example, that it had a number of notable villas either within or just over its borders, but these were seen – if considered in a wider context at all – essentially as part of the history of the cities of Cirencester and Verulamium, both far outside the county boundary. To an even greater extent the processes by which the county initially became part of the Roman province and the framework within which it was administered could only be guessed at by analogy from neighbouring regions and within broad general trends. Its military history was particularly obscure, with nothing that could be securely identified with the conquest and hardly a single unequivocally military site of any period within the Roman era.

What is now emerging is that there was a real cause underlying the apparent lack of coherent identity. The huge increase in depth and detail of knowledge of the archaeology of the county that – as will be explained in the course of this book – has been gained in recent years makes it clear that in aspect after aspect the essential character of Roman Oxfordshire was as a region in which the borders of different political, cultural and economic areas met. Such frontier areas tend to be extremely interesting, not only as potentially possessing great diversity but also permitting close inspection of the differences between neighbours and the ways in which they impacted on one another. It is clear, too, that in the case of Roman Oxfordshire this border character mirrored much of the situation before the Claudian conquest. Moreover, recent discoveries revealing the presence of the Roman army in the county beyond the conquest period have emphasised that even in military terms it retained elements of frontier character for a considerable time before finally settling into long-term civilian peace.

It has long been realised that the character of Roman Oxfordshire was strongly influenced by the pronounced topographical divisions within the county. The contrast between the Cotswolds and the gravels of the Upper Thames valley is the most obvious, but the chalk Downs, the Chilterns, the Oxford heights and the Corallian ridge which rise above the lowlands of the Oxford clay are all reflected in notable differences in the material traces of human activity in the Roman period. Recent archaeological research has produced environmental evidence of considerable importance in quantity and even more so in quality. It has also altered direction, no longer studying sites in isolation but in their relationship to one another and to the overall landscape in which they existed, operated and over time changed. This not only reflects changes in the methodology and underlying theories of archaeology but also the opportunities now afforded by the sheer quantity of information becoming available in a region which has seen a great deal of archaeological investigation of high quality in recent years, building on what went before.

It is easy to become so immersed in the remarkable degree of illumination that archaeology by itself can throw on ancient cultures that one is liable to overlook or downplay the importance of the fact that Roman Britain was not only a society in which literacy and the written word played a central part but also existed within a highly complex civilisation which has been and still is the subject of close academic study by classicists. It is true that the amount of Roman literature directly relating to Britain is small but much in the classical sources is highly relevant to it. Moreover Britain itself is by no means without writing, in the form of inscriptions of every sort – all the way from official dedicatory slabs, through gravestones and other private inscriptions, down to graffiti and manufacturer's stamps on pots – and now also in the form of substantial numbers of letters and other original documents which make up an outstanding scholarly resource of a size and interest not paralleled from elsewhere in the Roman Empire outside Egypt. Art history, too, has long been part of classics, and the output of Roman Britain in the visual arts was not inconsiderable. Bringing all these strands together and applying the techniques of scholarship to what survives in and about our county adds extra dimensions to what archaeology can produce, helping to bring alive the people – in some cases named individuals – who, however distant they often seem, are the ultimate target of archaeologists and historians alike.

INTRODUCTION

This is the first full account of Roman Oxfordshire apart from that which appeared in Volume I of the Victoria County History in 1939. It is true that Professor Peter Salway gave a memorable Tom Hassall lecture to the Oxfordshire Architectural and Historical Society in 1997, but its publication was too late for us to take proper account of its conclusions and, besides, we have preferred to take our own individual approaches. Apart from Tim Allen's masterly survey of the Iron Age in chapter one, the book breaks down into chapters two, five and eight by Martin Henig and three, four and six by Paul Booth. Chapter seven is the work of us both. Nevertheless we have read each other's contributions and satisfied ourselves that the volume remains a coherent statement.

It cannot, of course, be fully up to date. New discoveries are being made all the time and these will, no doubt, necessitate modifications to our statements. However, as can be seen in chapter eight, some observations stand the test of time and Eberhard Sauer has just confirmed that White Kennett's ascription of the Alchester fort to Aulus Plautius is likely to be right after all, while the map of Roman finds from the gravel terrace on which Oxford stands is in general terms little changed today from what it was a century ago.

The *Victoria County History* has already been mentioned. That volume, with its all-embracing inventory approach, the result of a prodigious search of the antiquarian and early twentieth-century literature and unpublished records, is a monumental piece of work which we have not attempted to emulate. The amount of data now available for Roman Oxfordshire is vastly greater than it was in the 1930s and a mere catalogue would be meaningless. Our aim has therefore been to be synthesise present information as effectively as possible. Such a synthesis involves many acts of judgement and interpretation and in some cases the statement of opinion rather than fact; not only will new information overturn some of our conclusions, but new approaches to the material may also result in very different interpretations.

Illustrations have been carefully chosen to reflect what is known about the distribution of sites and the wealth of objects that have been found throughout the county in the past 300 years or so. There was not space to show everything but the fact that there is so much of extraordinary beauty and interest shows the often unexpected quality of Romano-British culture in this part of central southern Britain. The museum legacy is largely divided between the Ashmolean Museum and Oxfordshire Museums. With regard to the latter our story has in effect formed the backdrop to a new,

imaginative display in which Carol Anderson and Sarah Hinds in the Museum and
Lauren Gilmour in the County Store at Standlake, among others, have transformed the
way in which we understand 'the Romans', not just as men in funny armour but as
people like us, with mixed origins but in many instances a large element of continuity.
Indeed the view of history we all seem to be espousing now is that what differentiated
Iron Age, Roman and Anglo-Saxon people from one another was less blood-stock than
customs, language and clothes. Men and women adopted or discarded the first two of
these as willingly (though not as frequently) as we all follow fashions in dress. If this
book is regarded as the 'book of the exhibition' that is fine by us.

Ours is, of course, a local book but it is intended to be more than that. Oxfordshire
provides a convenient sample of the south British countryside and contains all the
main settlement types except major cities. It is hoped that it will interest all students of
Roman Britain as well as those interested in the functioning of the Roman Empire,
especially its western provinces.

CHAPTER ONE

THE IRON AGE BACKGROUND

TIM ALLEN

Today's Oxfordshire is a modern political creation, dating from the reorganisation of 1974, but even the original shires came into being long after the end of the Roman period. While present-day Oxfordshire bears little direct relationship to the political or social realities of Iron Age and Roman Britain, the county nevertheless forms the administrative framework within which archaeology is carried out today. On this basis there is some justification for considering the Roman past of this modern political entity. Indeed in the sense that it includes within its boundaries parts of previously distinct administrative units, the present situation has parallels in the Roman period.

Geographically the county is diverse.[1] From the Bristol Channel north-eastwards to the Wash run successive geological deposits, all dipping south-eastwards so that they appear on the surface as bands, the earliest on the north and the youngest on the south (Fig. 1.1). Oxfordshire lies across these bands, which consist broadly of alternating limestone hills and clay vales, with lesser layers of sand. In the north are the ironstones of Banbury, then the lias clay lowlands, which only occur intermittently, and then the broad band of the Cotswold oolitic limestone hills. These give way to the Kimmeridge clay of the Oxford Vale. This vale is divided by a lower range of limestone hills, known as the Corallian ridge west of Oxford and the Oxford heights to the east, from the gault clay of the Vale of the White Horse to the south. The gault clay continues north-east from Dorchester-on-Thames to the Vale of Aylesbury. South of the gault clay rises the chalk escarpment of the Berkshire Downs and the Chiltern Ridge, capped by clay with flints.

Oxfordshire does, however, comprise most of the drainage basin of the Upper Thames. The river follows the Kimmeridge clay east as far as Oxford, before turning south across the grain of the land, weaving its way around/between the limestone hills to Goring, where the glacial meltwaters forced a gap through the Chilterns and Berkshire Downs into what is now the Middle Thames. Tributaries run into the Thames, particularly from the north and west, linking the different geological areas. During the four Ice Ages the Thames and its tributaries have been alternately

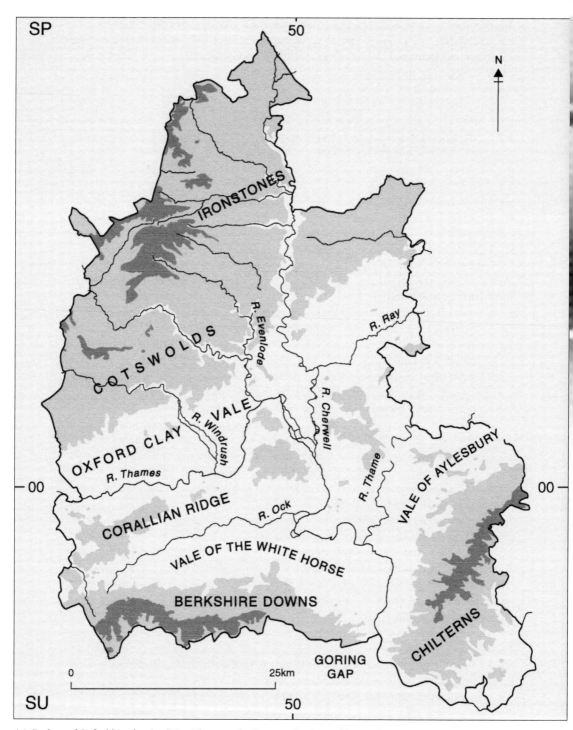

1.1 Geology of Oxfordshire showing River Thames and tributaries, the Cotswolds, Corallian Ridge and Berkshire Downs.

depositing terraces of limestone gravel alongside, and cutting down through them into the underlying strata. These gravel terraces, particularly the lower-lying and more recent second (Summertown-Radley) and first (Floodplain) terraces, provided a free-draining covering to much of the underlying clay vales, which proved particularly attractive to prehistoric settlers.

At the end of the last Ice Age the Thames was a network of small, rapidly shifting watercourses crossing the bare gravel terraces. As the climate warmed and soils and plant cover developed, the river stabilised into a smaller number of larger incised channels, which have remained relatively stable for the last 10,000 years. The floodplain of the Thames has, however, been transformed by alluvial deposition of fine sediments and by changes in water level. Excavations by the Oxford Archaeological Unit at Yarnton have shown that, up until 1000 BC, the floodplain was favoured for human occupation.[2] The work of Mark Robinson and George Lambrick has demonstrated the dramatic interaction between human activity and alluviation over the last 3000 years, most significantly in the rise in the water-table caused by clearance and agriculture.[3]

Geology has influenced not only ancient settlement but also archaeological investigation and knowledge within the county. The areas where stone is the underlying geology are more likely to have durable structures that survive the ravages of time, and in particular stone-robbing by later builders. Aerial photography, which has led to the identification of many buried sites owing to differential crop growth at certain times of the year, produces good results on some geologies (the gravel terraces in particular), but poor or no results on others (clay and areas blanketed by alluvium) except in unusual circumstances. The explosion of archaeological sites discovered by aerial photography in the 1970s[4] led to a concentration of effort on the gravels, a bias which has only been partially redressed in recent years.

In the nineteenth and early twentieth centuries archaeological discovery happened either by accident or as a result of research excavations. Since the early 1970s, however, administrative policy has had a controlling influence on the direction and scope of archaeology. The Oxfordshire structural policy for mineral extraction, for instance, has concentrated sand and gravel extraction in particular areas, largely around Stanton Harcourt, Yarnton, Abingdon and Dorchester, and in consequence these areas have seen much archaeological excavation, whereas the river valley upstream of Standlake has remained untouched except around Stanford in the Vale. The same geographical restrictions, paradoxically, have recently led gravel companies to extract the thinner gravels beneath the floodplain of the Thames, which has revealed a wealth of hitherto unsuspected archaeology.[5] Similar policies on new towns, housing, road construction and so on have also influenced where archaeology is likely to be found. The present concentration of archaeological work still means that much more is known about the areas around the largest towns such as Oxford, Banbury and Bicester than about the more rural parts of the county.

In considering the past it is also necessary to be aware of the limitations of archaeology, particularly before the Roman period. By definition, for prehistory there are no written records to give names to the people (except a few names that appear on coins at the very end of the Iron Age), to explain events (still less motives) or to link them in time, and archaeologists are dependent entirely upon material remains. This is

1.2 Early Iron Age angular pottery and middle Iron Age globular vessels. (Photo: Ashmolean Museum)

why the 800 years preceding the Roman conquest of Britain in AD 43 are known simply as the Iron Age. The dating of prehistoric sites relies upon typology, using changes in the shape, manufacture and decoration of artefacts (most commonly pots) in successive strata to provide a pottery sequence and a relative chronology, and scientific dating techniques such as radiocarbon to establish absolute dates.

At the beginning of the Iron Age people in Oxfordshire used handmade pottery with sharply angled shoulders, necks and flaring rims, and often coated their finest vessels with a red haematite (iron ore) slip, all in imitation of bronze vessels (Fig. 1.2). Fine middle Iron Age pottery in Oxfordshire is usually globular or fishbowl-shaped, and is mostly black or brown, possibly in imitation of leather vessels. In the south of the county fine pots are often straight-walled, and are known as 'saucepan pots'. Excavations in waterlogged deposits at Glastonbury and Meare in Somerset showed that finely carved lathe-turned wooden bowls were made in this shape,[6] and it is likely that the 'saucepan pots' are copying wooden prototypes.

Unfortunately, this represents only one significant stylistic change, from vessels with sharply angled shoulders and necks to round-bodied globular and bucket-shaped vessels (400–300 BC). A second major change occurs when the globular and saucepan-shaped hand-made pots are succeeded by wheel-turned vessels with an increasing variety of forms at around the beginning of the first century AD.[7] Dating by this means only provides accuracy to within 400 years. That the first stylistic change can be dated at all is due to radiocarbon dating. For most of the Iron Age, however, variations in the processes controlling radioactive decay mean that the date ranges obtained for each object span more than 200 years, which is not a great improvement.

In the last century and a half before AD 43 dating becomes more refined, largely owing to the appearance of coinage. Before the introduction of coins iron bars of standard size and weight (known as currency bars, though they were principally a form in which iron

1.3 X-ray of iron trade or 'currency' bar (370mm long) from Eastern England and Catuvellaunian late Iron Age coin of Tasciovanus inscribed 'Verlamio' (diameter 12mm), both from excavations at Abingdon Vineyard. (Vale of White Horse District Council and OAU)

was traded) may have been used as units of value, but these cannot be closely dated (Fig. 1.3). The first coins in Britain were struck on the continent, but from around 100 BC coins appear to have been minted in south-east Britain, though they rarely appear as far west as Oxfordshire at this time (Fig. 8.1). Until *c.* 50 BC these coins do not carry any legend, and can only be given a relative chronology by their associations in different hoards, but after that date names of people, and later places, appear.[8] With the expeditions of Julius Caesar in 55 and 54 BC we have the first written description of Britain,[9] although he did not reach Oxfordshire, and from 40 BC onwards other Roman writers mention people or events connected with Britain, which can be dated by reference to the Roman calendar. Some of these people also appear on the coins, and this has enabled the coinage to be given approximate dates.[10] In addition, some British coin issues appear to be based on Roman issues, which can be dated exactly.[11] It must be remembered, however, that coins can remain in circulation for long periods before being lost, and many Iron Age coins were still in use after the Roman conquest.

As for the names of the peoples of the area, these are preserved in those of the tribal groupings (*civitates*) subsequently defined and recorded by the Romans. Oxfordshire lay across the boundaries of three such groupings: the Dobunni, the Atrebates and the Catuvellauni. No names are recorded for any specific local native peoples.

Increased contact with their continental kinsmen in Gaul (modern France), particularly after Caesar had brought it under Roman control, led the British to adopt other practices that are useful for dating. Changes in diet were accompanied by the importation of Roman wine and oil in pottery containers, and other pottery vessels suited to the new foods. All of these can be much more closely dated (by association with Roman coins in Gaul) than is the case with native pottery. Once wheel-thrown pottery was adopted by British potters, forms diversified, and new forms can often be dated by reference to the continental imports they were copying. Safety-pin brooches become much more common, possibly indicating a change in dress. These brooches undergo a rapid metallurgical and typological development, and some authorities believe that they can be dated to within 25 years. The brooches are commonly found in cremation urns, aiding pottery dating. Coins and continental imports are, however, rare and are generally restricted to a small number of prestigious sites. These imports do not appear in any quantity in Oxfordshire, and the chronology thus remains based largely upon the pottery. The Iron Age is therefore divided into three: the early Iron Age (800–400 BC), the middle Iron Age (400–1 BC) and the late Iron Age (AD 1–50).

Despite these caveats, a great deal has been learnt about prehistoric Oxfordshire in the last millennium before the Romans arrived. The clearing of the land for grazing and for agriculture was a gradual process, but in some areas it accelerated in the middle Bronze Age. Large field and enclosure systems occur in the Middle and Lower Thames valley as early as 1400 BC, and traces of similar systems have been found around Dorchester-on Thames and Abingdon.[12] These organised landscapes all appear close to the Thames, and are believed to have developed in order to take advantage of the role of the river as a corridor of trade for bronze imported from the continent. Extensive clearance had also taken place further up-river, as at Yarnton, but was not accompanied by large-scale enclosure, and environmental evidence suggests that this clearance was solely for grazing.[13]

During the late Bronze Age (1000–800 BC) a number of high-status sites which can be interpreted as regional power bases appeared within these cleared landscapes.[14] One lies on an island in the river at Wallingford, and another may lie at the foot of Castle Hill at Long Wittenham, where a late Bronze Age midden has been found by fieldwalking.[15] Defended hilltop enclosures associated with field systems also appeared. One is known on the chalk of the Berkshire Downs at Rams Hill, and close by the chalk figure of the White Horse also appears to have been first made at this time.[16] Rams Hill sits on top of the chalk escarpment overlooking the Vale of the White Horse, and close to the ancient Ridgeway that runs along it.[17] In the north and north-west of Oxfordshire late Bronze Age defences, usually consisting of a palisade of timbers, have been identified at Chastleton Camp, Lyneham Camp and Madmarston hillfort.[18]

At around 800 BC this system of trade based upon imported bronzes collapsed, and the field systems were generally abandoned. It is still unclear whether the adoption of iron for weapons and tools brought about the collapse, or whether the volume of bronzes being produced itself devalued them to the point where the system could not be maintained. In any event, this ushered in the early Iron Age.

For the whole of the first millennium BC (late Bronze Age, early and middle Iron Age), most people lived in rural farmsteads, either scattered within field systems or in small hamlets. These settlements are generally characterised by circular houses based upon one or more rings of timber posts, ranging in diameter from only 6m to more than 13m, and by groups of four posts arranged in squares (2–4m across). The four-post buildings are generally interpreted as granaries raised on legs to discourage vermin, like examples used in Eastern Europe until very recently, and in support of this interpretation charred grain has been found in the post-holes of a number of examples.[19] Late Bronze Age settlements have been investigated at Tower Hill and Weathercock Hill close to Uffington, and another at Eight Acre Field, Radley, near Abingdon.[20]

The early Iron Age saw the introduction of below-ground storage in cylindrical pits. Experimental archaeology has confirmed that these pits are very effective silos for seed-corn over the winter,[21] and their numbers on most Iron Age sites indicate that arable agriculture was now a significant part of the Iron Age economy. Four-post structures continue to appear, especially on low-lying sites where below-ground storage is impossible because of the high water-table. Some of these settlements were enclosed by ditches, but the majority did not have continuous boundaries and are described as unenclosed or 'open'.

A typical example of the unenclosed settlement is that at City Farm, Hanborough, where a roundhouse lay close to the end of a linear boundary, with a cluster of pits on one side and post-holes marking fences on the other (Fig. 1.4).[22] There were substantial ditches on this site but they were separated by very wide gaps. Pits clustered along a semicircle of ditch, as if following the boundary. This surviving ditch did not lie on a steep slope, so cannot plausibly be interpreted as for drainage. Further pits and post-holes, however, appear to have marked a corresponding arc on the other side, forming a circle, and may have been following a boundary above ground that has left no trace. The distinction between enclosed and unenclosed settlements may therefore be somewhat misleading, though reflecting a clear difference in the form that boundaries took. Some settlements had both enclosed and unenclosed phases, as was the case at Rollright, where an unenclosed settlement, apparently with an associated system of fields and droveways, was succeeded by an enclosure.[23]

One of the best-understood groups of unenclosed settlements in Oxfordshire lies west of Stanton Harcourt, where a series of hamlets visible from the air as linear spreads of pits surrounded the earlier prehistoric stone circle of the Devil's Quoits and its satellite burial mounds.[24] A number of these sites have been part-excavated in advance of gravel extraction, and in the 1980s the settlement in Gravelly Guy field was fully excavated by the Oxford Archaeological Unit, revealing more than 800 pits.[25] This settlement was occupied throughout the Iron Age, lasting for more than 700 years.

Similar settlements with huge numbers of storage pits are also known from the gravel terraces of the Thames at Yarnton, at Stanford-in-the-Vale and at Faringdon.[26] Away from the Thames gravels air photography has recently revealed a very large linear cluster of pits alongside the Sor Brook below the hillfort at Madmarston (Fig. 1.5).[27] This, together with the pits and field system at Rollright on the Warwickshire/ Oxfordshire border, demonstrates that wide-ranging clearance had also taken place on the Cotswolds, as on the Berkshire Downs. The economy of these 'open' settlements appears to have been mixed farming, since pits and charred plant remains indicate arable and animal bones suggest the tending of livestock. Loomweights and spindle

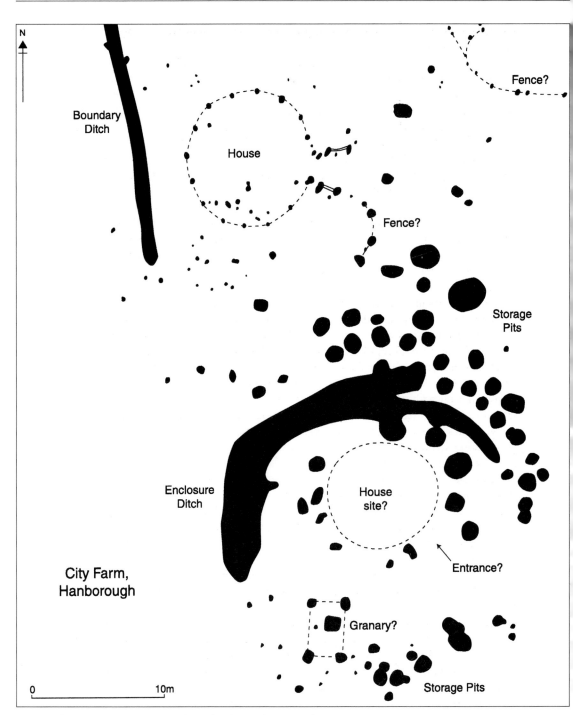

1.4 Plan of settlement at City Farm, Hanborough (after Harding 1972, pl. 26).

whorls are commonly found, showing that these communities were engaged in the manufacture of cloth.

Ditched settlements were uncommon in the early Iron Age, and very few of those in Oxfordshire were surrounded by substantial defences. At Allen's Pit near Dorchester an early Iron Age settlement was surrounded by a ditch 5m wide and nearly 3m deep, but this was exceptional. Generally enclosure ditches were between 1m and 1.5m deep, and only 2–3m wide. Other early Iron Age enclosures are known just north of Cassington, on Wytham Hill near Oxford and south of Fritwell.[28] In the middle and late Iron Age (after 400 BC) enclosed settlements became more common. Large numbers of enclosures are known from aerial photography, and many have been assumed to be Iron Age because of their irregular or polygonal shape. Examples have been investigated on the limestone at Rollright, on the clay at Bicester Fields Farm, on the first gravel terrace and floodplain of the Lower Windrush valley at Watkins Farm, Northmoor, and Mingies Ditch, Hardwick, respectively, on the second gravel terrace at Barton Court Farm, Abingdon, and at Mount Farm near Dorchester. Another was found just across the county border at Groundwell Farm in Wiltshire.[29] Although these are few, they come from a wide-enough variety of geologies to make it clear that the type was widespread, particularly north of the river valley on the Cotswolds.

There does not appear to be any distinction of status in either the buildings or the finds between enclosed and unenclosed settlements as a whole. These enclosures were not dug for defence, except perhaps against wild animals. There is little evidence for substantial banks inside the ditches; at Mingies Ditch, a double-ditched enclosure where the Iron Age ground surface was preserved, upcast from the ditch had been thrown out on both sides of the ditches. There was, however, evidence of bushes and trees in the waterlogged peats in the ditch bottoms, suggesting that hedges were growing on either side of the ditches, probably created by selective clearance of the pre-existing scrub. At Watkins Farm similar environmental evidence was recovered from waterlogged sediments in the ditch bottom.[30] This sort of evidence rarely survives, but confirms that above-ground boundaries of a variety of types were used in defining settlements and dividing up the landscape.

Many of the enclosures are of similar size, between 0.5 and 0.8ha in area. This may indicate that they performed a similar range of functions, and were occupied by similar-sized groups, but this is hard to prove as few of the sites have been completely excavated. In the middle Iron Age roundhouses were often built of stakes, which do not survive as well as the roundwood timbers of the early Iron Age, but fortunately middle Iron Age houses were usually surrounded by drainage gullies. At Mingies Ditch five roundhouses were found, of which only one or two are likely to have been in use at one time, suggesting a single family unit. A similar succession of single houses was found at Groundwell Farm, Wilts, and at Mount Farm, Dorchester, but at Watkins Farm there could have been anything between one and four houses in use at a time.

Several of these sites had trackways leading into the centre of the interior (that at Mingies Ditch had a gravelled surface), and also small paddocks or fields outside the main enclosure. There are, however, no ditched and surfaced roadways linking Iron Age settlements; trackways linking settlements together over any distance do not appear until the Roman period, and so interpreting how sites interacted is not easy. Within some of

1.5 Linear pit cluster settlement below Madmarston hillfort. (RCHME. NMR 15529/12, 18.7.1996)

the enclosed settlements there is evidence of zoning into living, storage and open spaces to varying degrees. There are, however, differences in internal organisation and structural elements depending upon location: some sites (particularly those with a high water-table) contained four-post storage structures while conversely pits for below-ground storage were present only in the drier settlements. Those sites with storage pits appear to have been mixed farms, but some in low-lying locations, such as those at Mingies Ditch and Watkins Farm, may have specialised in pastoral farming.

The middle Iron Age was a time of increased diversification and specialisation of settlement types. On the first gravel terrace and floodplain of the Thames and its tributaries pastoral settlements consisting of ditched house enclosures, sometimes with small annexes, appear, scattered within an open grassland landscape. These sites can be divided into two types. The first is best exemplified by the series of excavations carried out by the Abingdon Archaeological and Historical Society at Thrupp.[31] Occupation of this low-lying area began in the early Iron Age, but shifting settlement continued and intensified throughout the period. Environmental evidence is limited, but pits and deposits of charred grain have been recovered, suggesting either arable nearby or some form of exchange with other local settlements for cereals. More generally, by analogy with similar small groups of buildings at Claydon Pike, Fairford, Glos., the landscape is likely to have been cleared for open grazing for a considerable distance. Similar enclosures have been found beside the Windrush at Ducklington.

The second type of site, while morphologically very similar, is a summer encampment of transhumant pastoralists, and has been demonstrated unequivocally only at Farmoor.[32] Here the ditches of all of the small enclosures produced deposits containing domestic pottery and other finds in layers separated by sterile floodplain silts coming from the Thames. This showed that the sites were used between periods of flooding, probably seasonally. Mark Robinson was also able to show that the plant species were all those that colonise disturbed ground in the first five years. Those that establish themselves later (after seven years or more) were absent. These sites therefore appear to be shortlived and shifting, though the finds include fine ware decorated pottery. Similar enclosures are visible both as cropmarks and as surface features on Port Meadow west of Oxford.[33] Some have been investigated and confirm the evidence from Farmoor.

Close relationships between neighbouring settlements have already been suggested, but transhumance at Farmoor demonstrates that some settlements must have been part of larger groups working not at the level of the settlement but at that of the community. It also has considerable implications for understanding the fluctuations in numbers that may be present within the more permanent gravel terrace settlements.

The interaction between these various types of settlement, implied at Farmoor, can be seen in two areas where intensive archaeological investigation has taken place: at Abingdon and around Stanton Harcourt. At Abingdon, where the river Ock runs into the Thames, a series of Iron Age settlements has been identified on gravel terrace deposits, usually situated close to streams running down from the north (Fig. 1.6). Two early Iron Age mixed farming settlements are known within 600m of each other alongside the Stert and alongside another smaller stream under the town centre.[34] Two more lie on either side of the Larkhill stream between 1 and 1.5km to the west, at Spring Road and at Ashville/Wyndyke Furlong.[35] In the middle Iron Age settlement appears to have nucleated, one of each pair of sites expanding while the other was abandoned. East of the town were the first terrace gravels at Thrupp, with their spread of small house enclosures, which were probably one element of the community alongside the river Stert.

The settlement at Ashville/Wyndyke Furlong was over 400m long, and is the only one known that may merit the term 'village'. The settlement does not appear to have been divided into properties with static boundaries, so houses and pits cut across one another, and it is difficult to be certain how many houses were in use at one time. Nevertheless, it is possible that fifteen or more houses were contemporary. However, no evidence of specialisation in occupations was found, nor anything to suggest that the site was of higher status than its neighbours. It continued to flourish until the late Iron Age, when it appears to have dwindled when the Stert settlement was given defences (see below).

Given that gravel terrace deposits similar to those which developed these mixed farming settlements also existed east of the town, it is perhaps odd that there is little evidence of mixed farming settlements in this area. Much of the second terrace was, however, occupied by the Neolithic and Bronze Age ceremonial burial site of Barrow Hills, whose many mounds were still prominent landscape features.[36] This area would traditionally have been used for grazing, and it is possible that the continuation of earlier traditions of semi-nomadic pastoralism is evident in the Thrupp scattered house enclosures.

A clearer example both of the influence of earlier prehistoric traditions and of the operations of wider communities than single settlements can be seen around Stanton

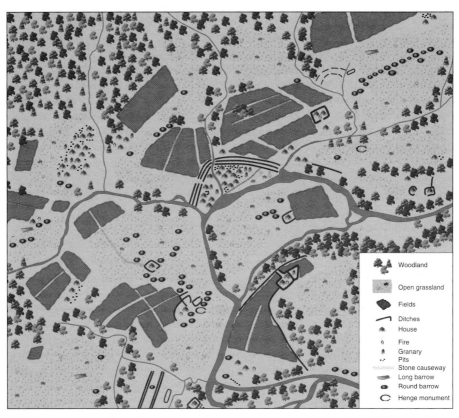

Legend:
- Woodland
- Open grassland
- Fields
- Ditches
- House
- Fire
- Granary
- Pits
- Stone causeway
- Long barrow
- Round barrow
- Henge monument

1.6 Reconstruction of the Iron Age settlement pattern around Abingdon. (Abingdon Town Council/Heritage Lottery Fund)

Harcourt, where the linear pit cluster settlement at Gravelly Guy was excavated (Fig. 1.7). This was only one of a group of such sites on the second terrace between the Windrush and the Thames, others of which have been investigated, in particular at Beard Mill. The Gravelly Guy settlement lay along a boundary which divided pasture on one side from arable on the other. Contrary to expectation, the grazing was on the well-drained gravel terrace, the arable in a narrow strip running down to the river Windrush. Extrapolating from the similarities between all of the sites known from cropmarks or excavations, Lambrick has plausibly suggested that all of the Iron Age linear pit settlements surrounding the Devil's Quoits ringed a vast area of common grazing, with arable fields lying on the outside, and generally occupying only a narrow band between the settlements and the river Windrush or wet clayey areas.[37]

The central area was probably both a focus for ancestral burial and traditional common grazing from the period when it was used for burial mounds, and livestock was probably more important than arable to these mixed farming communities. Although each of the settlements contains up to 800 storage pits, their longevity means that there need have been only a very few pits in use at any time. Most importantly, the organisation of this group of settlements surrounding the central grazing area suggests that they belonged to one community acting in concert.

This group of linear pit settlements is surrounded by enclosed settlements that occupy low-lying ground close to the Windrush and the Thames or wetter clay areas. Two of these are Mingies Ditch and Watkins Farm, both of which appear to be specialised pastoral settlements established in scrubland during the middle Iron Age, and which are probably importing cereals from elsewhere. This is probably another example of the increasing specialisation of farming by families within a single community, and the Ducklington small house enclosure may be another element of this. The discovery of foal bones at these low-lying sites has been taken to indicate that horse-rearing was one of these specialised functions.

These two landscapes are important evidence for the organisation of Iron Age society, which operated not simply at the level of the individual nuclear or extended family group, but also within wider communities, probably kinship groups that evolved out of the common use of Neolithic monuments and Bronze Age burial grounds. There is no evidence that the burial rites of the Bronze Age continued into the Iron Age; rather it is likely that traditional grazing areas, probably held in common, were the controlling factor in the organisation of these later Iron Age settlements. At Stanton Harcourt the Roman conquest did not materially affect the social organisation of the community. In the late Iron Age the focus of settlement at Gravelly Guy field shifted across the linear boundary into the edge of the grazing area. Circular houses and circular pits for storage disappear, and the characteristic structures of this period are sub-rectangular or sub-circular small ditched enclosures. Similar enclosures, all of first-century AD date, are also found on the other linear pit cluster settlements around Stanton Harcourt. In every case they lie on the other side of the linear pit boundaries, suggesting that a very similar shift occurred at most of the Iron Age settlements, and during a similar period. Despite significant changes in the character of houses and agriculture, all of the settlements show the same changes, demonstrating the continuity of community. These settlements developed along very similar lines into the early second century AD, and almost all of them were abandoned at much the same time.[38]

In a survey of cropmark evidence carried out in 1984, Hingley noted that unenclosed or 'open' settlements were characteristic of the gravels and floodplain of the Thames valley, while enclosed settlements were predominant off the gravels to the north.[39] He attempted to distinguish between enclosures as specialised components of larger settlements (such as stock enclosures), which he took to be the function of those in the valley, and self-contained individual farmsteads, which, in the absence of cropmark evidence for open settlements, was how he interpreted the cropmark enclosures elsewhere. He further linked these different settlement forms to different social structures. The societies of the valley (such as that around Stanton Harcourt discussed above) were clearly long-established, practised communal ownership and so were perceived as acting at communal level. In contrast the groups occupying the individual enclosed settlements of the Oxford Uplands were interpreted as newly established in the later part of the Iron Age and thus acting independently. The evident differences in the subsequent Roman settlement pattern, seen as reflecting this Iron

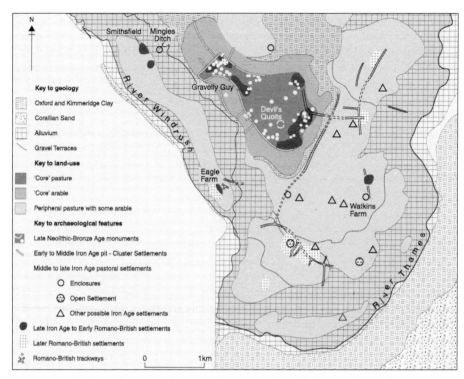

1.7 Map showing the development of the Stanton Harcourt area from the late Neolithic to the early Roman period.

Age pattern, were then suggested as indicating contrasting responses to the competitive opportunities offered by Romanisation (see Chapter four).

This is a stimulating hypothesis that needs testing by much more fieldwork. The greatest weakness of Hingley's argument is its reliance on cropmark evidence, which is undated. Work in the valley has since shown that some of his enclosures as components of larger settlements are later than the Iron Age settlements that appeared from cropmark evidence to surround them. Other enclosed settlements such as Mingies Ditch and Watkins Farm were newly established in relict scrubland in low-lying locations, and were probably semi-independent farmsteads, albeit specialising in pastoral husbandry. More significantly, excavation off the gravels has begun to reveal open settlements such as those at Deer Park Road, Witney, Slade Farm, Bicester, Glympton Park and Blackbird Leys, Oxford.[40] Taken together with the cropmark evidence from Madmarston, it would now appear that the distinction made by Hingley is gradually being blurred. It is still, however, true that the vast majority of possible Iron Age sites known from cropmarks in these areas are enclosed, though this may also be biased by the very visible nature of enclosures as opposed to 'open' settlements.

As well as these undefended settlements, hillforts also proliferated in upland areas in the Iron Age. Some have argued that this was the result of the dislocation and fragmentation of society consequent upon the disappearance of the late Bronze Age trading system. Along the Ridgeway these hillforts include Liddington, Uffington Castle (Fig. 1.8) and Segsbury Camp, while Rams Hill was enlarged. Blewburton was probably also constructed at this time.[41] All these sites share certain characteristics: they all have single defensive circuits consisting of a deep V-profiled ditch backed by a rampart made from the upcast spoil, usually revetted with stone or chalk at the front and held together by a framework of timbers; they all have two entrances; and all have produced the decorated pottery known as All Cannings Cross style. At Tower Hill near Uffington a hoard of bronze axes and other fragments was found in association with this pottery in an undefended settlement within a field system, underlining its transitional date between Bronze Age and Iron Age. It is also probably at this time that the Downs are divided up by large ditches.[42]

Hillforts used to be considered the 'towns' or 'central places' of the Iron Age, and the scale of their defences certainly suggests the efforts of large numbers of people. With the exception of Rams Hill, none of these forts along the Ridgeway has been excavated on a large scale, but limited investigations carried out in recent years have led Gary Lock to suggest that these sites were not intensively occupied at this time. There is at present no evidence from any Oxfordshire hillfort that these were chieftains' residences – indeed there is a lack of either settlement or burial evidence for much social differentiation in the Iron Age. Other interpretations, such as refuges in times of trouble, meeting places or sacred enclosures, have therefore been put forward.

Between 600 BC and 500 BC a new hillfort was constructed at Alfred's Castle, Ashbury, set back from the escarpment. This site does have evidence of significant internal occupation.[43] At some point, as yet undated, the defences of Uffington were strengthened, one entrance being blocked, while the ditch was deepened and the rampart heightened with the spoil. Both Segsbury and Rams Hill show the same modifications, but there is little evidence of increased occupation inside these modified hillforts.

Only Segsbury and Blewburton Hill have produced evidence for occupation after 400 BC (in the middle Iron Age), and at Blewburton there is some evidence from the defensive ditches of a possible break in occupation. Geophysical survey at Segsbury suggests that the interior here was much more intensively used than at some of the neighbouring hillforts. This pattern of some sites developing at the expense of their neighbours is one commonly found in Wessex, and the 'developed' hillforts are often viewed as central places whose many storage pits suggest a redistributive function.[44] Excavated evidence from Segsbury is still limited, but the pottery from Blewburton includes many decorated vessels which suggest wide-ranging contacts for the site, both southwards into Wessex and northwards into the Upper Thames valley.

On present evidence, neither of these sites appears to have continued in use after the introduction of wheel-turned late Iron Age pottery sometime between 50 BC and the end of the century. At Alfred's Castle, however, air photography has revealed a much larger enclosure surrounded by a ditch up to 3m deep, which trial trenching has shown is of late Iron Age date.[45] Whether this was simply a stock enclosure or represents domestic occupation on any scale is as yet unclear.

The development of these hilltop enclosures is significant in several respects. The appearance of four or five defended sites of the earliest Iron Age is supplemented by the

1.8 Uffington Castle hillfort and the White Horse during excavations.

appearance of linear boundaries such as the Berkshire Grim's Ditch at much the same time (Fig. 1.9). These form a virtually continuous system from the Thames at Streatley west along the escarpment to Segsbury Camp, and are possibly linked to the chain of hillforts along the ridge. The common characteristics of these early forts, and the common alterations to three of the four, could simply result from a shared knowledge of developments in hillfort design but could equally indicate a line of defensible sites built and later modified to protect the important route of the Ridgeway, and the physical boundary of the chalk escarpment of the Vale of White Horse, by one tribal group. Given the lack of intensive occupation, which suggests that the population who built each hillfort lived in the surrounding landscape, this latter interpretation seems more likely. The emergence of particular sites as centres of occupation in the middle Iron Age may also be interpreted as the common decision of this group.

The frequent redefinition of the White Horse, which lay adjacent to the highest eminence along this escarpment, suggests that the identity of this group, first defined in the late Bronze Age, persisted throughout the Iron Age, the Roman period and beyond.[46] Recently a discrete series of late Iron Age coin types has been identified in North Hampshire and the Berkshire Downs, centred around Marlborough, and extending into south-western Oxfordshire around Faringdon.[47] This could well be another manifestation of the same group. The choice of the horse as their symbol, and the persistence of the use of this area for horse-rearing today, may not be entirely coincidental.

If such patterning exists in the siting of other defended enclosures within Oxfordshire, it is not so easy to demonstrate. Early Iron Age defended sites along the

Corallian ridge are known at the extreme west of the county at Badbury and Little Coxwell. These sites may be an extension of those along the chalk escarpment, rather than a separate group. On Wytham Hill just west of Oxford a possible ditch terminal of defensive proportions was found, and a possible rampart has been observed in Wytham Wood. A close relationship between these hilltop sites and undefended settlements on the river gravels fringing the Thames below, particularly at Farmoor, was suggested by the similarity of the pottery.[48] Castle Hill at Wittenham Clumps opposite Dorchester could be considered another early Iron Age hillfort in this chain, and unusually it too has Iron Age settlement outside the ramparts.[49] Its position overlooking the Thames suggests that advance warning of river traffic, and thus control of the river, may have been important.

Roughly halfway between Wytham and Badbury there is a defended enclosure on an island in the Thames at Burroway Brook south of Bampton. This site was only investigated on a very small scale, but it did show that the rampart was raised upon a corduroy of halved timbers, with timber reinforcement to hold it together, which was subsequently burnt.[50] Behind the rampart was a thick black occupation layer, suggesting intensive use of the interior. The use of timber reinforcing is usually of early Iron Age date (800–400 BC). It is therefore possible that the line of the Corallian ridge was protected by a combination of widely spaced hillforts and valley forts. Too little is known of these sites at present, however, to be confident of their relative chronology.

There are no hillforts directly overlooking the tributaries of the Thames (that is, the Windrush, the Evenlode and the Cherwell) but an undated hillfort at Eynsham Hall Park lies midway between the Windrush and the Evenlode, and Bladon Castle near Woodstock occupies a similarly central position between the Evenlode and the Cherwell.[51] Applying geographical 'central place' theory to archaeology, it is possible that these defended sites controlled territories whose limits were the rivers that ran between them. Very limited trenching at Bladon Castle did not produce any firm dating evidence, except that the rampart had been burnt, like that at Burroway Brook. It is therefore likely that this fort is early Iron Age.

There are hillforts scattered over the limestone uplands of North Oxfordshire in clusters of two or three. Most have early Iron Age defences. Just over the county boundary, Rainsborough Camp, Northants, has revealed an early Iron Age impressive stone-fronted rampart with an elaborate gateway incorporating circular guardhouses.[52] This site was apparently abandoned for several centuries before being refurbished in the later middle Iron Age with a dump rampart. Most of the excavation at these sites was carried out by the Oxford University Archaeological Society and was concentrated on the defences; rather less is known of the organisation of the settlements that the defences enclosed.

In the middle Iron Age many of these hillforts appear to be abandoned. It must be remembered that hardly any of these sites have been excavated on any scale, and it is therefore possible that occupation of this date remains to be discovered. Where large parts of hillfort interiors have been dug, as in Hampshire, some like Danebury have occupation throughout, but others such as Winklebury have sparser activity, which is not evenly distributed. Nevertheless, on present evidence only a few sites (of which Blewburton and Segsbury have already been mentioned) continue. Madmarston is

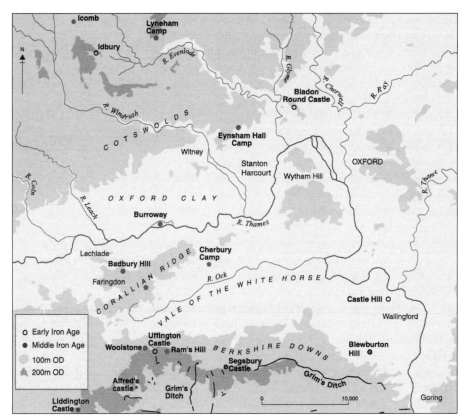

1.9 Map of early and middle Iron Age hillforts and linear boundary systems in Oxfordshire and north Berkshire.

another, and air photography has recently revealed a very large linear cluster of pits and a number of small ditched enclosures alongside the river below the hillfort, which is likely to represent a large and long-lived settlement. The apparent scarcity of hillforts used in the middle Iron Age suggests a period of peace, and this interpretation is supported by the many unenclosed settlements of the period, and by the modest size of the ditches of enclosed settlements.

Although it is called the Iron Age, iron artefacts are rare, only becoming common in the Roman period. Traces of iron-smithing slag are found on many settlements, however, indicating that most farmsteads either repaired or reused broken iron tools, rather than discarding them. Bronze-working crucibles are also common, suggesting either the reworking of scrap or the visits of peripatetic tinkers. The iron bars of various shapes, known as 'currency bars', occur at a number of sites. A hoard has been found at Madmarston hillfort in the north of the county, and smaller numbers of incomplete bars at Abingdon and at Gravelly Guy, Stanton Harcourt.[53] Iron tools include a complete adze found at Yarnton, a sickle or billhook from Ashville, Abingdon, and knives from a variety of excavations. Weapons, particularly swords or their scabbards, have been found in the river Thames at Newbridge and Standlake, in the Minster Ditch at North Hinksey near Oxford, and at Long Wittenham, while two swords and a scabbard chape have been found at Little Wittenham near Dorchester (Fig. 1.10).[54]

These weapons show the craftsmanship, and the artistic abilities, of Iron Age people. They are rare objects, and constitute the strongest evidence for the warrior elite in Iron Age society to which Caesar alludes in his narrative. Otherwise, in Oxfordshire only occasional pieces of metalwork such as brooches and the decoration on pottery attest to the artistic taste of Iron Age people.

The distribution of these weapons is believed to derive from their deliberate deposition in water as offerings. Deposition of objects, and of human and animal bones, in the river Thames is a tradition that began 3000 years earlier in the Neolithic. In the Bronze Age stone axes were replaced by bronze weapons and ornaments, but deposition of human bones and pots continued, as at Dorney in Buckinghamshire, and probably at Wallingford. In the Iron Age the metal of the weapons changed, but the tradition persisted, as the dating of at least five individuals at Dorney shows.[55] No human bones from the Thames in Oxfordshire have yet been dated to the Iron Age, but burial in the river might help to explain the lack of cemeteries and other burials throughout the Iron Age.

Considering the number of excavated settlements, burials dating to this period are very rare. There are no 'chieftain' burials beneath barrows, as had occurred in the Bronze Age. Where burials have been found the bodies are usually laid on one side in a foetal or crouched position. One burial was found within a stake-walled roundhouse at Frilford. Most settlements include occasional human burials in storage pits, as at Beard Mill and Gravelly Guy, Stanton Harcourt, Standlake, Dorchester, at City Farm and at Ashville, Abingdon.[56] Sometimes only selected bones are present, as with the skull on a pit bottom at Abingdon Vineyard. A scatter of bones came from the ditches around the central roundhouse at Watkins Farm, and stray bones from peripheral features at Mingies Ditch, Hardwick. The scarcity of formal burials and the common finding of stray bones have led to the suggestion that excarnation, where the body is left exposed to deflesh, was practised. An alternative interpretation would see the skulls and other bones found as trophies of war.

1.10 The Little Wittenham sword. Length 0.81m. (Ashmolean Museum)

Recently a formal cemetery of thirty-one individuals, none of whom had any grave goods, has been found at Yarnton.[57] It was only through the use of radiocarbon dating that the date of the burials was discovered, and the excavator has suggested that more Iron Age cemeteries may exist among the many undated burials recorded in the past. Nevertheless, it is likely that the numbers of Iron Age burials on land will remain low, and many Iron Age people may have been buried in rivers or pools. In the late Iron Age cremation burial accompanied by grave goods is reintroduced into south-east Britain from the continent, and a single cremation pit containing four whole vessels has been found at Watlington.[58] At present, however, no cemeteries of this period are known in Oxfordshire.

Evidence for Iron Age religious buildings or practices is virtually non-existent before the late Iron Age. We know from Caesar that the Druids venerated sacred groves and pools, and this suggests a religion focused upon natural sites, not upon artificial structures such as temples. Some probable temples have, however, been identified in recent excavations, for instance at Hayling Island on the south coast and at South Cadbury hillfort.[59] Unlike most Iron Age buildings, these are square or rectangular. In his 1972 survey of the Iron Age in the Upper Thames area Harding claimed that the Iron Age small sub-circular enclosure and stake-walled house that underlie respectively a Romano-Celtic temple and rotunda at Frilford represent Iron Age religious structures. A possibly votive iron ploughshare was found in a pit within the enclosure, and two crouched burials and a late Iron Age pit containing a sword-chape within the stake-walled house. More recently, however, Harding retracted that view, arguing that the ploughshare and pit were not votive, and the superimposition of the Roman buildings upon the Iron Age ones was coincidental.[60]

A large collection of Iron Age brooches and other objects, some of exotic origin, has been found at the site of the Roman temple at Woodeaton.[61] These are taken to indicate that the site was of particular significance in the Iron Age as well, though no buildings have yet been found. Possibly the most convincing ritual structure is one found at Smithsfield, Hardwick-with-Yelford, where a square of four post-holes was enclosed within a rectangle by a shallow gully or wall-trench, into one corner of which had been placed a virtually complete cow burial (Fig. 1.11). A similar four-post structure at Roughground Farm, Lechlade, Glos., enclosed a cremation burial in a Roman second-century pot.[62] The four-poster was surrounded by a horseshoe-shaped fence, and then by a square enclosure set diagonally to the four-post structure. Both of these structures are similar to the burial enclosures of the Champagne region of Northern Gaul, which often contain four-post structures such as these, interpreted as mortuary houses or shrines. In form the four posts surrounded by a larger square wall-trench is also reminiscent of Romano-Celtic temples later built in stone.

In the late Iron Age there were some significant developments in settlement character. Enclosed farmsteads like that at Barton Court Farm, Abingdon, show clear internal organisation.[63] The structural elements present were a deep-ditched enclosure containing an arc of post-holes (possibly representing a house), a rectangular pen surrounded by gullies, a group of pits of varying shape and size, some forming lines that appear to mark boundaries, and an open area. There did not appear to be any contemporary structures outside, and this can plausibly be interpreted as a self-contained single farm or family holding.

The same structural elements recur at Gravelly Guy field, Stanton Harcourt, where modest enclosure ditches indicate three similar-sized units, each containing a deep-ditched enclosure of similar dimensions, a rectangular pen, an assortment of pits of varying shape and size, and an open area. Two of the three also contain arcs of gully and rough ovals of post-holes possibly indicating houses. The parallel arrangement of some of these elements strongly suggests that they may have been laid out to a pattern representing all that was necessary for a single farming unit.[64]

At this site the enclosure ditches were also a secondary development, but there are stretches of earlier gullies on the same lines, and it is likely that the separate farmsteads were divided by boundaries above ground from the start. Other late Iron Age enclosures did not always conform to this pattern. At Old Shifford Farm, for instance, the settlement apparently began as a line of sub-circular small enclosures, which were subsequently replaced by a group of connected square or rectangular enclosures of larger size. Only in its third, Roman, phase does the farmstead take on a unified form within one enclosing ditch.[65]

At Bicester Fields Farm the enclosed settlement was of rather different character. Here a small square enclosure possibly containing a single roundhouse gully was later enlarged fourfold, the later enclosure being divided into two parts, one of which had the circular roundhouse gully (twice recut) approximately at its centre. There were few other surviving internal features, though outside the enclosure there were groups of pits and quarries, and other subsidiary enclosures.[66]

Unfortunately the function of the various elements of these late Iron Age farms is less clear. Some of the clearest elements of middle Iron Age settlements – the circular drainage gullies surrounding circular timber roundhouses – disappeared from most settlements, as did the cylindrical storage pits.[67] Houses may be represented by a number of incomplete ovals of post-holes, some surrounded by arcs of gully, but no well-preserved certain example has yet been excavated. The difficulty of identifying late Iron Age buildings may be due to a change in their construction materials from timber posts or stakes to mass-walls of cob or clunch, which do not require substantial bedding in the ground. Such buildings need not have been circular at all, and could have been built in virtually any shape; the deep-ditched small enclosures of oval, horseshoe or sub-rectangular shape that commonly appear on late Iron Age sites may have contained houses. The most unusual aspect of the Bicester Fields Farm site was the presence of roundhouse gullies, which are otherwise virtually unknown in late Iron Age Oxfordshire.

It is possible that timber buildings on sleeper beams now became common, as at sites in the south-east such as Gorhambury near St Albans.[68] At Abingdon a roughly rectangular platform of limestone cobbles of the late Iron Age was found, adjacent to which were patches of trampled floor and an oven. This may have been the floor of a building of sill-beam construction; similar floors cut slightly into the ground have recently been found in an early Roman enclosure in the Middle Thames valley.[69]

The gradual disappearance of cylindrical storage pits marks a significant change in farming practice. The pits of the late Iron Age are of very varied dimensions and sizes, many of them unsuitable for the storage of grain or other materials, and it must be assumed that grain was now stored in some other way. Storage pits had been used ubiquitously for 600 years and their abandonment, together with the change in house type, indicates a significant break with the past. Farming regimes were also changing. On most early and middle Iron Age sites sheep are the most numerous species, but cattle replaced sheep as the most numerous species at both Barton Court Farm and at Bicester Fields Farm. In addition, charred grain from a pit at Barton Court Farm suggests that bread wheat (similar to modern wheats) was replacing the hardier spelt as the main cereal crop.

A change in pottery also accompanied these other developments; hand-made middle Iron Age pottery was replaced by wheel-turned vessels in different forms. The chronology of this change-over is still being debated, and it is possible that it occurred at different times across the county. Sites such as Bicester Fields have at least three phases of roundhouse using late Iron Age pottery before the Roman conquest; around Stanton Harcourt middle Iron Age pottery appears to continue in use until the end of the first century BC, and at Abingdon middle Iron Age pottery may have survived even longer.

Defended sites became more important again towards the end of the Iron Age, when their defences were often refurbished, but new and much larger strongholds were also built in valley-bottom locations near rivers. The earliest known of these is at Cherbury, where a defended enclosure was constructed in the later middle Iron Age (sometime after 200 BC). This had more than one circuit of banks and ditches, the ramparts being faced with stone blocks. Its position is low-lying, and it can best be described as a 'valley fort'. Snail evidence showed that its defences were augmented by surrounding marshy ground. Only a few hundred metres away cropmarks show a concentration of smaller enclosures and circular house enclosures, which may indicate an extramural settlement, though the limited pottery recovered there is of late Iron Age/early Roman character, of later date than that recovered from the fort.[70] Cherbury lies close to the river Ock, and may have been positioned to control river trade.

This was certainly the case with Dyke Hills near Dorchester, where the massive banks and ditch cut off 40ha of low-lying ground in a bend of the Thames opposite Castle Hill (Fig. 1.12). The west and south sides of the site are bounded by the Thames, the east side by the river Thame running into the Thames, and the north side is defended by two banks on either side of a very wide ditch. The single ditch perhaps suggests that the ditch was intended to carry water, and was in fact a moat. Neither the defences nor the interior have been excavated in the twentieth century, and the nineteenth-century records are observations of the destruction of a large section of the banks, from which only a later Saxon burial was recovered. Air photographs of the interior suggest that much of it was densely occupied with roundhouses, pits and small enclosures, though the south-eastern part appears to have been covered by alluvium, and may always have been unsuitable for habitation.[71] This may, however, have been a grazing area for livestock.

It is generally assumed that this site is late Iron Age, simply because of its size: none of the earlier defended enclosures is more than 7ha in area. The development of very large areas surrounded by defences, often known as 'oppida', begins in central Europe in the fourth century BC, but in France appears in the later second century BC, and in Britain later still.[72] Outside Dyke Hills to the north trenching has revealed a settlement containing Roman fine ware pottery dated to just before the Roman conquest, but its relationship to the defended enclosure is unclear.[73]

Another late Iron Age valley fort, under the town centre at Abingdon, has been partly excavated by the Oxford Archaeological Unit. Here the defences ran in a

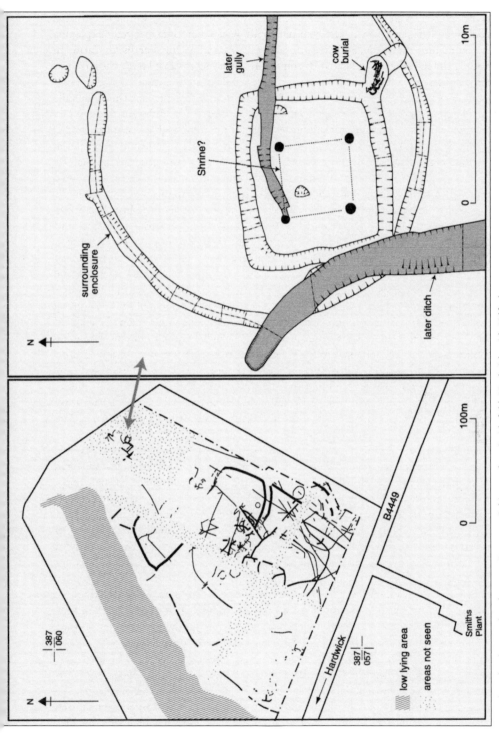

1.11 Plan of timber ritual enclosure or Romano–Celtic temple at Smithsfield, Hardwick-with-Yelford.

semicircle between the rivers Ock and Thames, and consisted of two (in places three) concentric ditch circuits, the outer and inner ditches being 10–12m wide and about 2.6m deep, the middle ditch only 3–4m wide and just under 2m deep. Both the outer and inner ditches held water, and were probably linked to the river Stert, making the ditch circuits similar to moats. A band some 10m wide inside the innermost ditch was devoid of late Iron Age or early Roman features, and is interpreted as the site of a bank.[74] In the second century AD this gravel bank was pushed back into the ditch to level it when more room was needed for the Roman settlement.

Only just over 1ha of the interior has been excavated in detail, but observations made in smaller trenches suggest that more than 15ha of the interior was densely occupied with Iron Age roundhouses, storage pits and post-hole structures, later replaced by a grid of rectilinear enclosures. The defensive circuit probably enclosed 33ha, the eastern part of which, as at Dyke Hills, was low-lying and may have been meadow or grassland. Radiocarbon dates from the lowest ditch fills show that the defences were constructed sometime between 200 BC and AD 55.[75]

Both Dyke Hills and Abingdon lie at the junction of the Thames with one of its tributaries, and a third ditched enclosure, called simply the 'Big Enclosure', is situated near the junction of the Thames and the Evenlode at Cassington, as close to the confluence of the two rivers as the topography would allow – further down-river is alluvial floodplain, liable to flooding in the winter months. The Cassington enclosure was only 10ha in area and was circular. Most of the site has now been destroyed by gravel quarrying, but limited excavations were carried out both in the ditch and the interior. The ditch was 10–12m wide and 2.5–4m deep, and was probably backed by a defensive bank. Pottery from the base of the ditch indicates that it was constructed during the first half of the first century AD. The interior contained a mass of cropmarks, but most of these belonged to earlier monuments and settlements, not to the late Iron Age.[76] This site does not appear to have been intensively occupied and there were a number of gaps or causeways in the ditch circuit, leading some archaeologists to the view that the enclosure was never finished.

Although there is a dense concentration of settlements of the late Iron Age around the Windrush on the Thames gravels and floodplain, there is no defended site close to the junction of this river with the Thames. The low-lying ground on either side of the river Thames in this area may have discouraged the building of such a site, and Cherbury lies only 4km to the south-west, but this fort is only 6.5ha in area. It is only much further up-river, at Salmonsbury near Bourton-on-the-Water in Gloucestershire, that we find a large defensive enclosure beside the Windrush. This site was rectangular and double-ditched. It covered 22ha, and limited excavations in the interior have revealed timber roundhouses surrounded by drainage gullies, and groups of pits. The pottery suggests that the site was first occupied in the first century BC, and continued in use into the Roman period.[77]

All four sites are situated in low-lying positions alongside rivers, and enclose larger areas than the hillforts earlier in the Iron Age. As at Cherbury, also in a low-lying situation, the lack of a high vantage point was compensated for by the use of concentric ditches and/or banks to provide defence in depth (except at the Big Enclosure at Cassington). The shift in location has plausibly been interpreted as the

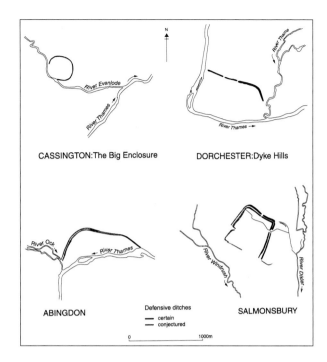

1.12 Plans of late Iron Age 'valley forts' on
rivers in Oxfordshire and Gloucestershire.

result of the increased importance of riverine trade during the late Iron Age, when
Roman imports from the continent were being traded via the Thames. The position
of three of these sites at the junction of major tributaries with the Thames may
indicate that they acted as collecting points for materials brought down-river from the
valleys of these tributaries, to be traded for exotic goods brought up the Thames.

There are, however, hardly any Roman imports in Oxfordshire that pre-date the
Roman period, and it is now becoming clear that regional trade with areas such as
Sussex via the Middle and Lower Thames was already occurring before Roman imports
arrived. At Abingdon, for instance, quernstones for grinding cereals into flour were
being imported from Lodsworth in East Sussex in the first century BC, and Lodsworth
soon became the largest supplier for the settlement. The shift to low-lying defended
sites may therefore have begun in the middle Iron Age, stimulated by regional trade.

Professor Barry Cunliffe has called these sites 'enclosed oppida', adopting a term
used by Julius Caesar to describe the native towns of Gaul and Britain during his
campaigns in the 50s BC.[78] To what extent they were truly towns is debatable. Towns
can be classified in a variety of ways, but generally include a high population, a market
function, an administrative role and usually a religious focus. They often also have
defences. The scale and the dense occupation that the Oxfordshire defended sites
appear to contain certainly suggest that they were significant centres of population.
Iron currency bars have been found both at Salmonsbury and at Abingdon, while
Dyke Hills and Abingdon have also produced more late Iron Age coins than most
other contemporary sites, suggesting either more wealth or a market function. As well

as the Sussex querns, Abingdon also has querns from May Hill in Gloucestershire and briquetage from Hampshire. The range of decorated pottery from Abingdon is much wider than that from other sites in the county, with imported vessels from the south and others imitating designs common in Wessex and the Middle and Lower Thames areas. All of this demonstrates wide-ranging contacts, reflecting either the high status or the market function of the site.

One style of decoration used on the globular bowls of the Upper Thames region is called 'Frilford style' after the site where it was first recognised (Fig. 1.13). This style is common to most of the sites in and around Abingdon, and is the most common style at the town centre within the defences. It was certainly made locally, although no production site has been discovered. None may ever be found, as these hand-made pots were not mass-produced, and do not require elaborate kiln-structures for firing. Ethnographic evidence shows us that such pottery may have been made seasonally by the women and then sold at local markets. Pots of this type are found north of the Thames around Cassington, and at a series of sites along the Windrush valley, most notably at Salmonsbury. There are also vessels from Abingdon which are exotic to Oxfordshire but are closely paralleled at Salmonsbury. This suggests routes of communication between the large defended enclosures. A Frilford-style bowl has recently been found at an Iron Age enclosure near the Thames at Reading, further demonstrating the significance of the river for trade links between Abingdon and the Middle Thames.[79]

One function that towns commonly perform is to provide specialist services that smaller settlements cannot support. The number of bronze-working crucibles found may be an indicator that a smith was resident in the settlement, though no moulds for casting bronze have been found. The charred plant remains from the many storage pits indicate that Abingdon may have been acting as a repository for grain from elsewhere in the area, and so may have had some redistributive function for the wider community. As yet, however, no public or chiefly buildings have been discovered, nor any religious focus.

Understanding such large settlements is difficult. They may have segregated certain activities or occupations into zones, and without very extensive excavation, which has not been achieved for any of the Oxfordshire sites, the role of these sites cannot be fully comprehended. It is also possible that the local aristocracy continued to live in farmsteads round about, as they certainly did around the oppidum at Verulamium. The late Iron Age farmstead at Barton Court Farm, less than 1km from Abingdon, may have been the home of a local aristocrat, as this farm became a villa soon after the Roman conquest.

The enclosed oppida have also been seen as the first stage in the development of very extensive systems of ditches or dykes which surround settlements at centres like Silchester, Verulamium (St Albans), Chichester and Camulodunum (near Colchester). One of the largest dyke systems in the country lies in Oxfordshire: the North Oxfordshire Grim's Ditch forms an incomplete ring up-river of the Big Enclosure straddling the river Evenlode, and ending on the east at the river Glyme (Fig. 1.14). A series of trenches have been dug across the dykes, from which it has been concluded that the system is of first-century AD date, and was built in two stages, perhaps originally enclosing around 200ha but later being enlarged.[80] A similar dyke system exists at Bagendon just north-west of Cirencester, and limited excavation in its interior has revealed currency bars, gold and silver coins and imported pottery.[81] So far no major late Iron Age settlement has been found within the 13 sq. km of the main circuit of the North Oxfordshire Grim's Ditch, but the enormous ditch circuit, and the fact that a group of wealthy early Romano-British villas later appears within it, has long been taken to indicate that it was a similarly important late Iron Age complex.

The Cherwell is the only major tributary of the Thames without a defended focus. Unlike the other rivers, the Cherwell has long been seen as marking a boundary between tribal territories, rather than as an artery of communication. This view derives mainly from consideration of the distributions of various late Iron Age tribal coinages. Oxfordshire lies at the junction of three major coin-using groups: the Catuvellauni, the Dobunni and the Atrebates. The coinage of each group bears different emblems, and we can identify to which group the coins belong from the abbreviated personal and place-names that appear on the reverse of the coins. In the main the Romans used the existing British tribal groupings as the basis for dividing up the administration of the newly established province of Britain, and retained the principal British settlements (and their names) for the capital cities of each tribal area. We can therefore identify Calleva Atrebatum (Silchester, Hants) as the British CALLE and CALLEV found on coins, and Verulamium (modern St Albans, Hertfordshire) and Camulodunum (Colchester, Essex) as the British VER and CAM, CAMV or CAMVL.[82]

Commius of the Atrebates is mentioned by Caesar, and his successors sometimes name him as father. The names of later rulers, Tasciovanus and Cunobelinus, appear on coins with the place-names VER and CAM. Coins are ascribed to the Dobunni purely on the basis of the broad correspondence of their distribution with the extent of the territory known to have been centred on Cirencester in the Roman period, though the tribe has plausibly been identified with the Bodunni who sent embassies to Aulus Plautius in the Claudian Expedition of AD 43.[83]

The three principal tribal coinages found in Oxfordshire are thus those of the Dobunni, whose coins spread from Gloucestershire across most of Oxfordshire north of the Thames as far as the Cherwell; the Catuvellauni, whose coins extend all the way from Essex to the Cherwell in the west; and the Atrebates, whose coins spread from Hampshire north into southern Oxfordshire. As mentioned already, a sub-group of the Atrebates has recently been identified from the circulation area of a variant group of coins around Marlborough, extending into south-western Oxfordshire around Faringdon. In general the distributions of coins of different tribes are distinct from one another, particularly the silver and bronze denominations, suggesting that they were indeed tribal currencies of sorts. The Cherwell appears to be a firm dividing line between the coins of the Dobunni and Catuvellauni.[84] There are, however, areas where coinage of more than one tribe is common; the area around Abingdon and as far south as Wallingford, for instance, is the meeting place of all three types.

Some numismatists have attempted to chart the political history of the tribes by plotting the coin distributions over time, assuming that the coins reflect the territory controlled by each tribe at any given time. It must be remembered, however, that many different types were minted by the British tribes during the 100 years before AD 43, and that, in the absence of any dates on the coins, their chronology is still

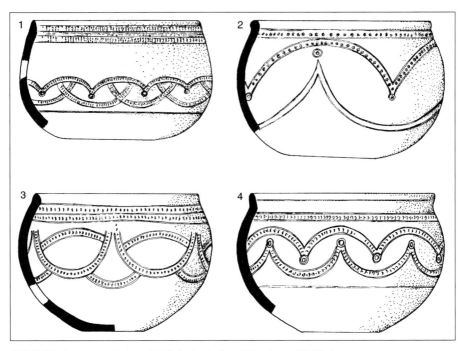

1.13 'Frilford' type swag-decorated globular bowls from Abingdon and Frilford.

uncertain. In some cases the order in which the various named rulers followed one another is unsure, and so plotting the chronological development of the coin groups is difficult. More importantly, excavations have shown that British coins continued to circulate for nearly 30 years after the Roman conquest, so that any patterns may be distorted by later events. While it may ultimately be possible to use coins in this way, at present it is best to lump the coins together and look only at broad differences.

Returning to the Cherwell and the North Oxfordshire Grim's Ditch, Eberhard Sauer has recently pointed out that the dyke system is largely missing on the east side (towards the Cherwell). He has therefore suggested that it may have surrounded a Catuvellaunian enclave established beyond the traditional tribal river boundary, and defended against the Dobunni living around it. Just east of the Cherwell, opposite the North Oxfordshire Grim's Ditch, is a straight dyke known as Aves Ditch running north-north-east for 10km. This has a bank on the east side, and recent trenching by Sauer has shown that it overlies an early Iron Age enclosure, and so has tentatively been ascribed to this same late Iron Age defensive system. Running east from the Thames opposite Wallingford for over 10km towards Henley is another linear ditch, the South Oxfordshire Grim's Ditch. This has a bank on the north side, suggesting that its function was to exclude the southernmost part of Oxfordshire, and Sauer has seen this too as part of a series of Catuvellaunian territorial boundaries.[85]

Sauer's view represents a plausible attempt to match the physical features with a commonly held interpretation of the political developments of the late Iron Age, that of Catuvellaunian territorial expansion, based mainly on coin distributions. One element of his hypothesis is supported by coin evidence, as the northernmost limit of Atrebatic coins in Oxfordshire lies south of Dorchester-on-Thames in the Wallingford area, and corresponds closely to the line of the South Oxfordshire Grim's Ditch. This may indeed have been a tribal boundary.

The other boundaries are not so clearly matched by coin distributions. There is no concentration of Catuvellaunian coins west of the Cherwell or within the North Oxfordshire Grim's Ditch, but they are clearly clustered east of the river Cherwell. In addition, there is a gap of several kilometres between the dykes and the river Cherwell, which makes its function as a bridgehead from this river difficult to sustain. While dyke systems at this time are commonly discontinuous, often making use of natural boundaries such as valleys or marshy ground as part of the defences, the most likely eastern boundary of the system is the river Glyme. The North Oxfordshire Grim's Ditch is better seen as connected in some way to the Big Enclosure at Cassington on the Evenlode. It is possible that Aves Ditch was a Catuvellaunian boundary similar to the South Oxfordshire Grim's Ditch, though it is unclear why it ran north-north-east so close to the line of the Cherwell, unless this was a second line of defence.

Sauer has included Dyke Hills at Dorchester in his system of defences, but not the Big Enclosure or Abingdon, though he notes that all three lay along the Thames between his two linear territorial boundaries. The Big Enclosure at Cassington lies on the east side of the Thames and the Evenlode respectively, and could conceivably have been a Catuvellaunian fort built in opposition to the North Oxfordshire Grim's Ditch. Abingdon lies on the west side of the Thames, but could have been a bridgehead. The distribution of Catuvellaunian coins shows a group extending westwards across the Thames to Abingdon and the Lower Ock valley, and it is possible that the occurrence of mixed coinages in this area is misleading, with the Catuvellaunian coins in fact superseding those of the Atrebates and Dobunni. We do not, however, know enough about the circulation of goods and money at these frontier settlements, whose market functions may have encouraged them to accept and circulate coins of different tribes.

Until the interiors of Dyke Hills and the North Oxfordshire Grim's Ditch have been more thoroughly excavated it will not be possible to substantiate or deny these hypotheses with confidence. The only defended site to have been excavated on any scale, that at Abingdon, shows strong links both with the north-west (Dobunni) and with the south (Atrebates), rather than with the Catuvellauni to the north-east. The concentration of valley forts may therefore represent the fortresses of rival groups facing one another across the boundary of the Thames and its tributaries.

The belief that late Iron Age society was organised into these very large tribal groupings may itself be a misconception. When Julius Caesar came to Britain in 54 BC he mentioned four kings (and presumably kingdoms) within what later became the circulation area of the coinage of the Cantii (Kent), which eventually formed a single Roman *civitas*.[86] The coin circulation areas may reflect confederations of smaller, largely independent tribes to facilitate trade, or even groups that recognised the leadership of particular individuals or dynasties for warfare in times of trouble, as Caesar implies was the case when he invaded. They need not imply permanent

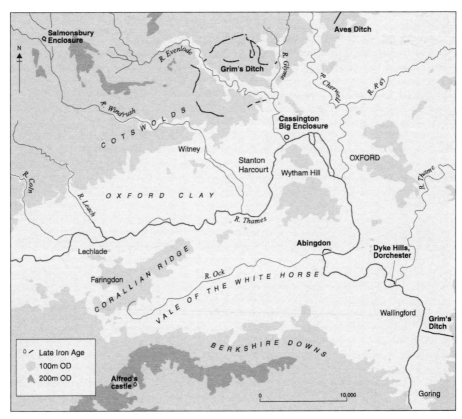

1.14 Location of forts and linear dyke systems of the late Iron Age in Oxfordshire and east Gloucestershire.

allegiances or alliances, and these defended sites in Oxfordshire may instead represent the foci of independent groups, each based around the catchment of a particular tributary of the Thames.

Cunliffe has seen the influx of Roman goods to the south-east as creating a 'core' zone of Romanising states, surrounded by a 'periphery' of others which were affected by the demands for exports from the core states in a variety of ways.[87] Among the commodities listed by the Roman writer Strabo were slaves, and it has generally been supposed that raiding by the core zone states to obtain slaves was common, resulting in increased insecurity in the periphery. In terms of the general settlement pattern there is little to suggest that 'open' settlements were now abandoned, or that individual farmsteads were now defended by substantial ditches. This evidence contrasts with that from Northamptonshire, where an increase in enclosed farmsteads is evident in the later middle and late Iron Age. Although the defences of a number of hillforts in Oxfordshire were refurbished late in the Iron Age, overall this suggests that Oxfordshire was not subject to significant dislocation of the middle Iron Age settlement pattern, as might have resulted from frequent raiding.

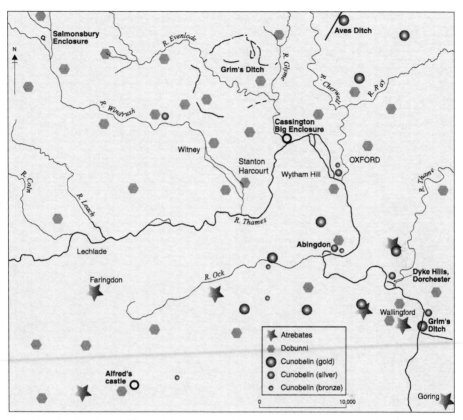

1.15 Map showing forts and linear dyke systems in relation to coinage distributions of the Dobunni, the Atrebates and Cunobelin of the Catuvellauni.

Whether or not a Catuvellaunian frontier defended by linear ditches and valley forts existed, the coin evidence certainly suggests that the Cherwell and the Thames below it represented a significant boundary between the Catuvellauni and the Dobunni (Fig. 1.15). Settlement evidence for Oxfordshire east of the Cherwell and Thames has until recently been slight, but in the last decade a number of important excavations, mostly around Bicester, have revealed a variety of Iron Age settlements. Bicester Fields Farm has revealed a late Iron Age enclosed settlement of two phases, while at Slade Farm close by there was a middle and late Iron Age unenclosed settlement. Aerial photography has recently revealed a probable 'banjo' enclosure (so-called because of the characteristic narrow ditched trackway leading out from the enclosure) just south-west of the Roman town of Alchester.[88]

One characteristic shared by the sites around Bicester is that their occupation appears to have ended at, or very soon after, the Roman conquest, in contrast to the rural settlements elsewhere in the county. This may indicate a different treatment of settlements close to the Roman fort at Alchester, or may possibly reflect a wider difference between the way in which the Catuvellauni, the Dobunni and the Atrebates were treated, the former being moved and resettled, the latter two being allowed to continue much as before.

To sum up, Iron Age Oxfordshire was a land of small and largely self-sufficient farms and hamlets, though these are often part of larger kinship groups acting in concert within larger territories, such as that around Abingdon, between the rivers Windrush and Thames around Stanton Harcourt or in the valley of the Sor Brook below Madmarston hillfort. Yet larger tribal groupings are evident from the very beginning of this period, as with the people of the White Horse on the Berkshire Downs. Similar groupings centred along the rivers Ock, Evenlode and Thame may be suggested from the emergence of much larger settlements, perhaps proto-towns, at their river mouths. These groups were part of large tribal groupings that appeared at the very end of the Iron Age, whose coins they used. Oxfordshire was the boundary of three such groups, and the Thames between Cassington and Wallingford was very much a frontier zone.

The late Iron Age in the south-east of England is really the result of the changes brought about by the influence of Rome, at first indirectly through the Gallic kinsmen with whom Roman traders came into contact, and after Caesar's conquest directly from the new Roman province of Gaul. Oxfordshire saw very little of the continental goods that are so significant in the development of an hierarchical society in the south-east, and the changes that characterise this period appear patchily and much later in time. Nevertheless, the people of this area were in contact through regional trade, and the indirect effects led to significant changes. New and larger settlement types appeared, while the roundhouse and the storage pit disappeared, and there was a shift in the crops grown and the balance of animals kept. These changes were also accompanied by the gradual introduction of coinage, of wheel-turned pottery in new vessel forms, and later the adoption of Roman dietary habits.

The 'enclosed oppida' had many of the attributes of the Roman towns that were to follow. Taxation may even have been introduced; the disappearance of the underground storage pit may have resulted from a demand that the harvest be visible for taxation purposes, since there is no evidence for improved storage arrangements in the late Iron Age. Much of the process of Romanisation had thus already begun before the Roman conquest.

NOTES

1. This geographical description is based upon Blair 1994, xv–xvi.
2. Allen et al. 1997, 120–5.
3. Robinson 1981; Robinson & Lambrick 1984b; Lambrick & Robinson 1988; Robinson 1992b.
4. Benson & Miles 1974.
5. Allen et al. 1997, 119.
6. Bulleid & Gray 1917.
7. Harding 1972; Lambrick 1984a, 173–6; Booth, Green & Allen in Lambrick et al. forthcoming.
8. The legends, their probable dates, the geographical locations of the coins that carry them and the Roman *civitates* or tribal groups to which they correspond are summarised in Millett 1990, 22, table 2.3.
9. Caesar, *de Bello Gallico*, iv, 20–38; v, 1–23.

10. See Millett 1990, Table 2.3, for the references in classical authors to names on the coins.
11. Haselgrove 1987, 201 and fig. 5.5.
12. Thomas 1980, 310–11; Yates 1999, 157–70.
13. Allen et al. 1997, 125.
14. Yates 1999, 160–2.
15. Thomas et al. 1986, 174–200; Cromarty et al. forthcoming c; Hingley 1983b.
16. Cromarty et al. forthcoming b.
17. Bradley & Ellison 1975; Needham & Ambers 1994.
18. Hingley & Miles 1984, 54–5.
19. Gent 1983.
20. Cromarty et al. forthcoming b; Mudd 1995.
21. Reynolds 1979, 71–82.
22. Harding 1972, pl. 26.
23. Lambrick 1988.
24. Grimes 1943; Harding 1972, 11–15 and pls 28–9; RCHME survey 1995.
25. Grimes 1943; Williams 1951; Hamlin 1963; Hamlin 1966; Mytum & Taylor 1981; Lambrick et al. forthcoming.
26. Hey 1991; Bell & Hey 1996; Sutermeister in Case et al. 1964; Saunders & Weaver 1999; OAU excavation in progress.
27. Eames 1998.
28. Harding 1972, 15 and pl. 27; Mytum 1986; Sauer 1999b, 67.
29. Lambrick 1988; Cromarty et al. forthcoming a; Allen 1990a; Allen & Robinson 1993; Miles 1986; Lambrick 1979; Gingell 1981.
30. Allen & Robinson 1993; Allen 1990.
31. Ainslie 1992; Everett & Eeles forthcoming.
32. Lambrick & Robinson 1979.
33. Atkinson 1942; Lambrick & McDonald 1985.
34. Allen 1991; 1993; 1998.
35. Allen 1990; Parrington 1978; Muir & Roberts forthcoming.
36. Barclay & Halpin 1999.
37. Lambrick 1992a, 89–93.
38. Lambrick et al. forthcoming.
39. Hingley 1984, 78–9.
40. Walker 1995; Hughes & Jones 1997; Cropper & Hardy 1997; P. Booth pers. comm.
41. Cromarty et al. forthcoming b.
42. Ford 1982a; 1982b.
43. Gosden & Lock 1999.
44. Cunliffe 1991, 533–4.
45. G. Lock pers. comm.
46. Miles & Palmer 1995.
47. Sellwood 1984, 198 and 200; Van Arsdell & de Jersey 1994, 8–12.
48. Mytum 1986.

49. Rhodes 1948; Hingley 1983.
50. Sutton 1966, 37; Lambrick 1984b, 104–5.
51. Hingley & Miles 1984, 54–5; Ainslie 1988, 94.
52. Avery et al. 1967.
53. Fowler 1960, 69–70 and fig. 18; Lambrick et al. forthcoming (Gravelly Guy).
54. Harding 1972, pls 78 and 79; Fitzpatrick 1984.
55. Allen 1997.
56. Harding 1972, 61–7 and pl. 33; Lambrick et al. forthcoming; Allen pers. comm.; Allen & Robinson 1993; Allen 1990.
57. Hey et al. 1999.
58. Case 1958; Harding 1972, pl. 72.
59. Cunliffe 1991, 510–16.
60. Harding 1972, 61–5; Harding 1987.
61. Kirk 1949; Goodchild & Kirk 1954; Harding 1972, 64–5 and pls 73 and 74; Bagnall Smith 1998. See also Chapter five below and illustration in Chapter eight.
62. Allen 1991; Allen et al. 1993, 52–3 and fig. 35.
63. Miles 1986.
64. Lambrick et al. forthcoming.
65. Hey 1995.
66. Cromarty et al. forthcoming a.
67. Allen et al. 1984.
68. Neal et al. 1990, 23–4.
69. S. Ford, interim report of excavations at Cippenham near Slough.
70. Harding 1972, 52 and pls 25a–b; Hingley & Miles 1984.
71. Hingley & Miles 1984, 65, 67 and fig. 4.9.
72. Collis 1984, 2–11.
73. Frere 1962.
74. Allen 1993; Allen 1997, 50.
75. Allen 1994.
76. Case 1982.
77. Dunning 1976.
78. Cunliffe 1991, 366–8.
79. Barnes et al. 1997, fig. 38.
80. Crawford 1930; Harden 1937b; Harding 1972, 56–9; Copeland 1988.
81. Clifford 1961.
82. See Mays 1992.
83. Dio Cassius lx, 20. For the distribution of Dobunnic coinage see Sellwood 1984; Van Arsdell & de Jersey 1994.
84. Sellwood 1984; Van Arsdell & de Jersey 1994.
85. Sauer 1999b.
86. Caesar, de Bello Gallico, v, 22.
87. Cunliffe 1991, 366–71.
88. Sauer & Crutchley 1998, 37.

CHAPTER TWO

OXFORDSHIRE IN THE ROMAN EMPIRE

It is clear that Oxfordshire was in no way a territorial unit in the Roman Empire; indeed as Dr John Blair shows the county did not come into existence until the end of the Anglo-Saxon period.[1] Politically Roman Oxfordshire was shared between three long-established *civitates*: the Catuvellauni, with their capital at Verulamium in the north-east, the Atrebates of Calleva (Silchester) south of the Thames and the Dobunni in the north-west, with their capital (from the end of the first century AD at least) at Corinium. Thus, while the people of what is now Oxfordshire possessed local market centres in small towns (notably Dorchester, Alchester) and other settlements secular or religious, including Abingdon, Asthall, Frilford, Swalcliffe and Woodeaton, administration at cantonal level was focused outside the county.

THE MAKING OF A PROTECTORATE

Despite this, in terms of the political geography of Roman Britain the region makes more sense as a unit than is popularly assumed, for it comprises a good deal of the northern section of that part of Britain which from the start, *c.* AD 43, embraced the Pax Romana. Of the three administrative centres mentioned above which all lie beyond the area of Oxfordshire, Calleva was an Iron Age oppidum, the northern capital of the Atrebates, allies of Rome. By the 50s it was probably controlled by the client king Tiberius Claudius Togidubnus. Verulamium, likewise partially sited on an Iron Age oppidum, was equally pro-Roman as is shown by recent excavations which again point to peaceful transition from pre-Roman to Roman times. The last king may have died in the reign of Nero and was given a lavish burial. By the time of the Boudiccan revolt of AD 60 it was a *municipium*. Here the Iceni and their allies exacted a terrible revenge on the Catuvellaunian population, precisely because of their alliance with Rome. But by AD 79 recovery was complete and the grand Flavian forum and basilica were inaugurated. A section of the tribe of the Dobunni, probably the eastern Dobunni of the Cotswold region, is mentioned by Cassius Dio as submitting to Aulus Plautius in AD 43. Here too a monarchy may have continued at least for a time.

Unlike Verulamium and Calleva, Corinium does not seem to have been founded until early Flavian times and the original settlement lay elsewhere, possibly at Bagendon.[2]

The version of the history of the so-called conquest of Britain recorded on the inscription on the Arch of Claudius at Rome and in Dio's much later epitome written in the third century was, of course, entirely angled to the needs of Roman propaganda in Rome and other parts of the Empire.[3] It is, in any case, far too concise to preserve anything much of the detailed diplomacy which must have gone on between Rome and the tribes and between the tribes themselves. Even so the main achievement recorded was merely bringing the tribes on the other side of Ocean under Roman control. The Atrebates – certainly that part of them under King Verica and his successor Togidubnus – were entirely supportive of the Roman forces which they would have regarded as liberators from the power of the Trinovantes of Essex, who under Cunobelin's sons Caratacus and Togodumnus had begun to threaten the security of their neighbours.

Diplomatic activity was perhaps centred on traditional meeting places and it is not fanciful to see boundary sanctuaries such as Frilford and Woodeaton as the sites where alliances were cemented, in the former between the Dobunni and the Atrebates and at the latter between the Dobunni and the western Catuvellauni, all of whom submitted to the Romans. By embracing the Roman side, most of Oxfordshire, along with neighbouring areas to west, south and east, saved itself from a heavy military presence. In contrast to the Norman conquest after 1066, there is very little indeed in the way of forts and hardly any stray finds south of Akeman Street. Professor Barry Cunliffe has noted that the army installation around Chichester and Fishbourne was 'significantly . . . the only military complex known within the Atrebatic domain' and nothing has since been discovered to challenge this observation.[4] At the important bridging point at the confluence of the Thames and Thame, Dorchester, there was possibly a fort but this would have been positioned to guard a key road from Silchester and the south. Essentially the Roman town of Dorchester, like Silchester and Verulamium, displays continuity from an Iron Age oppidum (here represented by Dyke Hills). Dorchester's strategic value is still evident in the presence of a *beneficiarius consularis* over a century and a half later.

The Thames today is often considered the boundary between southern England and the Midlands but, as John Steane has reminded us, it is a braided river separated in its middle section into many channels which run through its wide valley, and the best land route for east–west communications lies on higher ground to the north.[5] Akeman Street, running between Corinium and Verulamium, was constructed in the reign of Claudius, probably as early as AD 47 and like the contemporary Fosse Way, which passes close to the borders of Oxfordshire to the west, it has every appearance of being a frontier (*limes*).[6] As such it was the northern limit of what may be regarded as a Roman protectorate. Dio informs us that a garrison was left with the Dobunni (presumably to supply protection) and a fort has indeed been found on the site of Corinium. The evidence for a garrison at Verulamium is much less conclusive. There is certainly a quantity of finds of military metalwork from pits and graves and Professor Frere was convinced that there was a fort here, though its physical remains have proved elusive and the present excavator, Rosalind Niblett, explains the military objects found here as

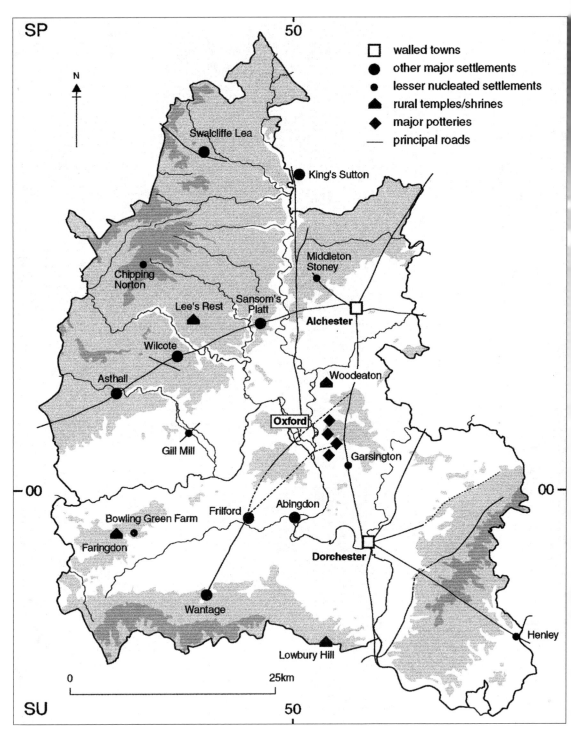

2.1   General map of Roman Oxfordshire showing principal settlements.

2.2 Roman military harness-
pendant of Neronian date
found just south of Alchester.
Height 60mm.

the possessions of members of the friendly Catuvellauni in many instances dedicated by
them to local deities.[7] Although one would not be surprised to find a fort like that at
Corinium in the vicinity, it would certainly be here to protect rather than to repress the
native population. Alchester, located centrally where the line of the road bulges forward
to its most northerly point, has recently yielded the most important evidence for a
military base on Akeman street. The first evidence is for a temporary camp but this was
followed by a vexillation fortress with associated parade ground, suggesting that it may
have been the pivotal point on this early frontier. For a short period Cirencester,
Alchester and (arguably) Verulamium probably supported vexillations of legionaries as
well as auxiliary units such as the ala Indiana and an ala Thracum attested by
tombstones from Cirencester.[8] There is also evidence for forts at other settlements on
Akeman Street including Asthall and Wilcote in Oxfordshire. Unlike the Norman
motte-and-bailey castles of a millennium later, these were not intended as strongpoints
from which to overawe the natives but rather to provide points of advance to subdue
the lands of less friendly tribes to the north, such as the Corieltauvi.

The Roman mission according to Vergil was 'to spare the meek and put down the rebellious' (parcere subiectis et debellare superbos) and Oxfordshire, together with the area of the modern counties of Berkshire, Surrey, Sussex, Hampshire and Wiltshire, would have been a beneficiary of the first of these options for control. Togidubnus' kingdom was probably enlarged after the Boudiccan revolt as a reward for his 'remarkable loyalty', to include the Belgae of Hampshire and Wiltshire, reaching the Fosse Way at Bath where the sculptural ornament of the Temple of Sulis Minerva extols Roman victory and culture through a wealth of imperial imagery including the great shield (*clipeus virtutis*), oak-leaf crown (*corona civica*), victories on globes, tritons indicative of naval victory and a star representing the deified Claudius. An inscription at Chichester gives Togidubnus the title *Rex Magnus Britanniae*, which he surely used with the favour of Rome; it may have been officially bestowed, possibly by Vespasian. The implications are that he was something like a 'High King' with over-seeing responsibilities throughout the region. The palace at Fishbourne was probably Togidubnus' main residence and there are contemporary villas along the Sussex and Hampshire coast, belonging it is thought to members of the local gentry.[9]

What happened in the northern part of this area, present-day Oxfordshire? Politically the county south of the Akeman Street line may have been administered for much of the later first century as part of Togidubnus' expanded realm. The population would have been very little disturbed by the coming of Rome except along the routes of Akeman Street and the north–south link from Alchester via the oppidum (and Roman small town) of Dorchester to Silchester and the south. Although a more profound peace now existed in the region, the virtual absence of the army or of any large concentration of settlement meant there was less stimulus for development than may have been found in some other areas. It would be a mistake, however, to think that there was anything very unusual in this. One of the topoi of Roman literature is the contrast between the sophistication of the town and the simplicity of the countryside as exemplified in the charming story told by Horace of the country mouse and the town mouse. The country mouse is in the end glad to leave the noise and violence of city life: 'I have no use for this way of life! Secure from dangers, my woods and my cave will comfort me with thin vetch.'[10]

At the top level the tribal leaders of the Dobunni and Catuvellauni were surely exposed to the benefits of Roman civilisation whether or not their monarchies remained, at least beyond the 50s. In the case of Verulamium the former tribal leaders are assumed to have become the town magistrates whose corporate identity is expressed by the municipal status of their city; this desire for status is likely to have been felt at Calleva and above all at Corinium. The centrality of the major settlement in the civitas, in Britain as in Gaul, would have tended to draw off local chieftains and their descendants, the 'sons of chiefs' mentioned by Tacitus, to the urban centres where they would have learned Latin and Roman ways and may, at least initially, have spent much of their time. Nevertheless the late first-century development of villas, including it seems Ditchley, Shakenoak and North Leigh, even if modest by Sussex standards, marks some spread of Romanisation into the rural landscape.[11]

As every local historian knows there is no such thing as absence of history, only absence of evidence. The inhabitants of Oxfordshire would have reacted to events, and known about the very different experience of enemies of Rome such as the Trinovantes and perhaps the eastern Catuvellauni who had suppressed them in the years before 43 and whose yoke they had thrown off with the arrival of the Roman army. They would also have known about the Roman campaign against the Durotriges and the Silures to the west. The storming of hillforts, dispossession of populations (for instance in the Colchester region for the fortress of legio XX and subsequently for the Colonia which took its place) and punitive taxation were experiences attested in the literary sources and sometimes confirmed by archaeology. In contrast, though there would almost certainly have been scores to settle between individuals in our region – and maybe some small elements of the population were dissatisfied – such minor dissent against Roman rule has left no mark.

The east of the county may have been affected, directly or indirectly, by Boudicca's revolt in AD 60, and news of the sack of Verulamium must have worried both the Romans and the natives of the area. Some of the military works and finds (Fig. 2.2) at Alchester date from this period. Boudicca's strategy would have been to cut off the Roman forces in Britain from the main port of entry and supply, still probably Chichester harbour. Certainly the route from Alchester to Dorchester, Silchester and the south coast must have assumed crucial strategic importance at a time when eastern Britain was in the hands of insurgents, and it is probable that links with the alternative entry ports in Kent, such as Richborough, had been cut. If Boudicca could only have sacked Silchester not only would she have punished the Atrebates for their support of the Romans but the position of the Roman army itself would have become desperate. It is just possible that the defeat of the rebellion occurred in the region of the Goring Gap, associated with the road just mentioned, though it is more likely that it lay much further east on the route between Staines and Silchester, perhaps at Virginia Water.[12]

The north–south road to the south coast and the east–west road (Akeman Street) were never the most important roads in the province, but they continued to have a role and were especially busy during imperial visits. Although such forays, notably those of Hadrian and Septimius Severus, were centred on northern Britain, many of the supplies were channelled through the south of the province, via London and from the south coast. It is no coincidence that the altar with screens set up to Jupiter Optimus Maximus at Dorchester by the *beneficiarius consularis*, Marcus Varius Severus (Fig. 2.3), seems to belong to the reign of Septimius Severus. It is likely that he had specific responsibility for securing supplies and expediting communications at the time of the *Expeditio Britannica* of 208–11. Another official with a similar task, perhaps more specifically concerned with supplying mounts to official travellers, was the *strator consularis*, one of whom is recorded on his tombstone at Irchester, Northamptonshire. Interestingly Silchester has yielded a cake stamp celebrating Severus' victories and a gem from a signet-ring depicting Caracalla as the Genius of the Roman people. The first of these in particular demonstrates local rejoicing at the successful outcome of the war in the north.[13]

For the inhabitants of Britain Roman roads served an even more important function. They were an essential part of the infrastructure of provincial life, allowing swift communications between major and minor towns as well as linking the villas and the villages of the countryside. The system in Britain was similar to that found in

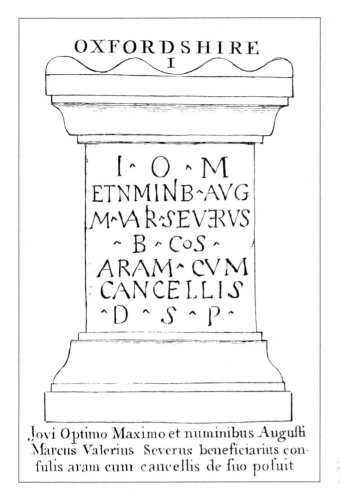

I · O · M
ETNMINB·AVG
M·VAR·SEVERVS
· B · CoS ·
ARAM· CVM
CANCELLIS
·D · S · P ·

Jovi Optimo Maximo et numinibus Augusti
Marcus Valerius Severus beneficiarius con-
sulis aram cum cancellis de suo posuit

2.3   Altar from Dorchester, after Horsley,
Britannia Romana.

other provinces, notably Gaul, though distances between towns were often rather greater here.[14]

It might be concluded that relative to many other areas the Oxford region was incorporated into the Roman Empire so quietly, decisively and painlessly that it condemned itself to remaining something of a cultural backwater within the province. The Romans, like the Greeks before them, thought of their culture in terms of towns, and where there was no *municipium* or even a *civitas* capital it was impossible to enjoy all the benefits of *humanitas*. Civilisation meant the sort of life that was enjoyed by a citizen; one could not be urbane outside an *urbs*. It is true that such towns needed the countryside for food and raw materials – clay for pots, stone for building, wool and flax for clothing – and that all of these were available in Oxfordshire; but these products were largely enjoyed in neighbouring cantonal capitals and even beyond, in the provincial capital of Londinium, for example. People living in what is now Oxfordshire would in other words have thought of themselves as Catuvellauni

(Verulamium men), Atrebates (Silchester men) or Dobunni (Cirencester men). As Greg Woolf wrote with regard to Gaul, 'there was no great gulf between Romanized cities and Gallic hinterland'. An inscription from Bath shows that Priscus son of Toutius was happy to designate himself a *civis Carnutenus*. Sculpture was a town-based craft and Priscus may have come from Chartres, but the tribal designation was sufficient.[15]

The towns that mattered administratively, and for those at the highest level socially, were these three large chartered cities. In the late Roman period Cirencester was evidently the capital of the province of Britannia Prima. It is not known in which province the others were then placed but it is possible that the Atrebates were in the same province (which would have kept intact the territorial integrity of the area once ruled as part of the first-century kingdom). The Catuvellauni seem most logically to have come within the province of Maxima Caesariensis with its capital at London.[16]

In a famous series of *topoi*, Tacitus cites 'Templa, Fora, Domos' as the necessities for urban life. Temples were to be found everywhere but what Tacitus had in mind was no doubt the official veneration of the gods of the Roman state and the imperial cult of deified emperors and of the 'numen' of the living ruler.[17] Classical-style temples were certainly attached to the Verulamium Forum and there is every reason to believe that State cults were established in the other civitas capitals. Certainly the basilica of such a city served as an assize-court and with its council-chamber (*curia*) was the focus of local administration which assumed a thoroughly Roman character. The shops and offices around the Forum were significant too, though commerce could find a home in smaller centres. The *domos* were not ordinary dwellings but grander houses, as used by town councillors, often with mosaic pavements and frescoes in the second century, and here again we find them in the tribal centres. The town houses with their second-century mosaics in Verulamium, Silchester and Cirencester demonstrate that the classes which produced the merchants, town councillors and administrators did well. Other *topoi*, the spread of oratory, of baths and of banquets, need not in theory have been so limited but in fact Tacitus was all the time thinking of his urban ideal. The 'sons of chiefs' he mentions as so adept at learning Latin were being groomed for the city lawcourts rather than for a life of rusticity.

Smaller towns like Alchester, Dorchester and perhaps Abingdon were technically *vici*, like the *vicus Salodurus* (Solothurn near Augst) or the *vici* in and around Rome. Undoubtedly such places served a market function and farmers from some small villas may have looked to them to sell their produce.[18] Presumably they had magistrates to regulate their own affairs. Inscriptions have been found in a few small settlements in Britain, and rather more in Gaul, which throw some light on administration. For example an inscribed panel from the small town (*vicus*) of Brough-on-Humber is the dedication of a theatre-stage by an *aedile*. Did some such official donate a stage-building to Frilford? In Britain, as in Italy and Gaul, *magistri vici* had a prominent religious function. For instance, the *magister* of the village of Vic-sur-Seille in Gaul set up a dedication to Mercury while at Old Carlisle the *magistri* collected money from the villagers to dedicate an altar to Jupiter and Vulcan for the welfare of the Emperor. There is a large altar from Cirencester dedicated to the local genius of the place. None of the uninscribed Oxfordshire altars comes from a small town and private dedication has been assumed, but it is possible that the Bablock Hythe altar, for example, was set up by the local community of the *vicus* or *pagus* at a river crossing.[19]

It is possible that, as village headmen, such officials may have had some responsibility for tax collection as their counterparts did in Egypt. However, the real leaders of British society would not on the whole have been found here, so far away from the centres of power, but rather in the cantonal capitals where they could aspire to the prestige of being *duoviri* (that is, local consuls). A small town had no need for lawcourts and offices (basilica and forum) and for the most part substantial public buildings such as temples are also lacking although, for both local needs and the ease of travellers, the provision of baths was another matter. Often planning was haphazard or non-existent. Alchester is exceptional in its orthogonal grid, large temple and public baths, evidently well appointed and arguing a status superior to most. It is just possible that in the course of time it became the administrative centre for the western

2.4   Altar showing a *Genius*, from Bablock Hythe. Height 685mm. Photo: Ashmolean Museum.

Catuvellauni. We are reminded that when the younger Pliny went unexpectedly for a brief visit to his Laurentine property, he would use the ample bathing facilities of the nearby small town rather than make his slaves fire the villa baths.[20]

Large and small towns were not the only settlement types in Roman Britain (or Gaul). Rural sanctuaries with ancillary buildings, often in effect large villages, are also known. Frilford has yielded evidence of temples but also of an amphitheatre or, more probably, a theatre-amphitheatre for meetings, presumably in connection with cult. A similar complex existed at Gosbecks near Colchester and such sanctuaries are well known in Gaul, for instance at Sanxay or Fontaines Sallées, where they provide the main settlement foci for dispersed rural populations. It is possible that there were originally other structures at Woodeaton and that it, too, was part of a religious centre. The word sometimes used for such a site is a *conciliabulum*, though this legal term for a centre of a country district or *pagus* is not actually used after the Republic.[21]

The typical 'villa' in the county, as elsewhere in Britain, was merely a farm like Ditchley, Shakenoak or Barton Court Farm which remained relatively modest in size and appointment through the Roman period (Fig. 4.2), though this does not mean that the Oxfordshire area was poor or did not produce a surplus. All these farms have yielded rich finds such as glass drinking cups, indicating the drinking of wine in Roman-style banquets. Larger villas with mosaic-floored rooms are a feature of the Cotswold region in the north-west of the county, perhaps suggesting that as in the Trier region and especially manifested by the reliefs of the Igel tomb, larger profits could be made from sheep-ranching. It is not certain that even luxurious villas such as North Leigh were necessarilly the preserve of a single nuclear family; they may have housed his dependants or clients as well. This has been suggested in the case of Thruxton in Hampshire where a mosaic gives the name of the patron, Quintus Natalius Natalinus, and his clients the Bodeni. Such continuity of traditional Celtic farming patterns has been suggested not only for Picardy but even in Aquitaine. But it has something in common with the paternalistic Roman ideal of farm management expressed by the Latin poets.[22]

Even so it is a truism of Roman life that material success was often easier for a slave than it was for a peasant, provided that he or she was ambitious or at least lucky and was able to obtain freedom and wealth. Petronius' Trimalchio is the notorious example in Latin fiction. The free peasant, after all, was at the mercy of the weather and of fluctuating prices whether he lived in Italy or Britain. While there is nothing to show where Regina, the Catuvellaunian freedwoman and wife of a Palmyrene merchant called Barates, originated within her natal *civitas* nor how she came to be a slave in the first place, her tombstone at South Shields (Co. Durham), the work of a Syrian sculptor, is one of the best from the province. The slave running the goldsmith's shop at Malton was surely making his way to a fortune; does the jewellery mould from Alchester (Fig. 5.20a) point to a similar upwardly mobile entrepreneur?[23]

Of course the urban rich could spend their money in the countryside, for the sake of prestige, embellishing public sanctuaries with further buildings such as theatres (who paid for the construction of the amphitheatre at Frilford?), arches and sculptures, and above all acquiring estates – a process which probably began fairly early and can again be compared with what was happening in Gaul.

LATE ROMAN OXFORDSHIRE IN THE ROMAN WORLD

The history of the county during this period is either mythical or hard to reconstruct. We cannot, for example, give much credence to Oxfordshire having an important place in the history of the British usurper Allectus. Largely because of a misunderstanding of the name Alchester, Allectus was long believed to have been defeated in Oxfordshire. However, it is not unlikely that both Carausius (AD 286–93) and Allectus (AD 293–6) passed through the area at some point in their progresses through their realm, though there is no evidence for this. The building of vital coastal forts at Pevensey and Portchester would certainly have enhanced the importance of existing north–south routes considerably. In 296 Constantius Chlorus' general Asclepiodotus seems to have landed near the Isle of Wight and defeated and killed Allectus, probably near the coast rather than as far north as the Thames.

The fourth century in Britain was a time of prosperity, at least for country landowners, as is well exemplified by such villas as North Leigh and Stonesfield, both presumably within the administrative area of Britannia Prima. There were signs of insecurity in late Roman Britain as provincials felt less in touch with an increasingly autocratic and militarised imperial court. Political events may be reflected in a coin hoard from Woodeaton ending in *c.* 340 because this was the year that Constans defeated and killed his brother Constantine II who had ruled in Britain. This may have triggered disaffection in the province and two years later Constans made a hurried trip to Britain in mid-winter. Britain was certainly the epicentre of the usurpation of Magnentius in 350 and another Woodeaton coin hoard consists of coins of Magnentius and Decentius. We know that Constantius II sent a commissioner called Paulus to root out former supporters of Magnentius after his fall in 353, and this hoard may have been buried then. Some villas in southern Britain, such as Thruxton in Hampshire, even appear to have been abandoned at this time as a result of estate confiscation, but as yet there is no evidence that any Oxfordshire villa was so affected.

In its essentials the relationship between town and country did not change in the later Empire even though, as we have seen, Britain was split into four provinces. Large houses with mosaic pavements in all three major cities show that the curiales still lived there in comfort, even if they also had country seats. Cirencester was much more successful than the other two cities because of its capital status but Neil Faulkner's suggestion that it was 'designed to bolster the military bureaucratic complex' can be refuted. Unlike Trier it was not the seat of emperors and its mosaic pavements are matched by those in its many satellite villas including those of the Oxfordshire Cotswolds which show every sign of organic development.[24]

There was, in fact, a new emphasis on country life throughout the Roman Empire. The larger sort of Roman villa was in many respects comparable with the eighteenth-century country house, sufficiently large to support a village-sized community of its own including (as has been suggested) dependants. Such palatial establishments as North Leigh, Stonesfield and Wigginton acted as centres of power for their owners. Although they could probably be reached in as little as half a day from Corinium, for most purposes they were self-sufficient. The same situation existed in Gaul as late as the fifth century as the writings of Sidonius Apollinaris attest.[25]

Such estates were major economic enterprises whose products may have included woollen goods such as the hooded cloak called the *birrus Britannicus*, depicted on a mosaic at Chedworth beyond the county border in Gloucestershire, and a rug known as the *tapete Britannicum*, both of them listed in Diocletian's Edict of Maximum Prices. In some ways the Dobunnic region called by Hingley 'the richest area for villas in the province' can be compared with the Moselle valley in the region of Trier, whose well-appointed villas producing both textiles and wine are described by the poet Ausonius, though they are best known to archaeologists from the vivid scenes of country life shown on funerary monuments such as the reliefs from Neumagen or the tomb at Igel. The Cotswold region corresponds to an area of great late medieval wool churches and it is tempting to see the villas of the fourth century and the churches of the fifteenth resulting from the same sort of surplus wealth.[26]

Such gentlemanly farming can be contrasted with the organisation of industry. Although there was at least one well-appointed house with a mosaic at Swalcliffe possibly associated with iron production, the largest-scale production of late Roman Oxfordshire was the pottery industry which, like that of the Nene Valley and the New Forest, stands out as having much more than a local significance. Although centred on modern Cowley and Headington, there was no town at Oxford to act as a market centre and the settlement that sprawled along the gravel terrace on which Oxford lies, along the Banbury Road to North Oxford, was profoundly rural. It is notable that excavation of graves in the area has produced plenty of pottery but nothing much that suggests refinement and culture. So far no large villas (though there are some smaller ones) are known here and, unlike the area of the Nene Valley, no sign of wealth going into mosaics, silverware or other luxuries locally. Many of the workers, including Tamesubugus, were assuredly British, but the financial capital which directed the potteries and creamed off their profits must have come from elsewhere. The best analogy may be the lead and silver mines in Britain and Spain which were leased out to wealthy businessmen, perhaps operating through local bailiffs. In the late Empire we know that British estates were owned by rich families of senatorial rank in Italy, for example those of the Christian heiress Melania, and it is just as likely that such estates were in part at least industrial than that they were agricultural.

The most significant change, empire-wide, in the fourth century was the shift from traditional religious practices to the acceptance of Christianity as the official religion of the Empire. The presence of Christianity in the Catuvellaunian civitas is suggested by the martyrdom of Alban, generally placed in the third century. Although there was possibly some conflation with a pre-existing pagan cult at Folly Lane on the next hill to the abbey, north of Verulamium, and although it could be argued that Alban met his death in the aftermath of the revolt of Albinus (under Septimius Severus) or the usurpation of Allectus (under Constantius Chlorus), there is no doubt that the Christian cult of the saint was well established by the end of Roman rule. At Corinium, the re-erection of a Jupiter column to the *prisca religio* perhaps demonstrates the attempt to restore the pagan cults under Julian, *c.* 360–3, but chi-rhos at Chedworth and an early Christian intaglio depicting the Good Shepherd from

Barnsley Park, also in Gloucestershire, show unequivocally that Christianity was present among the Dobunni. In the south the building at Silchester known as 'the church' is more controversial and is not well dated. It may be a church, though it has been proposed that it was used for a pagan cult or served the purposes of administration, after the basilica went out of use.[27]

The only overtly Christian object from the county (or rather formerly in the county as it comes from Caversham) is a lead font embellished with a chi-rho. Its findspot north of the Thames places it in the civitas of the Catuvellauni. Once Verulamium had its saint, it may have begun to attract a higher Christian population than the other neighbouring civitates. Even so, if Professor Charles Thomas's surmise that such tanks were carried about on ox-carts to be set up in temporary baptisteries is true, it contributes to the argument that, even here, Christianity was very much a minority religion. The name Pagan(us) implies someone from a *pagus*, a country dweller, and the lack of towns in the county would have rendered the advance of Christianity slow and uncertain, even in the fourth century when most of the emperors were Christian.[28]

At Dorchester the situation may have changed in very late Roman times. The large number of late Roman coins from the town, the silver hoard and significant graves suggest growing importance. Did it acquire an enhanced administrative role which perhaps originated with its long-established importance as a communications post? Unlike Silchester, for instance, it lay on the river system which was vital for the passage of men and goods. As proposed by Parker, this is suggested by its later history when Birinus, in the aftermath of the Augustinian mission, took the site as the seat of his bishopric. After the end of Roman political control Christianity provided a beacon of tranquillity and there is evidence from Dorchester (see Chapter six) that the Church made considerable headway, a phenomenon found elsewhere in Britain, for instance at Lincoln and Wroxeter, as well as widely in Gaul. The site of the abbey outside the East Gate could represent a cemetery church, the site of a *cella memoriae*, as was the case at St Albans (outside Verulamium) or at Vetera/Xanten (Ad Sanctos) in Germany. Briefly and intermittently one of the small towns of Roman Britain was to become one of the most important cities in Anglo-Saxon England.[29]

Despite the lack of documents we can thus suggest an outline of how Oxfordshire developed in the Roman period. Although we do not have the unity that an entire civitas would provide, and it lacks any urban focus, it provides an excellent sample of civilian Roman Britain, allowing us to study its rural economy, settlement and culture both on the uplands and in the river valleys. The study of Roman Britain does sometimes tend to be centred on military affairs which very largely passed Oxfordshire by. Central southern Britain had more in common with large parts of northern Gaul than we often think. The Roman Empire, whatever it may have meant at the level of senatorial propaganda, was basically a commonwealth, an arrangement allowing the peoples of central and southern Europe, western Asia and North Africa to live peacefully at the cost of limited outside interference such as tax collection. The gain for almost all was the spread of technology and luxury goods (in Britain including wine, oil and samian pottery). There was little reason to abandon this system until it broke down through the strains of economic and military demand elsewhere. The end of Roman Britain as a political event occured in the first decade of the fifth century with the sudden termination of the money supply to pay the troops. Such dislocation must surely have occasioned major disturbances but need not have been totally catastrophic. At first ad hoc arrangements and the use of old coin would have sufficed but it is touching to see how something of Roman organisation was preserved in the neighbouring cantonal capitals until the end of the fifth century at least, as it did also at Dorchester, which may have continued even longer and perhaps even assumed a higher status. As in Gaul, archaeology is tending to suggest continuity in terms of settlement and population through and across periods, not only in towns but in the farming countryside (as at Yarnton). However, from the sixth century, society can hardly any longer be called Roman in the way that term has been used in this book. Not only did an influx of populations from elsewhere, largely from north-west Germany and Denmark, introduce new settlement patterns and languages whose impact would have been decisive even among the descendants of the local Britons, but the whole province, including the Oxfordshire area, underwent a cultural change as profound as that which we designate 'Romanisation'.

In much of Oxfordshire, in the Thames valley for instance, there was never any landowner of the wealth and standing of Sidonius Apollinaris or his associates in Gaul. The great Cotswold villas had no ready markets after the collapse of the Roman trade system; they were too far along the lines of communication from southern Europe or even the Trier region to survive as flourishing concerns for any time. We do not know to what degree the owners of these estates became economic migrants or whether any stayed to sink to an economic level comparable with their peasantry or perhaps to become bandits or war lords joining groups such as the *Gewissae*, 'the chaps', ancestral to the West Saxons but containing in their lineage men like Cerdic (=Caradoc). If so, we are more than a little reminded of the Iron Age Britain of small fearful clans under powerful overlords from whom the coming of Roman literacy, organisation and law had delivered three and a half centuries of welcome relief.

NOTES

1. Blair 1994, 102–5.
2. Wacher 1995, 271–9 (Calleva); Wacher 1995, 214–27 and Niblett 1999 (Verulamium); Wacher 1995, 302–6 and see Cassius Dio lx, 20, 2 (Corinium).
3. Barrett 1991; Webster 1993, 170, 200–2.
4. Cunliffe 1991, 164–5.
5. Steane 1996, 14–16.
6. I am grateful to Roger Ainslie for sharing with me his views on this subject in advance of publication.
7. Wacher 1995, 219, proposes a very short military occupation but this is questioned by Niblett 1999.
8. G. Webster in Henig 1993, nos 138 and 137.

9. Vergil, *Aeneid* vi, 851. For the concept of southern Britain as a 'protectorate' after AD 43 see Henig in *British Archaeology*, Sept. 1998, 8–9; RIB 91 (Chichester inscription); on the meaning of the sculpture of the Bath temple see Henig 1999c and 2000.
10. Horace, *Satires* ii. 6, 77–117.
11. N. Faulkner in Holbrook 1998, 377–8. For the Oxfordshire villas cited see Hingley 1989, 109, fig. 59; Rudling 1998 for the Sussex villas.
12. Fuentes 1983 provides the evidence and suggests that the archers mentioned by Dio lxii, 12, 3–4, may have been Atrebatan allies.
13. For the *beneficiarius consularis* at Dorchester and *strator consularis* at Irchester see Burnham &

Wacher 1990, 33–4. Boon 1958 (cake stamp); Marsden 1997, 4 and pl. 1A (gem).

14. Woolf 1998, chapter 5.

15. Woolf 1998, chapter 6; Priscus son of Toutius, RIB 149.

16 Faulkner's view of late Roman Cirencester is to be found in Holbrook 1998, 379–84.

17. Tacitus, *Agricola* 21.

18. Burnham & Wacher 1990, 35; see Frederiksen 1976 on Italy.

19. Burnham & Wacher 1990, 39; for cults in Italy see Zanker 1988, 131–5.

20. Tax collection in Egypt, Bowman 1986, 76–7; for local bathing facilities see Pliny, *Letters* 2, 17.

21. King 1990, 91–2. See OCD, 3rd edn, 375.

22. For the Hampshire villas see Henig & Soffe 1993; for Gaul see King 1990, 92–4.

23. RIB 1065 (Regina); RIB 712 (Malton goldsmith).

24. See note 15 for Faulkner's view.

25. For Sidonius Apollinaris see Stevens 1933, chapter 4.

26. Hingley 1989, 137 and figs 61 and 66 (Cotswold villas). See Ausonius, *Mosella*, and Wightman 1970, 183–92 and pls 14–20 for country life in the Treviran countryside.

27. RIB 103 (Cirencester), 128 (Chedworth); Henig 1978, no. 361 (Barnsley Park intaglio). For doubts about the Silchester church see King 1983.

28. Thomas 1981, 220–7 for the lead tanks. See OCD, 3rd edn, 1091 for use of term pagan.

29. Thomas 1981, chapter 7 for extra-mural churches in Britain and on the continent.

CHAPTER THREE

THE PATTERN OF MAJOR SETTLEMENTS

COMMUNICATIONS

Among the most evident impacts of the Roman presence in the years after the conquest was the development of a network of major roads.[1] Initially, the more significant of these roads were important in strategic military terms. Later they came not only to provide local as well as long-distance communication but also to link the settlements of varying sizes which grew up alongside them. In many cases these sites developed in new locations along the roads, but in a smaller number of instances roads were directed towards pre-existing centres of settlement. This certainly seems to have been the case at Dorchester, where the major road north from Silchester was routed close to the important pre-Roman settlement and subsequent Roman fort. On a much larger scale it seems likely that the principal east–west axis through the county, Akeman Street, was deliberately aligned to run through the territory enclosed by the North Oxfordshire Grim's Ditch. This area, which was a notable focus of high-status rural settlement from the later first century AD onwards, was clearly of great significance in the immediately pre-conquest period, even though the exact nature of this significance is uncertain. For whatever reason, the Romans seem to have felt it important to route a major road right through the middle of this complex, but there is no firm evidence to support the view that the road followed a significant earlier route.

Akeman Street was probably one of the very earliest major Roman roads in the county and its line must have been established within a decade or so of the conquest, even if it was not surfaced until a little later. It ran westwards from Verulamium (St Albans) to Corinium (Cirencester), thus linking what were to become two of the most important towns of Roman Britain. From the east Akeman Street entered the modern county along the line of the present A41 just south of Bicester, passing north of Otmoor in the vicinity of the Roman town of Alchester. Here, in what was later to become part of the extramural settlement of the Roman town, the construction of the road was associated with the excavation of a large ditch parallel to it some 60m to the north, which served as a watercourse and would have formed a very pronounced boundary to the roadside zone – in itself a major piece of construction. At Chesterton, just north-west of Alchester, the line of Akeman Street turned slightly south of west to cross the Cherwell near Kirtlington and traverse the southern edge of the Cotswolds and the other tributaries of the Thames on its way to Cirencester. The road surface, generally of stone, is well preserved in places, but at Wilcote, for example, it is completely absent, probably as a result of later ploughing, the position of the road being marked by a zone defined on one side by large quarry pits. The very early Roman fills of some of these suggest that road construction was probably underway within a few years of the Roman arrival in Britain.[2]

The principal north–south road through the county lay in its eastern part, forming part of a route which linked Silchester in the south with Watling Street in Northamptonshire. This road ran up the west side of the Thames valley, though its precise course is not always clear south of Streatley, and crossed the river just south of Dorchester-on-Thames before also crossing the Thame in order to reach the Roman town. From Dorchester the course of the road northwards through the eastern margins of Oxford is fairly clear.[3] From about the end of the first century AD the road ran directly to Alchester across Otmoor, since a probable timber bridge structure on its line at Fencott is dated by dendrochronology to *c*. AD 95 or a little later.[4] Before this time, however, it probably followed a drier route, or routes, with perhaps one to the east of Otmoor and another to the west of it through Noke and Islip,[5] though it is less clear how the latter route then reached Alchester. North of Alchester the road ran roughly north-north-east towards Towcester on Watling Street.

Another important road line, aligned north-north-east/south-south-west, was more central to the county. This may have run across the Berkshire Downs from a point on Ermin Street (the road from Silchester to Cirencester), perhaps at Baydon in Wiltshire,[6] but is not confidently identified until it reaches the vicinity of Wantage. Thence the road ran through Frilford to a crossing of the Thames at Oxford. While the exact location of this has been debated it is likely that there were two crossing sites. The more southerly, marking the continuation of the road over Boars Hill, was probably at Redbridge, continuing thence north-eastwards, and presumably crossing the main channel of the Thames in the vicinity of the modern Donnington Bridge, before running through Headington towards the Dorchester–Alchester road.[7] A second route, perhaps crossing the Thames in the general area of the present-day approach from the west, then linked to a more confidently identified north–south line along the Banbury road through North Oxford,[8] crossing the Cherwell near Kidlington and the line of Akeman Street at Kirtlington. Later known as the Portway, this road headed up the east side of the Cherwell valley to the large settlement of Kings Sutton, just in Northamptonshire. A number of branches have been suggested running north-eastwards from the northern part of this route, but one of these, Aves Ditch, now appears to have been a pre-Roman earthwork rather than a Roman road.[9] In the same general area a road running north-westwards from Alchester through Middleton Stoney presumably linked with the main north–south route. Further north, part of a north-west/south-east aligned road is known near Swalcliffe. This ran into Warwickshire, to the Fosse Way and beyond, while to the south-east it probably headed to Kings Sutton and thence to the Alchester–Towcester road further east in Northamptonshire.[10]

Apart from its position on the Silchester–Alchester road, Dorchester was an important link in the road system in the south-eastern part of the county. One road ran to Henley, where it crossed the Thames to join the road from Verulamium to Silchester. Another road ran north-eastwards towards Akeman Street at Fleet Marston in Buckinghamshire. In the same area the line of the prehistoric Icknield Way along the edge of the Chilterns may have continued in use, though a 'Romanised' version, the Lower Icknield Way, lay to the north of the escarpment and is thought to have linked to Dorchester.[11] Other pre-Roman tracks may also have been perpetuated in the Roman period. Many lesser roads are known or suspected in the county, with varying degrees of certainty. Only the major roads would have been regularly surfaced, and detection and dating of minor roads, of which there must have been many, is extremely difficult archaeologically. In the Thames valley itself some minor roads are identified from the air, usually as trackways defined by ditches. Even so, these can rarely be traced for great distances and their courses are often irregular, in contrast with the relatively straight alignments of the more major roads. In some instances they may reflect pre-Roman alignments, but the majority of well-defined trackways which have been examined by excavation seem to date to the second century or later, rather than to the earliest part of the Roman period.

The river Thames was also presumably important for communication, though its use is much less easy to demonstrate archaeologically. It is generally agreed that the Thames would probably have been navigable at least as far upstream as Oxford in the Roman period and some aspects of the distribution of pottery from the major late Roman Oxford industry suggest that the river was used to transport products of this industry downstream, for example to London and north Kent. No concrete evidence of this in the form of wharves or boats has been found on the Thames in Oxfordshire, but wharves might well have existed, with potential locations perhaps near the crossing(s) at Oxford, or at Sandford and Dorchester. The extent to which any of the tributaries of the Thames might have been used for communication is, however, quite unknown.

SETTLEMENT PATTERN

Besides the relatively immediate impact of the major roads and the more short-lived military establishments the onset of Roman occupation brought both direct and indirect changes to the pattern of settlement. Most rural settlements, the base of the great majority of the population throughout the Roman period, were little affected by the conquest in the short term, at least as far as their location and essential physical appearance were concerned, though a few sites may have ceased to be occupied around the time of the conquest. New types of site soon appeared at points along the major roads and there was more gradual development of settlement forms in the countryside, of which the first and most conspicuous aspect was the appearance of villas, in some cases as early as the later first century AD, while in the second century there was significant disruption in the rural settlement pattern in a number of places. These issues are discussed in the next chapter. Overall, however, the Roman period saw a greater variety of settlement type and size than the preceding Iron Age, and some of the larger sites are discussed now.

While there were no examples of very large towns in the region, since the principal cities of the tribes within whose territories Oxfordshire lay (St Albans, Silchester and Cirencester) were all situated well outside the county, a wide range of types of Roman settlement can nevertheless be identified. These settlements can be arranged hierarchically on the basis of various criteria including size, morphology (settlement form), complexity of plan and function, and the nature and density of building types. This kind of analysis can be useful in aiding understanding of the relationships between sites, but there is no clear correlation between most stages of such a settlement hierarchy and, for example, any organised system of local government. Those sites generally accepted to have been the most important (the walled towns of Alchester and Dorchester) probably had a local administrative role, and similar minor functions may have been carried out at other settlements, but most variations in settlement type resulted from social and economic factors. Many of these centres were probably most important as markets and local service centres for the surrounding agricultural communities and some may also have had more specialised functions, for example as religious sanctuaries, as perhaps at Frilford.

Alchester and Dorchester were among the few settlements in the county which can be confidently described as 'small towns', a term used to distinguish sites with some urban characteristics but without the substantial public buildings and usually without the regular street grid typical of the large tribal centres mentioned above. The label 'small town' is also used for a variety of other extensive 'nucleated' settlements (i.e. those in which occupation is densely concentrated), defended or undefended, usually located on main roads and sometimes also referred to as 'roadside settlements'. The terminology for larger Romano-British settlement sites, including also 'minor settlement' and 'village', is often imprecise. A degree of overlap and uncertainty in drawing distinctions between one site type and another is often unavoidable given the state of the evidence – the confidence with which a particular site can be categorised is often in direct proportion to the amount of information available, as we shall see. Ultimately, however, it is more important to understand how individual settlements developed, functioned and related to one another than it is to be able to label them, so the careful use of models of settlement hierarchy can be an aid to interpretation but not a substitute for archaeological evidence.[12]

ALCHESTER

Alchester was the largest (and is the best understood) of the major settlements, though even here knowledge of many aspects of the town is sketchy.[13] Fortunately the excavated evidence, which is limited in quantity, particularly for the area within the walls where it mostly derives from work carried out in the 1920s, is supplemented by high-quality aerial photographs (Fig. 3.1). The town wall formed an almost exactly square enclosure of some 10.5ha, but there was extensive extramural settlement as well, so that the total occupied area may have been as much as 40 or 45ha.[14] It is now

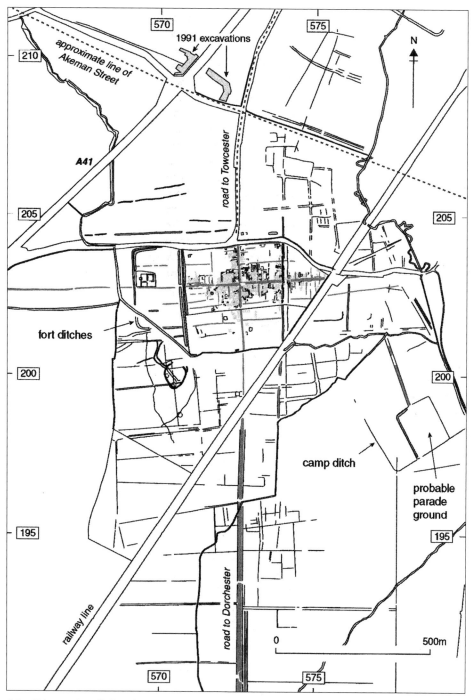

3.1 Alchester. Overall plan of the Roman town from aerial photographs. After RCHME with additions.

known that there was considerable military activity at the site, probably of several distinct phases, before the development of the town proper. Aerial photographs show the western part of a double-ditched fort lying west of and parallel to the west wall of the town. Excavation in 1999 has confirmed that some of these ditches probably belonged to a base for a substantial mixed battle group of infantry and cavalry, a type of site sometimes called a vexillation fortress. Coins and other evidence suggest that this dates to very early in the conquest period.[15]

Just south-east of the later town a substantial temporary camp, identified from the air, probably also belongs to the early years of the conquest period. This camp was succeeded on the same alignment by a smaller ditched enclosure approached from the north by a trackway defined by ditches. Recent work has resulted in the convincing identification of this feature as a parade ground – probably one of the earliest examples of this type of site from the Roman empire – which must have been associated with a fort. Whether this was the installation west of the walled town, or a later one beneath the town, is unknown. The overall distribution of military metalwork and other finds and features suggest that there may have been at least two forts in this general area. Further pieces of military metalwork have been found some distance south of the town and elsewhere, but their significance is less clear (Fig. 2.2).[16]

This evidence potentially transforms our understanding of the origins of Alchester as a town. There is as yet little indication of the detailed chronology of the various military phases but the presence of a branch road running towards them south-westwards and then west from Akeman Street suggests that at least one of the forts post-dated the establishment of the major road. It is possible that the military sequence lasted until after the revolt of Boudicca in AD 60/61. It is less clear what relationship the early stages of the town bore to the military activity. One well-established model of town development in Roman Britain sees military origins as particularly important. It is envisaged that a civilian settlement or *vicus* would have grown up alongside the fort, and although some of its inhabitants would have followed the army when the fort was abandoned, others would have remained to provide a nucleus of inhabitants as the town developed under civil administration once the army had moved on – an event which in this region is likely to have occurred in the 70s. More recently, many scholars have played down the importance of the army as a stimulus to settlement. It has been pointed out that there is relatively little hard evidence for early *vici*, and other factors have been invoked to account for the growth of towns. Nevertheless it can hardly be coincidence that the only two walled towns in Roman Oxfordshire were both located on certain or probable military sites, whatever the mechanisms that connected the abandonment of these sites by the army and their development as civil towns. In the case of Alchester, sited in an area where drainage was a recurring problem, the fact that the military may have already taken some steps to deal with the problem could have been a particular factor in encouraging reuse of the location for the civilian settlement.

Within the walled area of Alchester the earliest buildings associated with the town were dated to the later first century, and it certainly seems that the alignment of one or more fort phases – almost exactly north-south/east-west – determined the alignment of the central part of the town. The principal north-south road through the town,

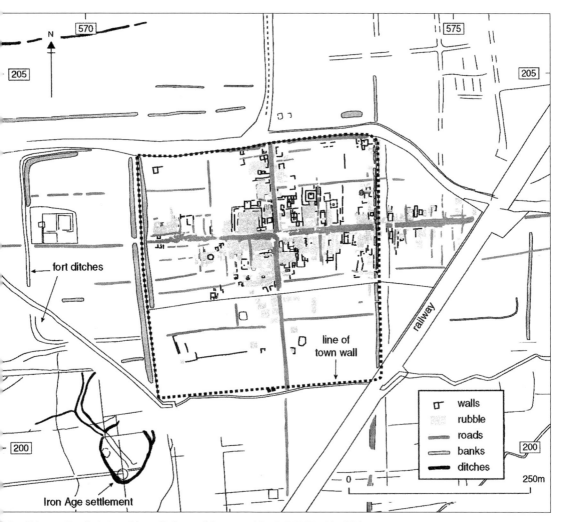

fort ditches

line of town wall

	walls
	rubble
	roads
	banks
	ditches

0 ——————— 250m

Iron Age settlement

3.2 Alchester. Detailed plan of the walled part of the town. After RCHME with additions.

which was established by the end of the first century, was probably later than the east–west axis which connected with the spur road to Akeman Street mentioned above. Once the north–south (Dorchester–Towcester) road was in place the stretch of Akeman Street between the two junctions – with the spur road to the east and with the north–south road directly north of the town – may have fallen into relative disuse, to judge from the paucity of physical evidence for it. Through (east–west) traffic may then have been mostly routed via the town.

The most obvious characteristic of Alchester from the air is the more or less regular street grid, which is most unusual among Romano-British small towns (Fig. 3.2). Elements of a wider rectilinear layout, including possible trackways or minor roads north of the walled area and an extensive arrangement of property boundaries to the south, can also be seen, but north of the junction of the Towcester road with Akeman Street, some 350m from the north gate of the town, the alignment of plot and probably field boundaries beyond was determined by that of Akeman Street, roughly north-north-west/south-south-east. The four-square outline of the defensive circuit is also evident from the air, but the town defences are relatively poorly preserved on the ground. Excavation on the eastern side has shown that they consisted of a stone wall some 2.5m thick fronting an earthwork bank up to 6m wide, with a wide shallow ditch outside which held standing water, in its early phases at least.[17] Somewhat unusually, the wall and bank were contemporary – in the majority of urban defensive circuits stone walls were a later addition to earthwork ramparts, as at Dorchester. Their construction, very likely in the last quarter of the second century AD, has been linked to that of a number of similar circuits in east central England at about the same time and it has been suggested that this campaign of defence building reflects a specific crisis in the region at this time.[18] However this may be, the defences formed a very substantial enclosure, within the region second only to those of the tribal centres in extent.

Despite excavation within the walled town, mainly in the 1920s, the best evidence for the general character of its structures comes from aerial photographs, recently plotted by RCHME. These show that the principal concentration of buildings lay around the central, slightly staggered, crossroads, with the frontages of the two axial roads fairly densely built up. On the east–west street this concentration extended for some considerable distance beyond the east gate, and beyond the walls to the west lay a substantial building, perhaps a bath-house, examined in 1766 and extensively damaged by stone-robbing around 1800.[19] Within the walls the most noticeable structure is a large walled enclosure in the north-west angle of the central crossroads, partly examined in the late nineteenth century. This is likely to have been a temple precinct enclosing a shrine which lay against its north side. A further typical Romano-Celtic temple of double square plan lay within the north-eastern quadrant of the town, set back from the main east–west road frontage, while south-west of the central crossroads a circular structure, perhaps with an associated colonnade, could possibly have been another temple. Other structures visible from the air are less easily interpreted in the absence of excavation, since in places elements of buildings of different phases may appear together. Nevertheless, buildings of the 'strip' type characteristic of small and larger towns – having a narrow frontage on to the street, and usually interpreted as shops or workshops with domestic accommodation either at the rear or perhaps on an upper floor – can be identified. All these buildings had stone foundations, and at least some may have had superstructures in stone, while the upper parts of others were probably timber-framed. Excavation in the 1920s revealed parts of some half a dozen stone-founded buildings of relatively simple rectilinear plan in the north-east quadrant of the town (one close to the eastern defences, the others in the north-east angle of the central crossroads) with the use of stone commencing perhaps as early as the late first century. Some had been preceded by timber structures, but because of the scale of excavation none of these is known in detail.

The concentration of stone buildings revealed from the air at Alchester is very much confined to the central area of the town and to the main road axes running through it.

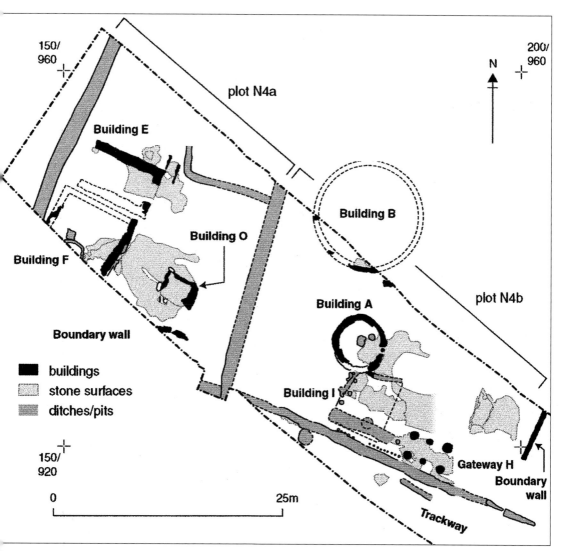

.3   Alchester. Part of the northern extramural settlement area, showing the early/mid fourth-century phase. The buildings, in two
istinct plots or property units divided by a ditch, probably belong to separate farms.

The significance of this is uncertain because of lack of excavation. It is possible that the
more marginal areas within the walls were not densely built up – they could have been
occupied by gardens, or perhaps by minor structures built of timber or other materials
which would not usually show up on aerial photographs. If these areas were not utilised
for buildings, however, it raises the questions of why extramural settlement was
apparently extensive, particularly in the area north of the walls, and why such a large
space was enclosed within the defences. Neither question can be answered at present.

Excavation in the northern extramural settlement area in 1991 produced evidence for an interesting sequence of development and a wide variety of buildings, many of which, however, were relatively poorly preserved.[20] A wide trackway or 'back lane' was established parallel to the line of Akeman Street and north of it, adjacent to the large ditch which had initially defined the road zone, by the late first century. Development of this area probably did not take place until a little later, however. The area between Akeman Street and the track was then divided into plots, and further plots were established north of the 'back lane' beyond the original line of the large ditch, these events and the construction of the earliest buildings probably not taking place before the mid-second century. Settlement north of the 'back lane' intensified from about the mid-third century, when one of the plots was subdivided, each half containing a farm with buildings and paved stone yards (Fig. 3.3). In the early fourth century one of these complexes was entered through a timber gatehouse and a stone wall divided this unit from one adjacent plot. In the middle of the farmyard was a small stone-built round structure, with a further, larger, round building or pen beyond. The first building had a timber outbuilding attached. These unpretentious structures were not particularly urban in character, but the establishments they represent would have been important in providing agricultural produce for the town and its markets. As such they may have been more characteristic of the margins of small towns than is sometimes realised.

Cemeteries were also typical of such locations. At Alchester, however, these are little known. Two small groups of east–west aligned inhumations (16 and 28 respectively) were found near the south-east corner of the walls in the nineteenth century, but it is unclear if these belonged to one of the principal cemeteries of the town. In the northern extramural area some thirty inhumations, comprising most if not all of a discrete group of burials immediately outside the settlement boundary, may have formed a family burial plot, or at most served a small sub-community of the town. This cemetery is important in that it had an adjacent and probably related post-Roman phase (see below).

DORCHESTER-ON-THAMES

Like Alchester, Dorchester was the scene of early Roman military activity, and was later walled, and it is also similar in having had only relatively limited investigation by excavation, for the most part located within the walls.[21] Since the walled town lies largely beneath the present village, however, there is nothing to compare with the aerial evidence from Alchester in providing a general view of the layout and character of the town. Unlike Alchester, Dorchester was probably a site of considerable importance in the immediate pre-Roman period, on the assumption that the site at Dyke Hills was occupied at this time and this factor and its significance for communications, at an important river crossing, would have made the location entirely appropriate as the site of a fort in the early years of the conquest period. The factors of good communications and a pre-existing settlement focus may have been more important in the development of the Roman settlement, however.

The extent and size of the fort remain uncertain, but buildings thought to be of military character were excavated in 1963 roughly in the middle of the western part of the walled area.[22] While some reservations have been expressed about the military origins of the town the cumulative evidence, including that of the coins and pottery, is strong, though it is notable that the main concentrations of early Roman pottery, including imported material, seem to lie south of the excavated military structures. As no certain evidence for military defences has yet been located, however, the significance of this possible distinction is unclear. It could be, however, that the material to the south represents settlement pre-dating the establishment of the fort, which is not thought to have taken place until after AD 60, though at least two ditches or gullies found in this area were on an alignment almost at right angles to that of the 1963 military buildings, and could thus reflect the same overall layout of the site.[23]

Despite the importance of its location, Dorchester seems to have been considerably smaller than Alchester (Fig. 3.4). There is relatively little evidence for extensive extramural settlement and while sites are known in the vicinity of the town – for example at Bishop's Court some 500m north-west of the walls[24] – these appear to be agricultural in character and, unlike the suburban farms of Alchester, do not form part of a continuum of settlement extending from the town centre. The size of the settlement focus itself is in some doubt, however, as the extent of the defensive circuit, which presumably enclosed the nucleus of existing settlement, is uncertain. As at Alchester these defences were probably constructed in the later second century AD, but here they initially took the form of an earthwork bank with an associated ditch. A stone wall was then added, probably in the later part of the third century, the front of the earlier bank being cut back to accommodate the wall. Presumably at the same time, though possibly later, the second-century ditch was replaced with a much wider ditch lying further from the line of the wall, the earthwork bank behind the wall being raised simultaneously. This pattern of modification of town defences is a common one in Roman Britain, and the resiting and enlarging of the defensive ditch is a feature often associated with the addition of towers to the wall perhaps, but by no means certainly, intended for artillery. Such towers were not always added to the walls of small towns, however, and there is as yet no clear evidence for their provision at Dorchester, the remodelling of the ditch being suggestive but not conclusive.

The line of the defences is well established on the west and in the western part of the north and south sides, but evidence for the location of its eastern side is ambiguous. It was most probably situated just to the west of the abbey, where a large wall was located in 1961, producing an elongated rectangular defended outline, but this leaves unresolved the questions of why the adjacent topographical high point (now occupied by the abbey) should not have been incorporated within the circuit or indeed why the abbey itself should have been sited outside the walls.[25] One possibility is that the later abbey was located within a Roman cemetery, to which a Roman building reportedly beneath the abbey might also have belonged.[26] An alternative view would see this area as also enclosed by the Roman town defences, but this seems less likely to have been the case. The failure to locate the eastern defences on their more widely accepted alignment at the Old Castle Inn in 1972[27] may be explained by the suggestion that the large ditch encountered there was in fact part of the town defences

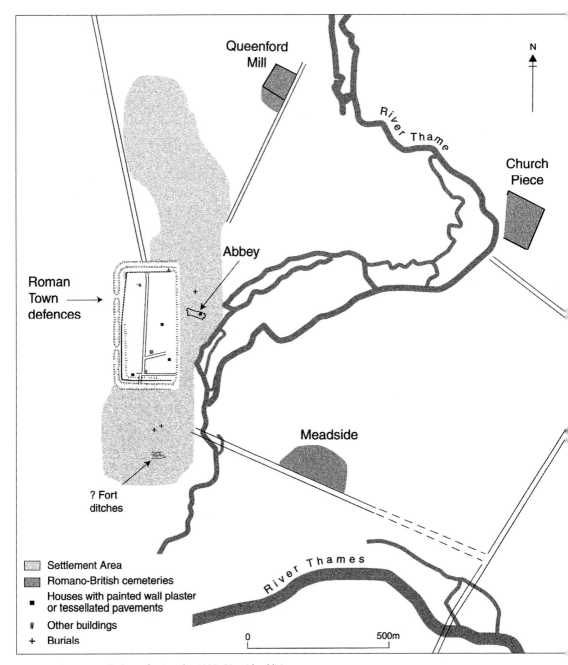

3.4   Dorchester overall plan. After Rowley 1985, 22, with additions.

which terminated at the edge of the excavation in line with a known east–west street alignment, thus marking the position of a gateway in the eastern defences which would have lain just west of the site. Assuming that the 1961 wall was indeed the east wall of the town the enclosed area would have been about 5.5ha.

This elongated rectangular defended area was roughly bisected by a north–south axial road, likely to have been established well before the defences were built. Curiously, however, this road did not extend immediately south of a side street which ran mainly eastwards from its line just inside and parallel to the south defences. A possible southerly continuation of the axial road here, offset to the west from its main alignment, appears to have been put out of commission by the earthwork defences. A little further north was another side street, not quite parallel to the southerly one.

The early development of the civilian town is not well understood. Military activity could have continued as late as AD 90. While this is about the time that civilian building construction was underway at Alchester, the earliest certainly identified structure here, of timber, is no earlier than about the mid-second century.[28] The overall plan of this building and of timber structures probably of comparable date (though thought to be later by the excavator) at the Old Castle Inn remain unclear, however.

There is rather better evidence for later Roman buildings, the majority of which at least had stone foundations if not stone superstructures. Such buildings include a possible aisled structure of mid-third-century origin, on an anomalous north-west/south-east alignment situated in the north-west corner of the town. In the late Roman period this was partly demolished and its site occupied by about a dozen hearths or ovens, apparently used for lime burning.[29] A not dissimilar building lay east of the axial north–south street close to the centre of the town, while further south and west of the street was another building with corridor or aisled elements, of late fourth-century date and containing traces of a tessellated pavement in its south aisle. A little further south again a simple three-roomed building, with its long axis parallel to the street line, was also of very late Roman date.[30]

The existence of further probable stone buildings can be inferred from earlier records of tessellated floors. Examples of the latter, suggesting substantial town houses, are recorded just west of the High Street, at a point which might have lain just inside the eastern defences of the town, and in the south-west corner of the defended circuit. Another stone building is noted from beneath the abbey. Painted wall plaster, recorded in several locations, could also have derived from such buildings but might equally have come from timber structures, as seems to have been the case at the Old Castle Inn, for example.

There is relatively little evidence for economic functions in the town, but the close connections between even settlements at the upper end of the regional hierarchy and the surrounding countryside is indicated by the presence of agricultural implements in two late Roman ironwork hoards from within the town.[31] The significance of the possible lime-burning kilns from the Beech House site is unclear – the development of this site in the late Roman period is seen as 'industrial', and certainly the number of kilns or ovens suggests fairly intensive activity, thought by the excavators to be possibly producing material for agricultural use, but there is no direct evidence for the nature of the activities involved here.[32] Less equivocal industrial activity in the immediate area is represented by a group of pottery vessels including production waste of late first- or early second-century date, from a well beneath the abbey.

An important eighteenth-century discovery may have some bearing on one of the roles of the town, however. This was an altar erected to Jupiter and the *numinibus Augustorum* (divinities of the Emperor(s)) by Marcus Varius Severus, a *beneficiarius consularis* (Fig. 2.3). This official, responsible to the provincial governor, probably had duties relating to control of military supplies and transport. The dedication also tells us that Severus had erected an altar (presumably that on which the inscription was cut) with screens, giving some idea of the shrine in which the altar would originally have been placed.[33]

One additional aspect of the archaeology of Dorchester which is particularly important is its cemeteries. A number of burials are known in the vicinity of the town, including an early third-century cremation with glass vessels from the Vicarage garden,[34] and a rather more extensive cemetery may have lain alongside the road running south-east from the southern end of the town. Dorchester is somewhat unusual among small towns, however, in having two substantial and relatively well-defined late Roman cemeteries associated with it. These were at Queenford Mill to the north, a site partly examined during construction of the Dorchester bypass, and at Church Piece, Warborough,[35] on the opposite bank of the Thame from Dorchester and about a kilometre distant, though on present evidence there may have been no direct road access from the town to the cemetery, which would have been approached by a rather circuitous route. Both cemeteries contained rows of orderly, roughly east–west aligned burials set out in defined enclosures. The burials were of fourth-century and (in at least some cases) later date, generally without grave goods, and may have been Christian. The evidence of the cemeteries, as indeed that of a number of the buildings within the defended circuit of Dorchester, is of particular significance in understanding the latest phases of Romano-British activity in the region, and is discussed further below (see Chapter seven).

The two walled towns are the sites most likely to have had official functions related to local or provincial administration. While there is no direct evidence for the former, the inscription of the *beneficiarius consularis* from Dorchester is confirmation of the latter. One of only two other inscriptions from the county is a fragment from the northern extramural area of Alchester, where it was presumably redeposited, having most likely originated in a building within the walled town (Fig. 8.9). Unfortunately the inscription is too fragmentary to be interpreted, but it is cut on Purbeck Marble with very high-quality letters, perhaps suggesting some form of imperial dedication. Such inscriptions are very rare from small towns and the presence of a local dignitary at least, if not a government official of some kind, is implied.

Both Alchester and Dorchester may have had official functions in relation to their positions in the communications network, and this may indeed be the context for the presence of the *beneficiarius consularis* at Dorchester (see Chapter two). None of the major roads through Oxfordshire appears in any of the Roman route books such as the Antonine Itinerary, however. One consequence of this is that the Roman names for the settlements are not known (with the possible exception that Alchester might have been the *Alauna* of the Ravenna Cosmography, though this is more likely to have been Alcester in Warwickshire).[36] Another consequence is that there is no external indication of the likely locations of the installations of the *cursus publicus*, the imperial post, which provided a network of posting stations for travellers, particularly those on government business. The establishment of such facilities, *mansiones* and *mutationes* (inns and changing posts), on the major roads has been seen as a major impetus behind the growth of many roadside settlements,[37] but some scholars see other factors as more important in many cases and most are agreed that the majority of such settlements were multifunctional, though generally with a variety of economic aspects to the fore.[38] It is uncertain how many of the through roads in the region might have been regular routes for the *cursus publicus*, and it is perhaps possible to argue from the absence of references in sources such as the Antonine Itinerary that none was, but Akeman Street at least seems a likely candidate, linking as it did two of the most important cities of Roman Britain. The scale of examination of the sites along this road is such that the present lack of evidence for official establishments could easily be changed. Moreover, Black's study of the *cursus publicus* in Britain has shown that buildings interpreted as being associated with it do not always conform to the 'typical' courtyard plan of the best-known examples, so the absence of buildings of the classic ground plan is not necessarily conclusive either. It may be noted that the courtyard complex in the north-west angle of the central crossroads at Alchester has been suggested as a possible *mansio*,[39] though this interpretation seems unlikely. Another large building closer to the west gate of Alchester may be a more viable contender, but again this is speculative.

OTHER ROADSIDE SETTLEMENTS

A number of other roadside settlements are now known or suspected within the county, though the evidence for some is quite slight, which makes their position in the regional settlement hierarchy unclear. On Akeman Street, for example, these sites include Grendon Underwood, east of Alchester and just in Buckinghamshire, which is very poorly known. West of Alchester, however, is a sequence of better-known sites. The first of these, some 12km from Alchester, is at Sansom's Platt, close to the crossing of the river Glyme north of Woodstock. This has been known for many years as an extensive scatter of surface material in fields south of Akeman Street, with limited evidence from a pipeline excavation for a substantial building interpreted as a possible villa.[40] Recent aerial photographs taken by RCHME have transformed our understanding of the site, showing that its focus was not apparently Akeman Street itself but a road diverging from it in a south-westerly direction (Fig. 3.5). Both frontages of this minor road are densely built up with substantial stone structures for a distance of at least some 200m. Closest to Akeman Street, within a roughly triangular walled enclosure between the minor road and a further lane, is a Romano-Celtic

3.5   Sansom's Platt, aerial view of settlement. Akeman Street runs across the top of the picture while the principal buildings front of to a minor road. To the right a circular temple can be seen within a walled enclosure. (RCHME. NMR 15456/16, 15.7.1996)

temple of concentric circular plan. The possible villa building can now be seen as one of the structures on the north-west side of the minor road. In total the settlement may have covered at least 4 or 5 ha, almost entirely to the south of Akeman Street. Features have also been located alongside Akeman Street at Sansom's Farm[41] and there was clearly activity in the vicinity of that road, but its relationship to the apparent focus of the settlement around the minor road, and the destination of the latter, remain uncertain.

A further 18km from Sansom's Platt there was a large settlement at Asthall, on the west bank of the Windrush.[42] The site has some similarities of character with Sansom's Platt, but was perhaps rather larger (Fig. 3.6). In contrast to Sansom's Platt, however,

Akeman Street formed the principal axis of the settlement, though aerial photographs show the presence of a number of rather irregular side streets running from the main road on both sides, three of those to the south being joined at their southern ends to form a loop through that part of the settlement. Here, as at nearby Wilcote, the settlement clearly developed once the line of Akeman Street was established. The extent to which an early military presence was a factor in the development process is uncertain, but a small camp, itself respecting the line of Akeman Street, lay some 500m south-west of the settlement, and a number of items of military metalwork and a bone *gladius* (sword) handle were found in excavations in 1992, though no military features were definitely identified.

The 1992 excavations provide the bulk of our detailed evidence for the settlement. In Site A, adjacent to Akeman Street, the road was shown to have been resurfaced numerous times and was fronted on its south-east side by a variety of buildings, most of which were probably of 'strip' type, but the relatively narrow excavated area, along the route of a pipeline, did not permit the recovery of complete building plans. The earliest buildings were of timber, only roughly datable to the mid to late first century. By the mid-second century two of these buildings were reconstructed with substantial stone foundations. A timber annexe to one of the buildings, facing on to a minor side street, contained a sequence of well-built ovens, perhaps for baking. On the other side of the side street a late third/fourth-century building was also stone-based, but with less solid foundations. Burnt deposits within this building produced crucible fragments, one of which had probably been used for refining silver from lead.

Metalworking was seen elsewhere in the settlement. Towards its southern edge, in Site B, a smithy of second/third-century date was identified. This marginal location was later used for a cemetery which lay within a ditched enclosure. Further burials are located on the north and north-west sides of the settlement, but it is unclear if these were part of a formal cemetery.[43] Other marginal activities included quarrying for gravel and building stone, with probable pits for the former located just south-west of the 1992 excavations,[44] and likely stone pits known from the air at the end of the north–south ridge which approaches the south-eastern fringes of the settlement from the south.

Even the 1992 Site A was probably quite close to the edge of the settlement. Nearer to the centre, evidence from aerial photographs indicates that the Akeman Street frontage was continuously built up on both sides, though this was not necessarily the case along the side streets running south from the main road. Details of the buildings are hard to discern and those which are identifiable mostly appear to have been of relatively simple rectilinear plan. One exception is a probable circular building located close to the line of Akeman Street on its south side. This could have been a domestic or agricultural building like those seen in the extramural area at Alchester, but a shrine is another possibility. At least one larger building lay within the southern part of the settlement. Here, the parchmarks of a substantial structure were noted on the ground in the dry summer of 1976.[45] It is unclear if this was a large town house or if it served some other function, perhaps even as a *mansio*. The field which contains the focus of the settlement is now pasture, but in the past has produced large quantities of Roman material including many coins. These indicate that while the marginal settlement areas examined in 1992 might not have been occupied up to the end of the Roman period – there is no conclusive evidence for occupation in Site A much after the middle of the fourth century – the central area saw continued activity at least to the end of the fourth century.

The next major settlement to the west along Akeman Street was at Coln St Aldwyn's/Quenington in Gloucestershire. This, like Asthall, was situated at a river crossing. It is relatively little known, however.[46] Between Asthall and Sansom's Platt a further roadside site lay at Wilcote, but this was apparently of rather different character, on the basis of the sample excavated to date.[47] As already mentioned, this site owes its location to the presence if not the actual construction of Akeman Street, as it appears to have been established very early in the Roman period. It may accurately be defined as a 'roadside settlement' since surface traces suggest that it consisted of a strip of activity only about 100m wide with the road in the centre. Although the road itself does not generally survive its line is indicated by a featureless band through the site. This was bounded to the north by a 'roadside' ditch, with another ditch some 26 or 27m north again, interpreted as marking the limit of the roadside zone. The earliest features examined were the roadside ditch itself and, to the south, a number of very large quarry pits, presumably linked to the extraction of material for the road. A number of these were at least partly filled in the Claudian period (AD 43–54). The extent to which the army might have been involved in these operations is uncertain, though its general concern with road construction is clear. There are no specifically military objects from Wilcote, but some other finds, including early coins and aspects of the pottery, are consistent with, though they do not conclusively demonstrate, a military presence. Structural evidence from the site is scarce,[48] but of three fairly slight timber buildings, reminiscent of some of the early buildings at Asthall and principally of post-hole construction, one was dated to the later first century. The dating of the other two is uncertain. No late Roman buildings are known and evidence for late Roman activity is sporadic, though the fact that this might have been intensive in places is indicated by deposits such as a very large group of fourth-century pottery and other finds from the upper fill of one of the quarry pits and the presence of quantities of late Roman coins from an area west of that examined by excavation. Since the excavator suggests that Akeman Street itself has been removed by later ploughing, this seems the most likely explanation for the absence of later Roman deposits, but the relatively scarcity of finds of any date in the topsoil does present a problem to this interpretation.

Dorchester, Alchester and the other Akeman Street settlements thus present a variety of types of nucleated site. A similar variety was found on the other major roads in the region, and there were further sites apparently of related types which did not necessarily lie on any main road. On the Dorchester–Alchester road there is evidence for settlement at Garsington, which is little known but likely to have been closely connected with the nearby pottery industry. North-west of Alchester a small settlement probably adjacent to a Roman road at Middleton Stoney[49] included a rectilinear stone-founded building probably of 'strip' type, a form not encountered in rural sites in the region, and implying that the site might have been more extensive than appears from excavation, since this sort of building is usually encountered only in

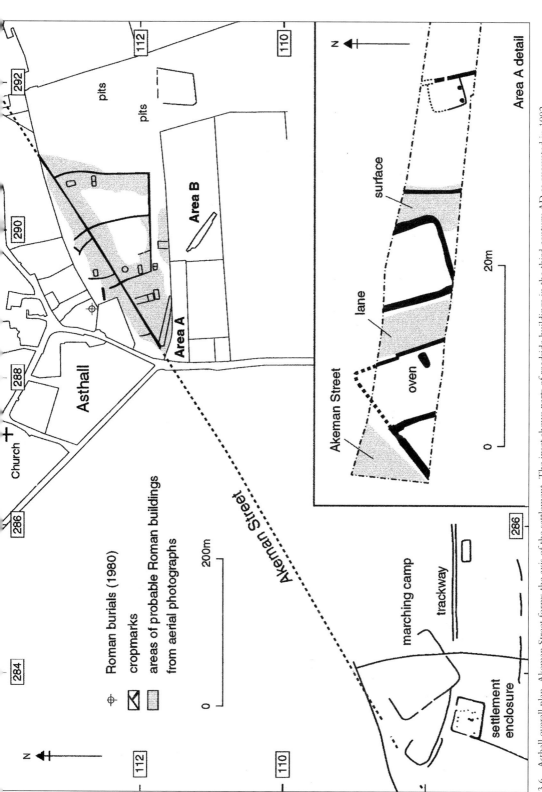

3.6   Asthall overall plan. Akeman Street forms the axis of the settlement. The inset shows parts of roadside buildings in the third century AD as excavated in 1992.

situations where road-frontage space was at a premium. The main period of occupation here was between the late second and late third centuries. Early Roman features did occur but first- and early second-century material was often residual, and very small quantities of fourth-century material were interpreted as deriving from a continuously occupied settlement to which the excavated site was peripheral.[50] It was suggested that the finds, including the pottery, indicated that the site was of higher status in the first to mid-second century than later, but a comparison of the pottery data from this phase with that from contemporary sites in the region does not support this conclusion.[51]

In the north of the county a more substantial settlement lay at Swalcliffe Lea, astride the road from Kings Sutton to the Fosse Way in Warwickshire and beyond (Fig. 3.7). This was one of relatively few sites of this type to be closely related to a substantial pre-Roman settlement, being situated adjacent to the hillfort of Madmarston Hill, within which there was at least some late Roman settlement, identified from surface finds. Activity on the lower ground to the south could also have been under way before the Roman conquest, however. The later Roman settlement in this area covered at least 24 ha.[52] It contained a number of stone-built structures, one of which had two very poorly preserved fourth-century mosaic pavements and was of 'small villa' character – in a later phase it had probable smithing hearths inserted into its floors.[53] At least one other building also produced evidence of ironworking in the late Roman period (Fig. 3.8), and there are consistent references to slag at several locations.[54] It is not clear if any of this derived from smelting, but this is possible given the location of the site in the ironstone area of the county.

Other large and potentially nucleated sites have been suggested at Bloxham and Chipping Norton, but the evidence for both of these is limited and does not allow their character to be clearly judged. Neither site lay on a main road, however. Bloxham is sufficiently close to Swalcliffe Lea for it to be doubted that it was a major centre in its own right. Surface finds suggest that the site at Chipping Norton might have been quite extensive. The discovery of a fine carved head, probably of Jupiter, may indicate the presence of a shrine within the settlement.[55]

Further south, the best-known major settlements are at Frilford and Abingdon. The site at Frilford lay astride the road running south-south-west from Oxford, close to the point where this crossed the river Ock (Fig. 3.9). A major focus of this site was its important temple complex, complete with amphitheatre, but while the site was much more extensive than this, these are the only components of it which have been examined by excavation in relatively recent times.[56] Evidence for its extent is based mainly on surface finds, however, with a little information from aerial photographs. As plotted, the surface finds suggest a number of discrete concentrations of activity, perhaps covering a total area of 30 ha, but it is uncertain if this represents a true picture – i.e. whether these concentrations were distinct or whether they were linked components of a single major site. Because of these limitations it is not possible to determine the role of the temple complex in relation to the rest of the settlement. In Burnham & Wacher's study of the small towns of Roman Britain Frilford is grouped with a number of sites which are considered to have a specialised religious function.[57] This view results from the prominence of the temple complex, but the evidence from

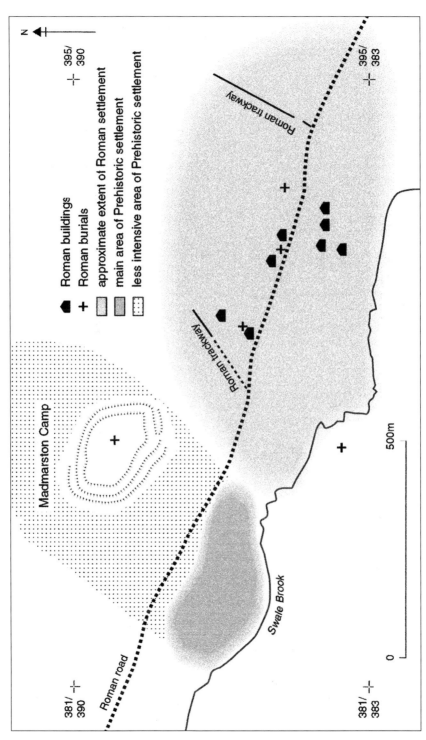

Roman buildings
Roman burials
approximate extent of Roman settlement
main area of Prehistoric settlement
less intensive area of Prehistoric settlement

Madmarston Camp

Roman road

Swale Brook

Roman trackway

Roman trackway

381/
390

395/
390

381/
383

395/
383

N

0   500m

3.7   Swalcliffe Lea overall plan. After Eames 1998, fig. 1.

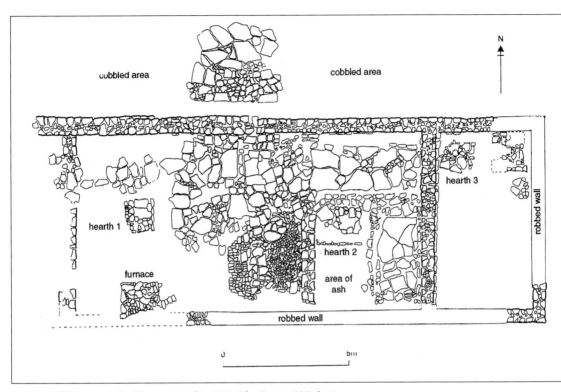

cobbled area

cobbled area

N

hearth 3

robbed wall

hearth 1

furnace

hearth 2

area of
ash

robbed wall

0　　　　　　　　　　5m

3.8　Swalcliffe Lea, 'strip' building excavated in 1966. After Eames 1998, fig. 6.

other major settlements in the region (e.g. Alchester, Sansom's Platt and Gill Mill,
Ducklington) shows that temples were a normal component of such sites and the
extent to which they provided the essential *raison d'être* for settlements of this kind can
be debated.[58] An important aspect of the Frilford site was the late Roman cemetery
located in the north-western part of the settlement. Unfortunately much of this was
recorded in the nineteenth century during quarrying and many details are obscure, not
least the exact relationship with an early Anglo-Saxon cemetery in the same area,
some burials of which appeared to cut Roman inhumations.[59]

South of Frilford there is growing evidence for a settlement adjacent to the Roman
road at Wantage. While the character of this site is still rather uncertain an increasing
number of finds can be interpreted within the framework of a roadside settlement.[60]
At Stockholm Way/Denchworth Road, close to the probable line of the Roman road,
first- and second-century features were succeeded in the third century by a fairly
substantial 'villa-style building' which was occupied until the late fourth century.[61]
Some 200m south-east of this site, features at Mill Street included ditched enclosures
on an alignment which could be seen as reflecting approximately the line of the
Roman road roughly 200m distant to the west. Associated structures consisted of a
probable domestic building and two further buildings, one probably of second-century

date in timber and a fourth-century one, roughly 10m square, with stone foundations, both interpreted as granaries.[62] The site appears to be of an agricultural nature, but as it lies some distance from the anticipated line of the road this would not be inconsistent with marginal activities related to a roadside settlement. A number of isolated discoveries over a fairly wide area would, if all related to the same site, certainly suggest a fairly extensive settlement.[63]

East of Frilford lies Abingdon, the importance of which at about the time of the conquest has already been discussed. The subsequent development and the function of this site in the local settlement pattern is far from clear, however, but among other factors which may be relevant is the apparent absence of any major road link, though there was presumably some sort of road between Frilford and Abingdon, and the position of the latter adjacent to the Thames at a possible river crossing may have been more important in terms of communications. Within the area of the probably late Iron Age earthworks no first-century Roman buildings have been certainly identified. A substantial building with herringbone masonry excavated in the nineteenth century in East St Helen's Street is not closely dated, though it has been tentatively associated with a nearby building for which an early second-century *terminus post quem* is possible.[64] A single, potentially large stone structure at The Vineyard may have been built as early as the second century, but the clearest evidence shows it still in use in the fourth century, when with a number of associated high-status burials it seems more rural than urban in character.[65] The large quantities of finds, particularly pottery, from the excavations at The Vineyard contained a preponderance of first to mid-second-

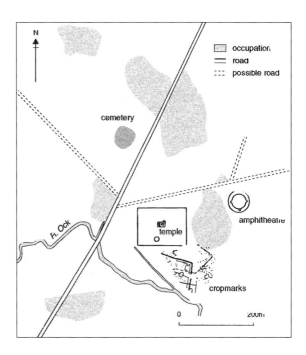

3.9 Frilford overall plan. Some of the cropmark features south of the temple enclosure may be of pre-Roman date. After Hingley 1989, fig. 49, with additions.

century material and there was a clear suggestion of a break or at least a very significant change in the nature of occupation in about the mid-second century. Late Roman pottery and other finds are present in reasonable quantities, but are generally less common than late Iron Age and early Roman material, and it has frequently been remarked that later Roman material concentrates outside the likely area enclosed by the late Iron Age earthworks.[66]

Another site with a river association should probably be included with this group of larger settlements. This was at Gill Mill, Ducklington, near Witney, where a minor road ran roughly south-west to north-east across the Windrush valley and presumably linked eventually with Akeman Street (Fig. 3.10).[67] The location of the Roman settlement in the valley bottom between the two arms of the Windrush appears curious, but the site seems to have been extensive and occupied over a long period, with the earliest activity thought to be of the later first century AD though the majority of finds are of the second century and later. Unfortunately, detailed excavation at this site has been relatively limited, despite continuing gravel extraction, though widespread trenching and more recently salvage recording have given an increasingly clear indication of its character. It was probably of linear form, based on the road, and in one area the rear of ditched plots laid out alongside the road was observed, with scattered cremation and inhumation burials lying just outside them. Since the frontages were not seen the nature of any buildings within the plots is unknown, but a lack of surface evidence suggests that most if not all were of timber. Two pieces of sculpture – relief fragments of a *genius* (Fig. 5.10) and a warrior horseman – from the site indicate the existence of a temple or shrine somewhere within the settlement, however.[68] Another striking feature of the finds is the relatively large number of coins recovered in work carried out in 1988. These might have been related to the shrine, but since the location of the latter is uncertain and the coins were relatively widely distributed this is by no means certain. The site is certainly distinct from other rural settlements in the vicinity of the Thames/Windrush confluence and may be presumed to have had at least a local market function.

There is one final site which probably belongs most comfortably with those just discussed, though it is enigmatic in many ways. This was at Bowling Green Farm, Stanford in the Vale, just south-east of Faringdon.[69] The site did not lie on any known Roman road, but was nevertheless extensive, covering an estimated minimum of 12ha. It seems to have developed in the second century, and a building of that date has been described as a villa. The scale of the site and the presence of a number of buildings, some of timber and some with at least dwarf wall foundations, combined with evidence for a relatively wide range of activities suggested by hearths and ovens among other features, nevertheless led the excavator to describe Bowling Green Farm as a possible small market town. Apart from this potential function, the presence of large numbers of late Roman coins and a variety of copper alloy objects prompted the suggestion that a shrine or temple was also present. Such a presence, though not proven, would be entirely consistent with the interpretation of the site as a major nucleated settlement, as we have seen.

A number of general observations can be made about the settlements considered above. In terms of origin, their backgrounds are diverse. Abingdon and Dorchester

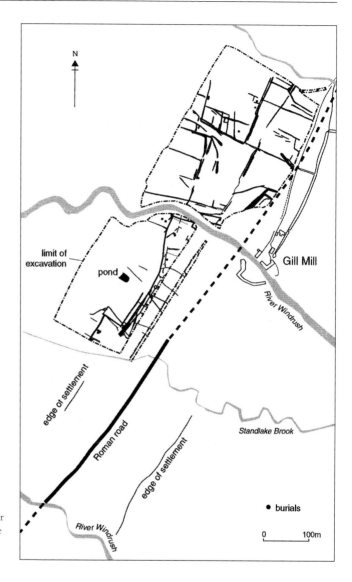

3.10 Gill Mill, Ducklington, overall plan. Only the principal excavated linear features are shown. The focus of the site was a narrow strip each side of the Roman road.

were both sited on or very close to significant centres of late Iron Age date and the same may have been true at Swalcliffe. Elsewhere, evidence for underlying pre-Roman occupation, as for example at Alchester, is insufficient to demonstrate that its presence was a significant factor in determining the siting either of the later settlement or (again in the case of Alchester) of the military establishment which must in some way have influenced the location of the later town. At Frilford, where the Roman temple complex directly overlay Iron Age structures, the excavator thought that there was no direct sequence linking the two.[70] Nevertheless the coincidence of Iron Age and

Roman circular structures is striking and might suggest a significant association, even if there was a chronological break. The significance of Iron Age settlement for other aspects of Roman Frilford is unknown, however. Other nucleated settlements, particularly those along the principal Roman roads, show little or no evidence of Iron Age antecedents, which is unsurprising since the function of the roads on which they lay was only in part to connect pre-existing settlements – in particular those (such as Dorchester) which might be seen as important bases of local or regional power.

Only at Dorchester, therefore, is the pre-Roman settlement apparently succeeded by a fort (though on present evidence this was not established until after about AD 60), which is perhaps a pointer to the status of the place in the late Iron Age. Elsewhere, early Roman military sites may have been located with relation to wider issues of communications – which may explain the location of a series of military establishments at Alchester, midway between Verulamium and Cirencester, and to a lesser extent the smaller scale activity at Asthall, at one of a number of crossings made by Akeman Street over tributaries of the Thames. As already mentioned there are also hints of a military connection in aspects of the artefact assemblage from Wilcote, but their significance remains uncertain.

Further 'official' factors in the siting of nucleated settlements in the county, such as the location of possible *mansiones* or *mutationes*, have also been discussed but cannot be quantified at present. More general economic factors and the economic and social concerns of local landowners also probably played their part in promoting growth at particular sites, but in the absence of specific structures or evidence from inscriptions again cannot be evaluated meaningfully. In their developed form most of the larger nucleated settlements were probably multifunctional. Market aspects may have been to the fore, but the presence of temples in most of these settlements should not be forgotten, as well as local administrative functions at Dorchester and Alchester. With regard to market function the spacing of nucleated settlements is important. It certainly appears that sites of this type in Oxfordshire were sufficiently closely spaced to provide a network of local market centres which would have been readily accessible to the surrounding rural population. This has been discussed by Hingley, who points out that such a pattern of settlement implies a relatively high population density and also a partial absence of self-sufficiency among the communities supporting the market system.[71] Ideally distances of no more than 10–15km between local centres would have been required for this kind of market network to operate effectively, and this can be observed for at least some areas of the county. It cannot be assumed that such a pattern was completely regular, but apparent gaps in the distribution of the larger nucleated settlements can at least be examined with the possibility in mind that further local centres remain to be discovered or their character demonstrated. On this basis the interpretation of Bowling Green Farm, Stanford in the Vale, as a local market centre is plausible, and it is even possible that another such site should be sought in north Oxford, or perhaps associated with the well-known temple at Woodeaton. The existence of nucleated settlements has been postulated for both sites, but a possible concentration of occupation in north Oxford is perhaps better seen as a rural complex. More evidence may yet overturn this assessment, however. Finally, the possibility that a significant settlement existed at Henley on Thames, on the road from Dorchester perhaps to Staines, should be considered. Part of a substantial building was examined at Bell Street in 1993–4 in what would have been a logical location (at the river crossing of a fairly important road) for such a settlement.[72]

Almost all the sites discussed so far lay on known Roman roads of varying importance. Where the evidence exists most can be seen to have been established by the end of the first century AD, but in the case of those sites with a military presence the status of civilian settlement before this time is unclear, even though some such settlement can be presumed to have existed. Once established, most of the settlements seem to have developed in the second century and continued through the third and fourth. The exceptions to this rule are interesting. They seem to include Wilcote, at least in part, though here it is not certain how far the absence of late Roman activity is a consequence of subsequent plough damage, since some very substantial fourth-century deposits survive, albeit patchily. The absence of stone structures, in an area where good-quality building material was abundantly available, is more puzzling, however. A different situation prevails at Abingdon. Here was a site which may have been most important right at the end of the Iron Age and which, after intensive occupation (though with little clear structural evidence) in the early Roman period, then saw a change in character. It is possible that it was supplanted as a local centre by Frilford, only 5–6km distant astride a major Roman road, with Abingdon becoming little more than a dispersed rural settlement, but much more evidence is required from within the modern town before this can be established beyond doubt.

In structural terms there is insufficient evidence to characterise these settlements in the early Roman period – the timber buildings of this time are poorly known and, if the early structures at Wilcote are at all typical, often sufficiently irregular in plan to have evaded elucidation in relatively small trenches cut into the lowest levels of site sequences. Timber structures were widely, but by no means universally, replaced by buildings with stone foundations – though a variety of superstructure types is possible on such foundations. Alchester may have some stone-based buildings by the end of the first century, though it may be that such early dating (based on the 1920s excavations) should be reconsidered in the light of evidence from Asthall and elsewhere which tends to suggest that such buildings did not appear much before the mid second century. At Dorchester, stone-founded buildings are not apparent before the third century at the earliest. The building plans of the late Roman settlements mostly appear to have been relatively simple, such as the strip buildings at Asthall and Alchester and the cottage and possible aisled types at Dorchester. A few more complex building plans are present, however. They are found at Alchester, though there may be no more than two or three examples there, at Asthall (one certain, but poorly known, example), at Swalcliffe Lea and also at Sansom's Platt, where a number of the buildings known from the air appear to have relatively complex plans, though it is possible that in some cases the complexity arises from the superimposition of buildings of different periods. Generally, however, it is clear that large town houses are effectively absent from these settlements.

Timber buildings continued to be constructed throughout the Roman period, and there is some evidence from the northern suburbs of Alchester and from Asthall that such buildings, particularly of post-hole construction, may have become slightly more common at the end of the period. The best example of such a sequence comes from Asthall, where a second-century building with substantial stone foundations was succeeded in the fourth century by an apparently simple post-hole building on the Akeman Street frontage. Elsewhere, evidence of such a trend in building technique is lacking, and at Dorchester the contrary trend appears to be indicated, with the construction of a number of very late stone buildings. This site may, however, have been exceptional.

As already indicated, there is some evidence of settlement contraction at Asthall in the late Roman period, and perhaps of a substantially reduced settlement at Wilcote in the same period, while elsewhere the evidence is either lacking or equivocal – and will be discussed in a later chapter. It is worthwhile, however, briefly considering the population of the major centres. Such estimation is speculative, but the problem can be approached from a number of different angles. The overall extent of settlement can rarely be converted into reliable population statistics because of the absence of complete settlement plans and variations in occupation density across sites. For example, the population of the centre of Alchester, where buildings were densely clustered, was presumably much higher per hectare than that of the sites of more rural character such as those seen in the northern suburbs, where probably only a handful of a relatively large number of structures spread across a considerable area were domestic in function.

Recent general discussions of the problem include those of Hingley[73] and Millett, who compiles figures showing the range of multiplication factors used by various scholars in the calculation of nucleated settlement populations.[74] These range from about 62 to 283 persons per hectare, though Millett's preference is for figures in the middle part of this range. These give an estimated population of roughly 1,400 for the walled area of Alchester alone.[75] Even allowing for a much-reduced density in the extramural settlement areas the extent of these might indicate a total population of at least 3,000, if not more, though if so this is well within the range which has been suggested for a number of the larger towns of Roman Britain.[76]

In addition to this general approach there is more local evidence which can be deployed. The regularity of the late Roman cemeteries at Dorchester permits an assessment of the total number of graves in these cemeteries at about 2500, extrapolating from the limited excavated samples. On the basis that the cemeteries were in use for 150 years or so, that they represented the only or at least the principal late Roman cemeteries of the town, and that the average age at death was thirty, a population of roughly 500 can be estimated for fourth-century Dorchester.[77] This is not impossibly different from the figure of about 750 which would be arrived at by applying the formula discussed above in relation to the walled area of the settlement, and it may be remembered that evidence for extramural settlement at Dorchester is relatively slight.

One further indication of population levels might be provided by the amphitheatre at Frilford. Amphitheatre sizes have sometimes been used as a guide to urban (adult) populations on the basis that there was a correlation between their capacity and those populations.[78] A possible capacity of some 4,000 has been calculated for the Frilford amphitheatre.[79] It is not suggested that this represents directly the population of Frilford itself, particularly given the likelihood that the temple complex to which the amphitheatre belonged was of significance beyond the confines of the Frilford settlement itself, but it certainly hints that the population of Frilford was not necessarily to be measured in the low hundreds. Some of the smaller nucleated settlements may indeed have been of that order of size, but the suggested figures for the larger sites are readily consistent with those for typical medieval market towns in the region. A final point in relation to medieval towns may also have a bearing on the Roman period. If in the later medieval period demographic statistics suggest that urban populations were not self-sustaining, but relied on immigration from the countryside to maintain their levels,[80] could this have happened in the Roman period also? Such a situation could have been a factor in promoting mobility within rural society. Overall, however, the great majority of people remained in the countryside. A recent estimate indicates that the proportion of the Romano-British population living in towns and cities was about 6.5 per cent.[81] This figure may be over-precise, but a value between 5 and 10 per cent, and perhaps nearer the former, seems likely. For an area like Oxfordshire, without major urban centres, the figure may have been rather less.

NOTES

1. The following is a selective summary of evidence for some of the principal Roman roads in the county. For the standard account see Margary 1973, 128–83 passim. See also Lambrick 1969 and for more recent work Malpas 1987 and Cheetham 1995.
2. Hands 1993, 11. A date '*c.* AD 47' is assigned by the excavator principally on historical grounds. The archaeological evidence cannot sustain such a precise date, though it is not necessarily inconsistent with it. Understanding the sequence of road development at Cirencester is crucial to the broader picture, but there is no consensus on this, Akeman Street being seen as earlier or (more usually) later than the line of the Fosse Way by different authorities (see e.g. Darvill & Holbrook 1994, 51–5). The evidence from sites such as Wilcote supports the former possibility.
3. The classic account is by Hussey (1841).
4. Chambers 1986.
5. Cheetham 1995, 422–6.
6. Smith 1987, 244.
7. Cf. Blair 1994, 87–9.
8. Hassall 1972, 46–7.
9. Eberhard Sauer pers. comm. Cf. Margary 1973, 168.
10. See Margary 1973, 153–5 and 168 for this and other roads in North Oxfordshire around Swalcliffe.
11. For this and other roads in the Dorchester area see Malpas 1987.
12. Millett 1995, 29.
13. The archaeology of Alchester has a long antiquarian tradition and has been summarised on numerous occasions, most notably in *VCH* I, 281–8, and then by Rowley (1975), Foster (1989), Burnham & Wacher (1990, 97–102) and in the introduction and discussion sections of Booth et al. forthcoming. For the main excavations see Hawkes 1927; Iliffe 1929 and 1932; Harden 1937; Young 1975; Foreman & Rahtz 1984; Booth et al. forthcoming; Sauer & Crutchley 1998.
14. Rowley (1975, 118) gives a remarkably precise estimate of 43.6ha.
15. Eberhard Sauer pers. comm.
16. Sauer & Crutchley 1998; Sauer 1999a; Booth et al. forthcoming for other metalwork finds.
17. For the eastern ditch see Young 1975, 154 and 166–7.
18. Woodfield 1995, 133 and 143–5; Young 1975.
19. *VCH* I, 284.
20. Booth et al. forthcoming.
21. Summaries of the archaeology of Dorchester include *VCH* I, 288–96; Rowley 1975 and 1985; Burnham & Wacher 1990, 117–22. The most significant excavation reports for sites within the town are Hogg & Stevens 1937; Frere 1962 and 1984; Bradley 1978; Rowley & Brown 1981.

22. Frere 1984, 94–8.
23. Hogg & Stevens 1937, 51; Frere 1962, 117.
24. May 1977.
25. Aston 1974b, 4.
26. Rowley 1985, 28.
27. Bradley 1978.
28. E.g. Frere 1984, 113–14.
29. Rowley and Brown 1981, 8–10.
30. Frere 1962, 121–3.
31. Manning 1984.
32. Rowley & Brown 1981, 8–10 and 24.
33. RIB I, 235, see also Burnham & Wacher 1990, 33–4 for a brief discussion of *beneficiarii*.
34. Illustrated in *VCH* I (pls xiiic–d) and the glass in Rowley 1985, 23.
35. For these cemeteries see Durham & Rowley 1972; Harman et al. 1978; Chambers 1987.
36. Rivet & Smith 1979, 244.
37. Black 1995.
38. E.g. Millett 1990, 144–7; Burnham & Wacher 1990, 43–50.
39. Smith 1987, 14.
40. Chambers 1978.
41. Parsons & Booth 1996.
42. The principal references are Cook 1955 and Booth 1997, with further references in the latter.
43. Taylor & Collingwood 1921, 214–15; Chambers 1981.
44. At Orchard House, Booth 1996.
45. Booth 1997, 151.
46. See RCHME 1976, 36–7 and 95–7. The coins from this site are now usefully summarised by Reece in Timby 1998, 400–21 passim.
47. Hands 1993; 1998.
48. For a convenient summary, Hands 1998, 23.
49. Rahtz & Rowley 1984.
50. Ibid., 49.
51. Ibid., 38; for the contrary view see Booth forthcoming.
52. The extent of the settlement was first noted in the 1920s (*VCH* I, 308–9) and subsequently plotted by Webster (1975, 59 and 61). The only significant excavation to have been reported is that of Fowler (1960), within the hillfort. The archaeology of the site has been recently synthesised in a dissertation for OUDCE by Barry Eames (Eames 1998), who kindly made a copy available. Much of what follows is based on this summary.
53. Shawyer 1998; 1999, 53–9.
54. Shawyer 1999, 58–9.
55. Eddershaw 1972. For discussion of the head, Henig 1993, no. 46.
56. Harding 1987, 1–16; Hingley 1982. A small-scale evaluation was carried out by the Oxford Archaeological Unit adjacent to the Noah's Ark site in 1987 (Miles & Wait 1987).
57. Burnham & Wacher 1990, 178–83.
58. Cf. Booth 1998, 12.
59. The principal references are Rolleston 1869 and 1880; Buxton 1921; Bradford & Goodchild 1939.
60. Holbrook & Thomas 1996, 171–4.
61. Barber & Walker 1999.
62. Holbrook & Thomas 1996, 117–24.
63. Mapped in ibid., 172.
64. Akerman 1865; Wilson & Wallis 1991 for the second building. The 'late 1st- to early or possibly mid 2nd-century occupation' (ibid., 8) is misconceived – this is the earliest possible date for the construction of the building. There is no basis for the interpretation of Akerman's building as a temple.
65. Allen 1990b.
66. The evidence from many small-scale excavations in Abingdon has not been synthesised recently.
67. Lambrick & Wallis 1988; Booth 1990; Lambrick 1992b, 213–14; Lambrick 1996.
68. Henig 1993, 14–15, 41–2.
69. The site has been extensively examined, though formal excavation has been limited in scale. Only very brief interim notes have been published; the principal ones are Chambers 1988; 1989b; 1990; and Mudd 1993.
70. Harding 1987, 15–16.
71. Hingley 1989, 112–16, but note the spurious road alignment south-west of Alchester on the map on p. 113.
72. Moloney 1997, 113–15, 129–30.
73. Hingley 1989, 78–80.
74. Millett 1990, 181–6.
75. Based on the calculations of Hassan 1981. The latter's lower figure (137 per ha) is considered by Millett to indicate a likely minimum population density per hectare for nucleated sites.
76. Cf. Frere 1987, 252–3.
77. Harman et al. 1978, 15.
78. E.g. Frere 1987, 253.
79. Hingley 1989, 116.
80. E.g. Bassett et al. 1992, 1.
81. Millett 1990, 185; the urban population of Roman Gaul has been put at about 10 per cent (Woolf 1998, 138).

CHAPTER FOUR

RURAL SETTLEMENT AND ENVIRONMENT

As in any pre-industrial society the great majority of the population of Roman Oxfordshire lived on and worked the land. A fairly dense pattern of settlement is evident and it shows a number of interesting differences of character across the county. The view we have of rural settlement has a number of imbalances, however, being skewed towards the rich villas of the Cotswolds on the one hand and the gravel terrace sites of the Thames valley itself on the other (Fig. 4.1).[1]

Until fairly recently excavation has been specifically site-focused, but increasingly the emphasis of study, particularly in the Thames valley, is on the wider landscape, as seen for example in the Stanton Harcourt area, in the recent programme of work at Yarnton and also just outside the county in the Cotswold Water Park sites in Gloucestershire. All these are areas where the presence of gravels has resulted in the availability of widespread background evidence in the form of aerial photographs and, through the process of gravel extraction, has provided opportunities in some cases for large-scale examination of sites and their hinterlands. In general, therefore, the Thames gravels have been studied disproportionately in relation to rural settlement in other areas of the county, though without excavation or surface collection of finds it can be very difficult to distinguish between sites of different periods, and particularly between settlements of Iron Age and Roman date. The aerial evidence for the Thames valley was first assembled in 1974 and has been re-examined since. This work has been supplemented by field survey, both within and south of the valley, and by excavation, in some cases on a large scale. An important aspect of these excavations from the 1970s onwards has been the integration of environmental studies with archaeological evidence to try to understand the workings of the broader landscape. In contrast, while the northern part of the county is known as the location of a number of wealthy villas, very few of these sites have been examined systematically from either archaeological or environmental perspectives. Apart from the structural sequences of a small number of villas, evidence for chronological development of rural settlement comes almost entirely from the Thames valley. The extent to which this was representative of the county as a whole is therefore unclear.

For most of the late Iron Age rural population of the region the immediate impact of the Roman conquest may have been slight, but the influence of Rome would soon

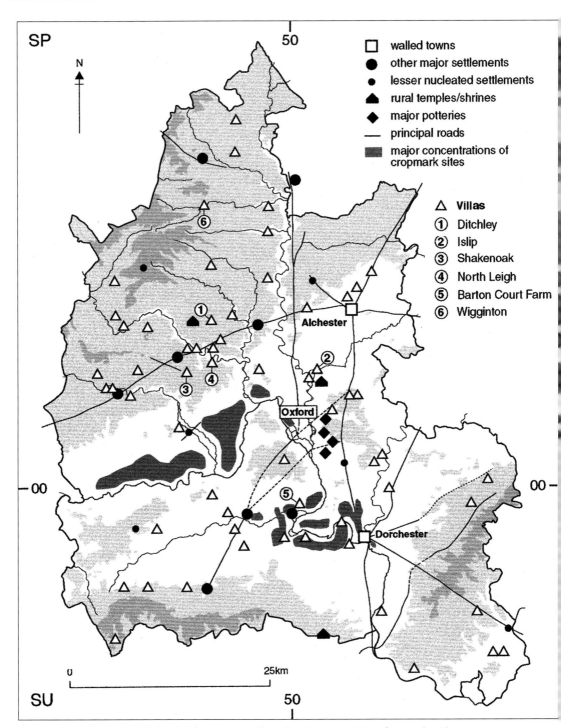

□ walled towns
● other major settlements
• lesser nucleated settlements
▲ rural temples/shrines
◆ major potteries
— principal roads
▥ major concentrations of cropmark sites

△ **Villas**
① Ditchley
② Islip
③ Shakenoak
④ North Leigh
⑤ Barton Court Farm
⑥ Wigginton

Alchester

Oxford

Dorchester

N

0   25km

SU

4.1   General distribution map of rural settlement types: villas and main concentrations of cropmark evidence.

have made itself felt through the demands of tax collection, perhaps initially as levies of produce in kind to provision the occupying forces, but later as taxation in cash. This development ultimately brought most of the rural population into the Roman monetary economy, but for many this was a very gradual process, clearly detectable archaeologically only from the later third century. Tax collection would have been carried out in large part by local élites and their agents.[2] The focus of this activity was most probably the civitas capitals (i.e. Verulamium, Cirencester and Silchester), and the extent of the involvement of lesser centres such as the small towns is unclear.

The exact scale of the impact of Roman taxation on the rural population has been the subject of considerable debate. It has been thought that the need to produce an agricultural surplus in order to raise cash to pay taxes stimulated agricultural production, perhaps leading to improvements in agricultural practice and in crops and animals.[3] Alternatively, some scholars have calculated that the requirements of the Roman army, at least (at provincial level), could have been met relatively easily by the existing population with little need to boost production.[4] On this view, it can be argued that levies on resources which were already being made by the local élites were simply (for the most part) reassigned to the Roman state, without the need for the overall level of payments to have been increased significantly.

The extent to which the nature and intensity of agriculture within the region would have changed simply to meet new demands from the state in the aftermath of the Roman conquest is therefore uncertain, though the most recent regional review sees the late Iron Age and Roman period as one of increasing intensification of exploitation of the land, characterised at least in part by the changing dynamics of pastoral vis-à-vis arable agriculture.[5] Agricultural intensification in the Iron Age was clearly not a direct consequence of Roman influence and presumably reflects the pressures of increasing population and, to an extent, changing environmental conditions, though it is possible that developments in the political structures of the late Iron Age also had implications for changes in the agricultural regime. Population growth is generally agreed to have been maintained in the Roman period, so the continuing pressure on land can potentially be assigned to at least three major factors: Roman imperial demands, population growth, and perhaps reduced yields in some cases as over-exploitation (and possibly also environmental changes) lessened returns.

Initially, developments in the physical appearance of the countryside were gradual and can be related to the late Iron Age pattern: there is almost no evidence for disruption of settlement patterns in the conquest period. In many places, fields and trackways were already well defined by the late Iron Age and remained in use for some considerable time with little significant change. The associated settlements, whether located on the Thames valley gravels or elsewhere, are commonly (but not always) defined by ditches, which are readily identified in excavation, from the air or by geophysical survey. The ditches would have had associated earthwork banks, though these do not usually survive, and in some cases they mark quite substantial enclosures which, though probably not for the most part defensive, would have served to define domestic accommodation and farmyard areas and to enclose stock when necessary.

There are some difficulties in reconstructing the internal physical appearance of individual rural settlement sites, however, owing to the very limited evidence for buildings, a problem which on some sites prevails throughout the Roman period. The most likely explanation for this lies in the character of the buildings themselves, since other evidence indicates continued intensive settlement at sites across the county. It seems probable that there was a major change in building tradition in the region, probably in the later Iron Age, with circular buildings of middle Iron Age type no longer regularly constructed using a technique that leaves traces readily detectable by archaeologists (such as the digging of holes for timber uprights). It is likely that the new tradition involved the use of a mass walling technique, probably cob construction, which in the great majority of cases was simply built from ground level and did not require holes for posts or gullies for wattle and daub walls to be dug into the subsoil. As a result of the adoption of this new tradition, the origins of which are unclear though it was probably established before the Roman conquest, many rural buildings which must have existed (and perhaps some 'urban' ones also) simply become invisible in the archaeological record.[6] They can occasionally be identified where surrounded by clearly defined drainage gullies or where, as for example in one case at Yarnton, an unusually well-preserved floor surface survived to indicate the location of the building. Here the identification as a potential dwelling was aided by the presence of relatively high concentrations of pottery and other domestic debris in a surrounding gully.[7]

VILLAS

Not all rural building types were as elusive as these, however. Some of the more wealthy occupants of Roman Oxfordshire chose to live in houses with walls constructed partly or wholly in stone, buildings which are often referred to as villas. Such sites, which appeared particularly from the second century onwards, were a regular feature of the landscape, interspersed among other settlement types with less easily identifiable structures, and the large villa at North Leigh is Oxfordshire's most important currently accessible Roman site (Fig. 4.2). The term villa is usually taken by archaeologists to refer to a Romanised farm, though such Romanised buildings need not automatically have formed estate centres with a primary interest in agriculture (nor is this implied by the Latin term). In Oxfordshire, however, it is likely that the great majority would have done so. At most sites, therefore, agricultural structures may be expected in addition to the principal domestic building or buildings, though in some cases both may have been combined under a single roof. The exact characteristics which qualify an individual site for villa status have been much debated by archaeologists. Here the term is used as a convenient abbreviation for a rural building of more than two rooms (though in reality rarely fewer than six) with stone foundations and often with other 'Romanised' characteristics such as mosaic pavements, heated rooms (hypocausts) and painted wall plaster. These last three attributes potentially enable such sites to be identified from surface evidence as well as in excavation or from aerial photographs. None of these, nor the presence of other features such as window glass, need automatically qualify a rural building for villa status, though these criteria have usually been followed here. There is clearly an overlap in building type between these structures and some of those found in larger

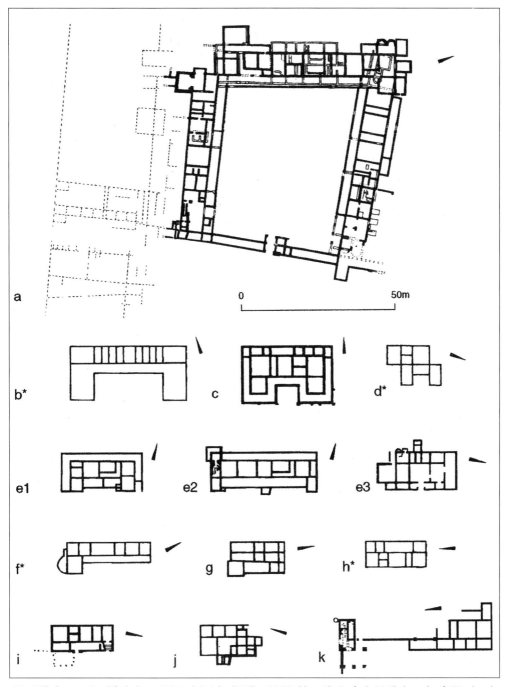

4.2   Villa houses, simplified plans: (a) North Leigh; (b) Islip; (c) Ditchley; (d) Garford; (e) Shakenoak; (f) Woodstock; (g) Frilford; (h) Little Milton; (i) Barton Court Farm; (j) Worsham; (k) Harpsden. Asterisked sites are recorded from aerial evidence. After Miles 1982, fig. 3, with minor additions.

nucleated settlements, for example at Swalcliffe Lea. Such buildings, though in some cases comparable in plan and potentially similar in function to their rural counterparts, are not regarded as villas here.[8]

A small number of sites appearing in the late Iron Age or early Roman periods have been seen as potential or proto-villas (Fig. 4.3). The case has been made most strongly at Barton Court Farm, Abingdon, where the late Iron Age rectilinear enclosure was overlain, probably in the later first century AD, by a similar enclosure on a different alignment. This was divided into two parts, within the southern of which lay a rectangular timber structure 8.5m wide and some 28–30m long, with plastered walls, and two probable granary buildings, each based on six upright posts. The site was unusual among contemporary rural settlements in producing a few coins, but there was little evidence which would allow reconstruction of its agricultural economy, though it was suggested that the principal building could have accommodated animals as well as humans.[9] A comparable site is found further down the Thames at Appleford. Here a more strictly rectilinear double-ditched enclosure covered an area almost identical to that of the Barton Court Farm enclosure (c. 0.5 ha). Limited examination again indicated the presence of probable timber structures, and the pottery included unusually high-status material within a very similar mid/late first- to early/mid-second-century

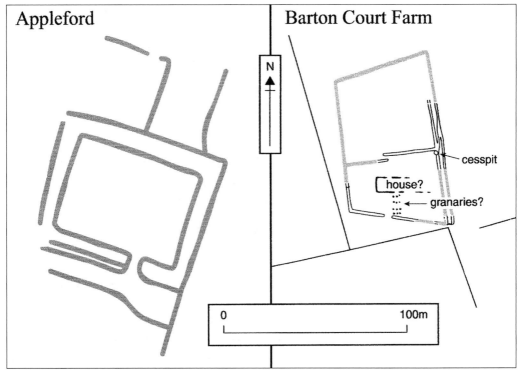

4.3 'Proto-villas'. Barton Court Farm (after Miles 1986, fig. 7) and the Appleford enclosure. Features shaded grey are known from aerial photographs.

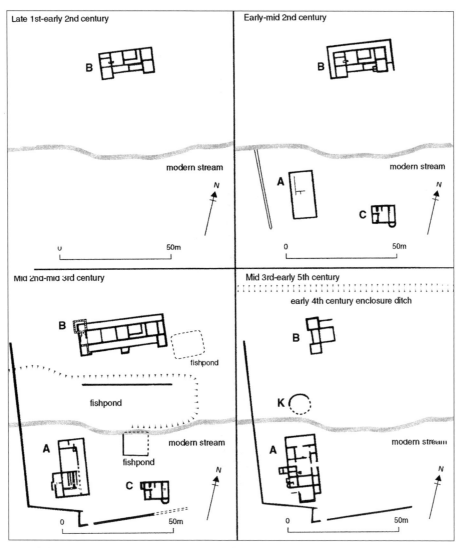

4.4 Shakenoak villa, the main stages of development. After Miles 1982, fig. 5.

date range.[10] This enclosure seems to have been linked to an extensive area of rectilinear fields. These, however, apparently continued in use while the settlement site, like its fellow at Barton Court Farm, was abandoned at a time of major settlement relocation in the first half of the second century AD, which is discussed further below.

The extent to which these sites were distinct from others defined as villas may be debated. On the criteria discussed above some sixty-two villas are currently known in Roman Oxfordshire, of which approximately fifty seem reasonably secure in their identification, but beyond this there are many for which there is little further meaningful information. Only two sites, Shakenoak and Barton Court Farm, have seen extensive excavation in relatively recent times. In both cases this work was completed in the 1970s, but these remain the only sites for which complete plans are known from excavation (Fig. 4.4).[11] Evidence for most of the other sites ranges from antiquarian excavation to surface finds, with limited excavation of more recent date in a few cases, but with the important addition of aerial photographs. Antiquarian excavation invariably concentrated on buildings, preferably those with mosaic pavements. The layout of villa complexes, as opposed to the plans of individual buildings, can therefore only be determined in very few cases, except for those sites known from the air. With plans based on aerial evidence, however, there is always the possibility that the picture is incomplete.

A pioneering Oxfordshire example of the combination of aerial and excavated evidence is seen at Ditchley Park (Fig. 4.5). Here excavations in 1935, based on new aerial photographs,[12] examined part of the ditched (and later, walled) enclosure within which lay the main house, a well and one or more associated round buildings, with further structures, including a probable granary, in a subsidiary enclosure. The whole formed for a long time one of the best-known villa plans of Roman Britain,[13] though it may doubted if the plan is absolutely complete, since excavation within the main part of the enclosure was limited in extent.

The excavated sites discussed so far were all relatively modest establishments. Perhaps coincidentally none had a simple sequence of development through the Roman period. Both Shakenoak and Ditchley appear to show a degree of disruption in their domestic accommodation in the third century, and Barton Court Farm was only reoccupied in the later part of that century, after an apparent break in occupation of perhaps as much as 150 years. By the fourth century there were certainly more grand establishments, though for the most part these are known only from their principal houses. North Leigh, close to both Ditchley and Shakenoak, is by far the best known. In size it ranks alongside the largest villas of Roman Britain, particularly so when the aerial evidence for additional ranges of buildings adjoining the principal courtyard complex exposed today is taken into account. These additional buildings are imperfectly understood, but may perhaps have formed the 'home farm' component of the late Roman complex.

Such a large site inevitably had a complex history.[14] In its initial form the villa was much more modest than later, but even about AD 100 it consisted of at least two adjacent buildings – a dwelling and either an agricultural building or a hall (the latter as well as the former soon acquired a mosaic pavement, so the agricultural interpretation is less likely) with a further detached bath suite. All these were located under the later north-west range. In its developed form North Leigh was the county's only certain example of a courtyard villa – i.e. one in which all four sides of a courtyard area were surrounded by continuous ranges of buildings or enclosure walls. It is conceivable that other large villa sites, such as Stonesfield and Wigginton (Fig. 4.6), were also of this type, but there is no firm evidence.

In plan most of the known villa houses conform reasonably well to established types, consisting often of a simple range of rooms to which corridors and other features may have been added. Another essentially simple type, the aisled building, is

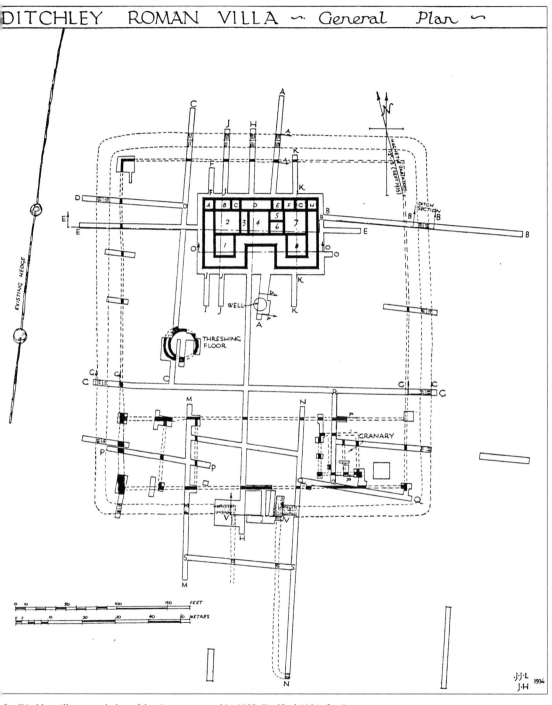

DITCHLEY ROMAN VILLA ~ General Plan ~

5 Ditchley villa, general plan of the site as excavated in 1935. Radford 1936, fig. 8.

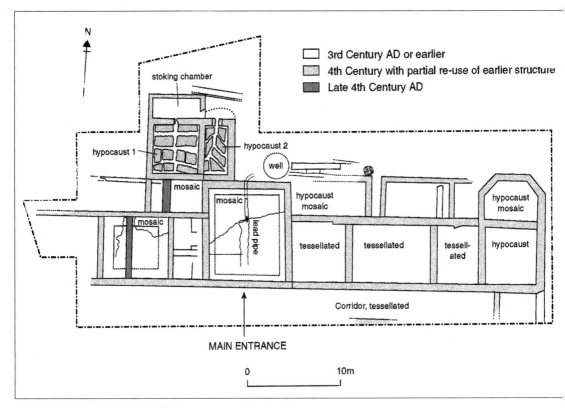

4.6   Wigginton, the late Roman villa house as excavated in the 1960s.

not so common among the known Oxfordshire villa plans, with Shakenoak Building
A the best known example while one component of the site at Harpsden Wood might
have been of this type. Characteristically, the Shakenoak building combined
agricultural and domestic use under the same roof. One of the clearest examples of an
aisled building, again probably accommodating domestic and other uses, is a building
currently under investigation at Gatehampton Farm, Goring.[15] More common, as at
Ditchley, is the winged corridor type, in which projecting wings at each end of the
façade, usually linked by a corridor, give symmetry to the main frontage of the house.
This concept was used in successive versions of Building B at Shakenoak, for example,
and also at Islip. Here the overall arrangement of the site, with the house placed
towards the rear of a rectangular ditched or walled enclosure, is strongly reminiscent of
that at Ditchley. The parallel is emphasised by the presence in both cases of circular
structures in front of the wings. At Ditchley one of these structures, in front of the
west wing, was excavated, and it seems clear that it was contemporary with the main
house. A possible corresponding feature in front of the east wing was not examined.

At Islip the evidence derives primarily from aerial photographs, but again there are hints of a circular structure in front of each wing.[16] While the Islip round buildings are not completely symmetrically placed the similarity of their location with that of the comparable structure(s) at Ditchley is striking and suggests that these relationships were part of a planned scheme, rather than merely accidental.

This juxtaposition of circular 'native' and rectilinear 'Roman' building types, which occurs also at Shakenoak, has interesting implications for the relative status of the individuals accommodated in them.[17] While the former type may have been perceived as being of lower status than the latter, these buildings, with stone foundations, were still of some standing. In Northamptonshire, where they are more common, they occur at villas and other rural settlement sites. In Oxfordshire we have already seen their occurrence as probable domestic structures in the extramural settlement at Alchester. Elsewhere the type occurs as a 'specialist' building – either a workshop, as at the pottery production site of the Churchill Hospital, or as a probable or possible shrine in a number of contexts, at Frilford, at Sansom's Platt on Akeman Street west of Alchester and perhaps in the south-west quadrant of the walled area of Alchester itself, at Woodeaton (Fig. 4.7), and most recently in a site at Faringdon.[18] It is notable,

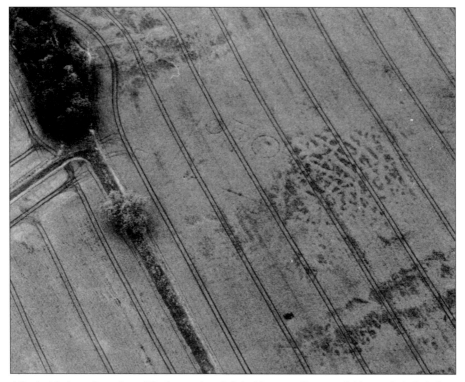

4.7   Aerial view of temples at Woodeaton. A typical double-square Romano-Celtic temple is flanked on each side by circular buildings. (RCHME. NMR 15284/54, 14.6.1995)

therefore, that in Oxfordshire at least stone-founded circular buildings are not found in low-status rural settlements.

The general lack of excavation makes it difficult to say much about the range of buildings encountered in villa complexes. The earliest villa phase at Shakenoak seems to have consisted of a simple winged corridor house, associated later with an aisled building and a separate bath house and most probably other features as well. Elsewhere evidence suggests the presence of two stone buildings, as for example at Little Milton and Lyneham, seen from the air, or Frilford, where the second building was a small bath suite.[19] Clearly a number of sites where there are extensive surface remains may have contained several buildings, and at South Farm, Bicester, for example, at least six buildings were noted, though the villa status of this site is not absolutely certain, nor are individual building plans known.[20] What was in fact probably a typical situation is seen at the excavated site of Barton Court Farm. Here the principal house was accompanied by a small 'cottage' with stone-founded walls but thought to have had a timber superstructure (Fig. 4.8).[21] Apart from a well and two corn drying ovens no other structures were evident in the late Roman phase. Here, as also at Little Milton and probably elsewhere, the only stone-founded buildings on the site were both probably domestic in function, though functions could of course have changed through time. In the smaller villas, therefore, subsidiary buildings might often have been relatively modest and/or perhaps of timber. It follows that, in most cases, it was only in the principal house (and in separate bath houses, where such features existed) that there was any suggestion of architectural pretension or of elaborate decoration. Such aspects of these buildings are discussed in Chapter five.

VILLA DISTRIBUTION

Traditionally, rural settlement in Oxfordshire has been seen as divided between a 'villa zone' in the northern part of the county and an area further south with a high proportion of 'peasant' settlements, the latter being particularly noticeable in the Thames valley itself, where aerial photographs have revealed many such sites. Inevitably such a contrast is too simple, though it is true that there is a concentration of villas in that part of the county where high-quality building stone is most readily available. The reason for this goes far beyond mere raw materials, however, and may ultimately have much to do with the underlying pattern of settlement here in the Iron Age, and specifically with the suggestion that this area was focal for a particularly large number of high-ranking members of the Dobunnic aristocracy.

Villas are distributed right across the county,[22] but on present evidence they are less well represented in the south-east than elsewhere, though this may reflect levels of fieldwork as much as anything else. Apart from the well-known concentration in the North Oxfordshire Grim's Ditch area the most noticeable variation in the distribution of villas seems to be in the Thames valley itself. At the upper end of the valley villas are seen just across the county boundary at sites such as Claydon Pike (Fairford) and Roughground Farm (Lechlade),[23] whereas the upper part of the valley in Oxfordshire appears strikingly devoid of such sites. Below Oxford itself, however, there is a marked

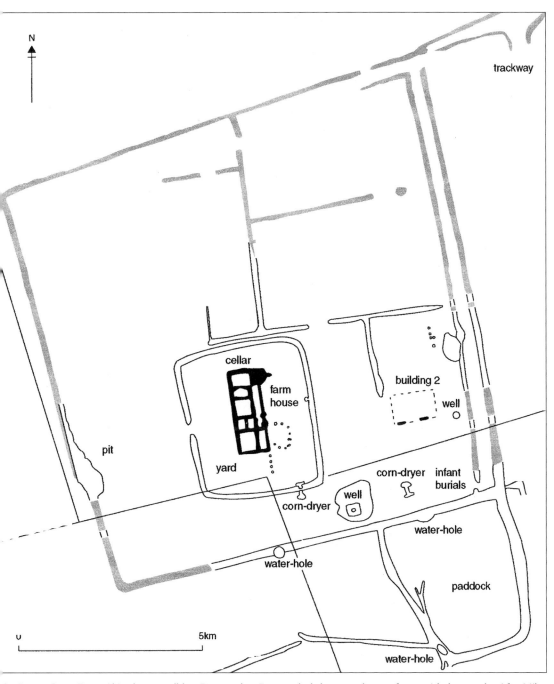

8 Barton Court Farm, Abingdon, overall late Roman plan. Features shaded grey are known from aerial photographs. After Miles
)86, fig. 8.

change, with a number of villas, of which Barton Court Farm is the best known, occurring on or close to the river gravels in the stretch between Abingdon and Dorchester. Below Dorchester again there are relatively few villas in the valley, but examples are known at South Stoke, Gatehampton Farm (Goring) and Whitchurch. In the south-west of the county there are suggestions of further (but less numerous) associations between topographical zones and villa distributions, with a row of sites (Woolstone, Fawler and East Challow) at the foot of the Downs west of Wantage and others such as Stanford in the Vale and Kingston Bagpuize possibly within a 'villa zone' related to the Corallian Ridge.[24] Further east the sites at Frilford, Garford, Chilswell and even Barton Court Farm could perhaps also be seen in this context, though all except Chilswell appear to relate more readily to the Thames valley and that of its tributary, the Ock.

OTHER RURAL SETTLEMENT

Non-villa settlements are of several different types, and there is no suggestion that rural settlement can simply be grouped into two categories – villas and 'the rest'. It is likely that some sites shared many of the characteristics of villa complexes but simply lacked – for whatever reason – the architectural elaboration which forms the basis of our somewhat arbitrary classification. Equally, there is no reason to see the agricultural regimes of villas as necessarily distinct from those of other settlement types,[25] though there certainly were distinctions in some cases (as is discussed below).

Where there is clear evidence it can be seen that most villas were set within well-defined enclosures, delimited by a ditch or a wall, or both. The presence of such an enclosure was seen as a characteristic feature of Ditchley Park, and by extension, of other villas, to the extent that the *Victoria County History* survey of Roman Oxfordshire listed a number of sites, particularly in the north of the county, as potential villas purely on the basis of the identification of a roughly rectilinear 'Ditchley Park type' enclosure. Such enclosures are in fact characteristic of many rural settlement sites, though they are perhaps particularly likely to have surrounded those sites which in other respects most closely resembled villas.

A number of late Iron Age or early Roman farmsteads of the Thames valley lay within ditched enclosures. The size of these early Roman enclosures varied considerably, and while many were at least roughly rectilinear, like that at Old Shifford Farm, measuring roughly 60 x 65m in its developed form (Fig. 4.9), some, such as Watkins Farm, Northmoor, were quite irregular in plan.[26] Most seem likely to have contained an individual farmstead and while on some sites several similar units were grouped together (as at Gravelly Guy (Stanton Harcourt) in the first century AD), there is no good evidence for large agricultural 'villages' in the region in the early Roman period, though sites such as Bowling Green Farm, Stanford in the Vale, discussed in Chapter three, as well as other sites, for example near Cote in the Thames valley, might best be seen in this way in the later Roman period.[27]

The extent to which ditched enclosures were characteristic of the county as a whole is unclear for want of good evidence, though their importance in north Oxfordshire

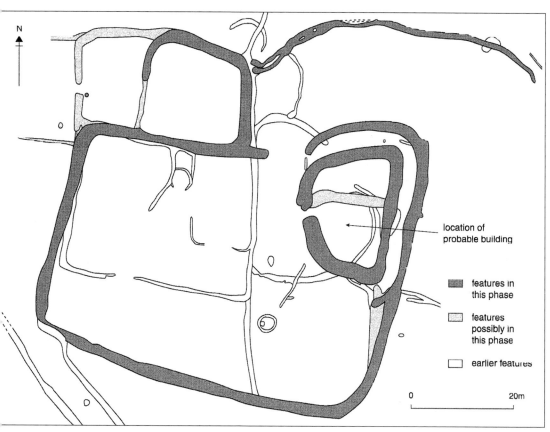

9   Early Roman farmstead enclosure at Old Shifford. After Hey 1995, fig. 8.

has been noted above. While not all such settlements were necessarily so well defined, however, there are few convincing examples which do not incorporate some kind of ditched component. There are, for example, no obvious counterparts to the unenclosed (and probably seasonally occupied) settlements seen in the middle Iron Age at sites such as Farmoor.[28] Equally, however, the prolific cropmark evidence for the Thames valley between the Windrush confluence and Oxford contains relatively few very distinct enclosures which stand out from the general pattern of features. Here, where blocks of apparently coherent Roman landscape can be seen (and it has to be accepted that their date, while likely, is often not certain), ditched trackways often lead to or are bordered with small enclosures which may have been paddocks or closes but in some cases are likely to have contained settlement, as can be seen from excavated examples such as Old Shifford or (further down-river) Appleford.[29] Another extensively excavated site in this area, Gravelly Guy (Stanton Harcourt), occupied into the second century AD but not later, similarly has no significant structural evidence, though there must have been occupation areas within the excavation. There is no clear indication of a hierarchy of settlement suggested for example by the presence of 'dominant' enclosures with abnormally well-defined ditches. This has been taken to indicate the presence of a particular type of social grouping, in which much land was held in common.[30]

Sites such as Yarnton may be characteristic of this landscape. Here the late Iron Age/early Roman phase saw a much increased emphasis on ditched enclosures, compared to the middle Iron Age, but these (generally irregular) features were of a size that might have contained individual structures or activity areas rather than enclosing entire farmsteads (Fig. 4.10). Some comparable elements were retained in the late Roman period but there was also more evidence for rectilinear ditch systems defining a trackway and possible paddocks or small fields. Within these successive layouts there is only slight evidence for structures (see above) but one sub-circular building is indicated by a surviving floor and stone post pads suggest a possible aisled rectangular building.[31]

The general invisibility of structures on these low-status rural sites remains a

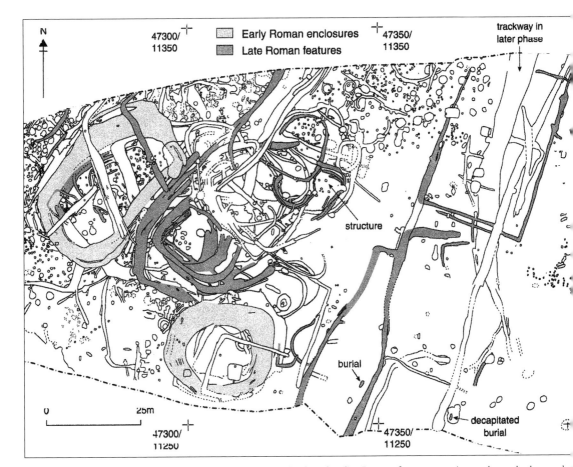

4.10   Yarnton, general plan of the late Roman settlement, with selected earlier Roman features, superimposed on a background of intensive Iron Age activity. The plan is quite irregular.

problem even in the late Roman period. The existence of stone-based round buildings, discussed above, may provide a clue to the nature of such structures. It is quite possible that some of these foundations supported walls of mass construction technique, such as cob, rather than stone superstructures. It has already been suggested that such a technique became widespread in the region in the late Iron Age. The fact that circular buildings in an identifiable, stone-based form continued to be built through the Roman period (buildings at the Churchill Hospital and the northern extramural area of Alchester were certainly of late third- and fourth-century date, for example) suggests that other, less visible circular structures may also have remained in use. This evidence, and that of the Yarnton building, for example, is slight, but taken together supports the view that a widespread building tradition, 'native' both in construction technique and in building form, might have remained dominant in low-status rural settlements across the region, and perhaps particularly in the Thames valley itself. In some cases these structures could easily have existed alongside more 'Romanised' rectangular building forms, as is seen at the villa sites already discussed.

The physical traces of the layout of the landscape in the Stanton Harcourt and Yarnton area contrasts interestingly with that seen a little further downstream, for example between Abingdon and Dorchester. Here a number of the same features are present – in particular the trackways with associated enclosures – but the arrangement seems, subjectively, slightly less dense and a little more regular. It may be significant that villas do occasionally occur in this landscape, whereas they are (so far) noticeably absent from, for example, the Stanton Harcourt area.

Further north in the county there is little detailed evidence for the nature of non-villa settlement. The existence of a number of enclosed sites has already been noted, but none of these has been systematically examined. Fieldwalking has located low-status settlement in the north-west of the county, for example at Shipton under Wychwood and Great Rollright, but the character of these sites, and whether or not they were enclosed, remains unknown.[32] In the north-east of the county recent surface collection has examined a number of rural settlements probably of non-villa type, some previously unknown, but again beyond their extent and potential date range little can be said without further evidence. At least one of these sites, at Drayton Park Farm, was apparently enclosed by earthworks, and this site and several others had one or more buildings with tiled or slated roofs. If not villas, these were fairly substantial farmhouses and in several cases the associated artefact scatters cover some 1.5–3ha, making them rather more extensive than, for example, the Shipton under Wychwood site, which, though densely covered with finds, occupied barely a quarter of a hectare.[33]

FIELDS AND TRACKWAYS

All rural settlements were directly and intimately linked to surrounding field systems, but these are much less often examined and thus less well understood than the settlements themselves. Much of the evidence comes from the Thames valley, though

4.11   Roman trackway and enclosures at Northfield Farm, Long Wittenham (some earlier features, particularly Bronze Age ring ditches, can also be seen). Ashmolean Museum, Allen collection.

here the contribution of aerial photography is less marked than might be expected, because while settlement sites are very apparent from the air (although without other evidence it is not always possible to distinguish between sites of Iron Age and Roman date) the intervening areas are sometimes less well defined and there are problems with dating the features which do appear. A good example can be seen at Long Wittenham (Fig. 4.11), where settlements and some of the trackways linking them are clearly defined though the indications of field systems between them are very limited, yet it is almost certain that they must have existed here.[34] Broadly, however, much of this landscape seems to have been divided into fields, the majority of which were defined by ditches that vary considerably in size, as a result of which some at least may not have survived modern agricultural practices. It may be presumed that in many cases the ditches were supplemented by hedges. This can rarely be demonstrated, but the presence of thorn hedges has been suggested, for example at Farmoor, on the basis of environmental evidence.[35] Another 'hedge' species, box, is also indicated at Farmoor,

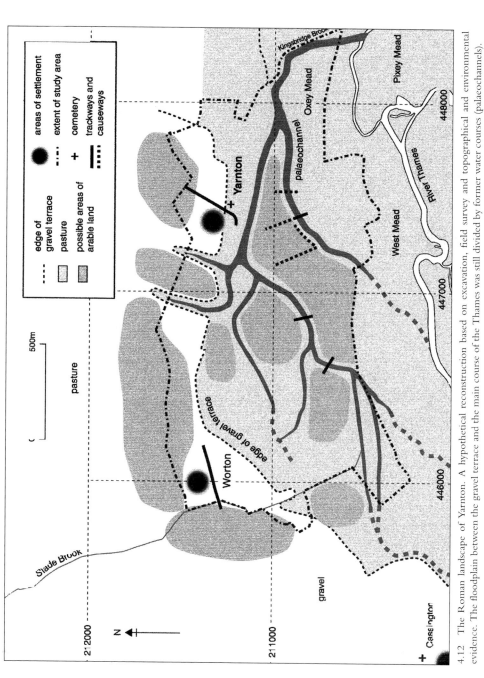

4.12 The Roman landscape of Yarnton. A hypothetical reconstruction based on excavation, field survey and topographical and environmental evidence. The floodplain between the gravel terrace and the main course of the Thames was still divided by former water courses (palaeochannels).

as well as at such disparate sites as Blackbird Leys and Roden Down, the latter just in Berkshire, though it may be that in all cases it derived from hedges directly associated with domestic sites.[36]

Large-scale fieldwork projects, or aerial photographic evidence supplemented by excavation to give chronological precision, enable us to see these field systems in operation. At Gravelly Guy (Stanton Harcourt) in the early Roman period a linear arrangement of roughly rectangular enclosures containing domestic and other settlement components, some possibly small paddocks, separated a zone of arable fields on the second gravel terrace from a very extensive area of long-established and arguably communal grazing land. The location of the latter, interestingly, was dictated not principally by agricultural logic but by its historic use for burials and other monuments, thus initially rendering it inappropriate for disturbance by arable farming, though at the Neolithic henge monument of Devil's Quoits nearby the upper fills of the ditch appear to consist of Roman ploughsoils, indicating that this landscape was eventually encroached upon for arable use.[37] At Old Shifford Farm evidence for early fields is scarce, though the grassland setting of the early Roman site indicated by the environmental evidence need not have been extensively divided up.[38] Elements of an early Roman field system may, however, have lain a little to the north of contemporaneous settlement. The alignment of these features was maintained in the later Roman period, when a substantial droveway ran through the site. Associated boundaries defined fields and activity areas at the edge of the late Roman settlement.

Slightly further down the Thames some of our best evidence comes from Yarnton, where a large area of gravel terraces and floodplain has been examined extensively (Fig. 4.12). Here areas of arable cultivation on the second gravel terrace south of the settlement site were not apparently defined by ditches, but there is extensive evidence for arable fields on the lower-lying floodplain, indicated both by drainage ditches and by ploughsoils, while the plant remains include arable weeds of wetter ground as well as those appropriate to cultivation on the gravel terraces. Field boundary ditches on the floodplain can be seen to cut earlier, pre-Roman deposits and to be sealed by later alluvial soils, probably of medieval date. In the lowest-lying areas the ground was too wet for arable agriculture but was instead exploited as pasture. These areas were accessed by droveways running between the arable fields. Elsewhere in the Yarnton area the extent of arable agriculture in the Roman period can be identified on the basis of the thin scatter of well-worn Roman pottery which probably derived from the manure heaps of the settlement, distributed in the fields as fertiliser. In the early Roman period at least these scatters extend into the floodplain but are less common here later on and it is possible that the floodplain ceased to be used for arable fields in the later Roman period.[39]

On the right bank of the Thames, at Farmoor, a ditched trackway ran in a rather similar way across the lowest gravel terrace to the edge of the floodplain, at which point it may have linked with a further track running along that topographical boundary, parallel to the line of the river. Whether this was the case or not, the two areas were separated by a ditch. Beside the trackway running across the gravel terrace lay ditched enclosures containing wells and waterholes. These are plausibly interpreted as paddocks for animals, an interpretation which is broadly supported by environmental evidence for grassland. Two corn drying ovens were also present, however, indicating arable agriculture not far away. An area with some (principally late Roman) occupation debris, most probably associated with a farmyard, was also identified in a marginal location just on the upper side of the boundary between the floodplain and the gravel terrace.[40]

Direct evidence for arable cultivation of Roman date, sealed beneath later alluvial deposits, was found at Drayton, south of Abingdon, revealed in the course of examination of earlier prehistoric features. Here a Neolithic cursus monument was overlain by Roman fields, linked to a settlement to the north. In one field, again defined by ditches, plough-marks and a ploughsoil of early Roman date were revealed, preserved by the overlying alluvium.[41] The ploughsoil contained a moderate quantity of very fragmented Roman pottery which indicated that it was probably of second-century date, and again suggests the use of farmyard refuse as manure.

Some 3.5km further east at Appleford contrasting evidence is revealed. At Appleford Field a substantial trackway first defined in the second century remained in use through the Roman period (Fig. 4.13). This formed one arm of a Y-shaped plan of tracks, the junction area of which was quite large and has been described as being like a village green in plan.[42] A number of very similar configurations of tracks have been noted in the Appleford area and elsewhere in the Thames valley, for example at Stanton Harcourt. The identification of all these distinctive features as Roman in date is very likely. Linked to this system of trackways were small fields or paddocks of various size, those closest to the trackways containing a variety of features relating to agricultural and domestic activity.[43] Barely half a kilometre to the north lies the probable villa site at Penn Copse, while a similar distance to the south an area of some 15ha of gravel terrace at Appleford Sidings has recently been planned after the removal of topsoil ready for gravel quarrying. Here, as at most of the sites already discussed, were quite small approximately rectilinear fields, associated at one point with a trackway, at another with a small enclosure which contained a cremation burial, and at another apparently integrated with a double-ditched rectilinear enclosed settlement of early Roman date (Fig. 4.3). The date of the establishment of this system relies largely on dating from the settlement enclosure, which is broadly of first/mid-second-century date but was probably not established until after the Roman conquest.[44] The extent of truncation of the deposits by modern ploughing means that no evidence of the type seen at Drayton survives here, but these may have been arable fields, unless the waterholes associated with this landscape can be demonstrated to be of Roman date (present indications are that these are prehistoric), which might suggest that the enclosures were intended to hold stock. At Appleford Field, however, a number of waterholes were definitely of Roman date.

Rectilinear field systems demonstrably of Roman date are less well known north of the Thames valley, but there are good examples closely associated with the town of Alchester. South of the town, rectilinear plots/fields are clearly seen from the air on both sides of the Dorchester road and aligned upon it. Ditches parallel to the road and apparently defining the limit of these fields lie some 400m west and 500m east of the road (Fig. 3.1). There is no close dating for this field system, though on the basis of its association with the Dorchester road it cannot have been established before the end of

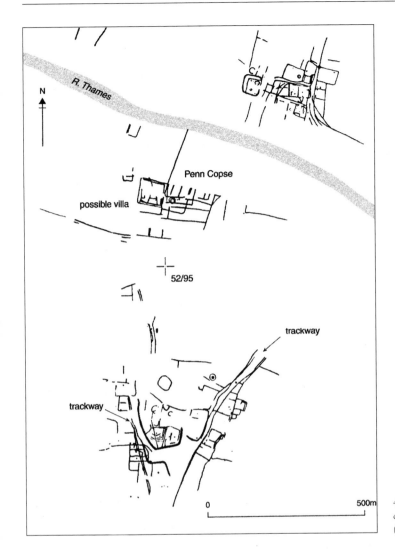

4.13   Rural settlement: plan of cropmarks around Appleford. (RCHME)

the first century AD. North of the town a further system of ditched boundaries, here laid out at right angles to the line of Akeman Street, was established in about the mid-second century. These later came to define property units some 55–60m wide, but in their original form seem to have been part of a more extensive field system; a ditch on exactly the line of one of these boundaries was located some 380m to the north and similar alignments have been recorded further north again in geophysical survey. The similarity of these alignments may perhaps have been coincidental, but seems to support the view that there was a substantial block of regularly laid out fields lying north of Akeman Street.[45] There is some evidence that a similar pattern might also have existed south of Akeman Street. These field systems around Alchester are notable in comparison with those other examples already mentioned in being rigidly regular, to the extent that their layout may be seen as a single act of policy, probably on the part of the governing body of the town, which may therefore have had the power, if not to appropriate land, then at least to reorganise it. The overall area covered by these very regular systems was relatively small, however, and there is no indication that this scheme was extended beyond the immediate vicinity of Alchester.

While there is little significant evidence for the form of fields in the northern part of the county – the small rectangular enclosures attached to the villa compound at Ditchley are among the few known examples – there is evidence of a very different kind from its south-western margins. On the Berkshire Downs are the surviving earthworks of so-called 'Celtic' fields, which vary in size, shape and regularity of plan but can be characteristically elongated and approximately rectilinear. Significant concentrations of these fields, first studied in the late 1940s, straddle the Oxfordshire/Berkshire border (Fig. 4.14).[46] The wide extent of their use in the Roman period has long been recognised, and recent fieldwork has suggested that many of these earthworks may have formed at this time as a result of intensification of arable agriculture,[47] a suggestion supported by environmental evidence which appears to indicate a relatively low level of arable use of these areas in the Iron Age.[48] While the evidence strictly relates to sites outside the county they are close enough to be directly

4.14   Rectangular Roman field system at Streatley Warren, Oxfordshire/Berkshire border, seen as earthworks in 1935. These features, typical of Roman field systems on the Downs, no longer survive. Ashmolean Museum, Allen collection.

relevant. Excavation at Tower Hill, Ashbury, inside the county also indicates a Roman (or possibly late Iron Age) date for a lynchet (earthwork field boundary) there.[49]

There is equally some evidence to support the view that parts of these field systems originated before the Roman period, as at Rams Hill, and at Lowbury Hill, where the temple enclosure, which could have originated in some form as early as the first century AD, appears to have been laid out over earthworks belonging to a pre-existing field system.[50] At least some of the colluvial (hillwash) soils of the area, likely to have formed as a consequence of arable agriculture, are almost certainly of pre-Roman date.[51] Nevertheless, even if parts of the system belonged to the first millennium BC the evidence for the use of most of it during the Roman period, and its expansion at this time, is overwhelming. These were of course arable fields, a fact indicated by the regular occurrence of (usually small) fragments of Roman pottery again derived from spreading farmyard manure. The apparent absence of these fields from some areas of the downland landscape, such as some of the more exposed parts of its northern fringes, might suggest that these locations were preferred for pasture, for which small fields were not appropriate. The expansion of arable in the Roman period is likely to have been at the expense of sheep pasture. The change of emphasis in the agricultural economy which this represents may reflect new opportunities for disposal of arable surplus in the Roman period.[52]

In the Thames valley and elsewhere differences in size, shape and frequency of field enclosures will have related to the type of agriculture practised within them. Pastoralism, often encountered on the lower terraces or the floodplain, required few field boundaries, as at Old Shifford (on the first terrace) and at Yarnton and Farmoor on the floodplain and as seen on Port Meadow, Oxford, even today. Defined trackways would have been required, however, for the movement of stock from these locations to other sites, and small enclosures related to such trackways and sometimes occurring in close proximity to settlements can be interpreted as paddocks for the enclosure of stock (or possibly in some cases as market garden plots). Larger fields defined by ditches or other features may generally indicate arable agriculture, therefore, as was probably the case on parts of the Berkshire Downs. Arable fields need not always have been defined in this way, however, and the 'boundary free' area of Long Wittenham mentioned above might possibly reflect a genuine absence of these features in a landscape that was nevertheless devoted substantially to arable rather than pastoral agriculture.

THE BROAD LANDSCAPE: THE ENVIRONMENT AND THE CHARACTER OF AGRICULTURAL PRACTICE

The landscape of the Downs was distinctive and for the Roman period is more readily characterised than that of almost any other part of the region, despite the quality and quantity of evidence for parts of the Thames valley and the lack on the Downs of some detailed evidence, particularly for settlement sites. The concentrations of 'Celtic' fields here indicate relatively intensive arable agriculture, supplemented in places by

4.15   Alfred's Castle, Ashbury. Substantial Roman building, possibly a villa, under excavation inside the Iron Age hillfort on the Downs.

pastoralism. A range of settlements was supported in this way and linked by trackways. They included modest villas, such as Maddle Farm (just in Berkshire) and perhaps the recently discovered site at Alfred's Castle, situated within a substantial Iron Age earthwork (Fig. 4.15), as well as non-villa sites, most of which seem to have been enclosed.[53] At least some of these sites were probably closely integrated, like the Maddle Farm villa and the nearby settlement at Knighton Bushes. Rather further east there was a temple at Lowbury and non-agricultural economic activities included pottery production at Compton (again just outside the county). This landscape was utilised right through the Roman period, and included probable domestic reuse of the Uffington Castle hillfort in the later fourth century and the contemporaneous insertion of burials into a nearby long barrow.[54]

North of the Downs, in the clay vale and along the Corallian ridge, the overall picture of rural settlement is much less clear. A few villas are known, though none has been examined in detail, but the density and in particular the character of other settlements is relatively poorly understood, despite fieldwork in the 1970s and 1980s, and the evident potential which these surveys revealed.[55] The Vale of the White Horse survey carried out in 1984 showed that Roman material was widespread in the sample area examined,

though generally significantly less densely distributed than in the corresponding Maddle
Farm survey on the Downs.[56] Again in contrast to the pattern observed in the Maddle
Farm area later Roman pottery appeared to be much more common than distinctive
early material. The very few low-status settlement sites examined by excavation,
however, like Hatford and Coxwell Road, Faringdon, seem to have been principally
occupied in the early Roman period, but this is probably an accident of the sample
size.[57] The large settlement at Bowling Green Farm, Stanford in the Vale, was clearly
occupied throughout the Roman period, but this extensive site, if not an agricultural
'village', arguably belongs with the nucleated settlements discussed above.

North again the Thames valley presents a complex picture, dominated by the aerial
evidence indicating for the most part a dense pattern of lower-status settlement. There
may have been considerable variation in landholding arrangements, but in one area at
least, around Stanton Harcourt, the presence of a very large area of common grazing
land has been suggested, utilised by the inhabitants of a number of adjoining
settlements with similar distinctive characteristics of plan and location.[58] As already
discussed, villas are very scarce here, while in the north of the county they form the
most archaeologically visible, though not necessarily numerically dominant, settlement

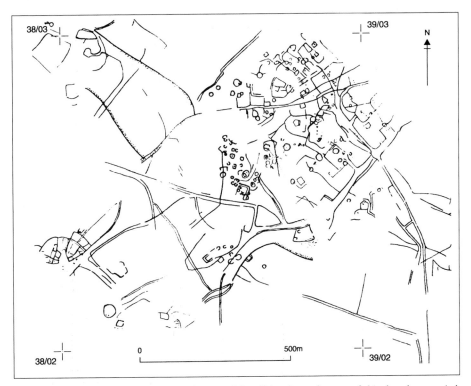

4.16 Rural settlement: plan of cropmarks around Standlake. Some features of this densely occupied
landscape may be of Iron Age date, but many are likely to be Roman, including most of the trackways
defined by ditches. (RCHME)

type. There may, however, have been a genuine distinction between the Thames valley and the uplands in terms of frequency of settlement sites. For the Iron Age Hingley has suggested that differences in settlement pattern between the Thames valley (particularly in that part of the valley centred on the Stanton Harcourt area) and the Cotswold area reflect very different organisations of society, with the former area characterised by dense, closely interrelated settlements and the latter by more widely spaced sites, frequently more clearly defined (by enclosure ditches) than their valley equivalents.[59] This pattern is seen as continuing into the Roman period. The 'Ditchley type' enclosures in the Cotswold area, whether or not they contained villas, could perhaps be seen as the Roman counterparts of the dispersed upland settlement pattern, but it is not clear that the situation is as straightforward as this. Certainly more recent work has increased the number of known Iron Age settlements in the Cotswold area, and the distinction in settlement density between the two zones may be less pronounced than Hingley thought. Equally, there appears to be (as yet limited) evidence for unenclosed sites, both Iron Age and Roman, in the Cotswold area. It remains true, however, that the characteristic Iron Age and Roman settlements of the area seem to be discrete, enclosed ones, and the existence of some unenclosed sites here does not in itself invalidate Hingley's model.

An extension of this view of the differences between the two areas is found in the suggestion that the contrasting social structures involved responded differently to the Roman conquest. In the upland area, where a more competitive social environment was already in place, active involvement in Romanisation resulted, while the valley settlements 'stagnate and fail to develop'.[60] The evidence of early villa development in the uplands would fit with this view, but such a development was arguably less a consequence of the broad social structure of settlement in the area than perhaps of the very specific social and political identity of the individuals concerned.

The Roman settlement pattern of the south-eastern part of the county, in contrast, is insufficiently known to provide evidence for such speculation. It has some of the characteristics of the Upper Thames valley, with a number of sites on the river gravels known from the air. East of the Goring Gap the chalklands are more wooded than those of the Downs to the west. There is, unfortunately, insufficient evidence to discern distinctive differences in settlement pattern north and south of the Grim's Ditch, which is likely to have been a boundary of late Iron Age date. A number of villas are known, including examples at Gatehampton Farm, Goring, at Bix and Harpsden Wood, all partly excavated at various times.[61] A typical flint and tile built structure at Harpsden High Wood, only a kilometre from the last site, is of uncertain character but might have been another villa. Non-villa settlement must have been widespread but is not well evidenced beyond finds scatters. At Cold Harbour Farm, Crowmarsh, a second/fourth-century settlement appears to have lain within a ditched enclosure, but the only structure so far identified is a probable corn drying oven and there is at present no clear evidence that the enclosure contained buildings of villa character. The site is of interest, however, for its close association with two coin hoards of third-century date and a small cemetery of north–south aligned inhumations of fourth-century date, one in a lead-lined coffin.[62]

THE CHRONOLOGY OF RURAL SETTLEMENT

Over a period of some 350 years there were inevitably changes in the character and patterns of rural settlement. A number of trends can be identified, particularly in the Thames valley, where the majority of excavation has taken place. Rural settlements of the post-conquest period were essentially of two types in terms of their earlier history: those which had been occupied through a considerable part of the Iron Age, and those which seem to have been newly established in the late Iron Age, though in some cases sites of the latter type grew up in close proximity to their predecessors, as for example at Gravelly Guy, where the late Iron Age and early Roman site lay immediately north of the early/middle Iron Age settlement. There is, as already mentioned, very little direct evidence for the disruption of the settlement pattern at the time of the conquest, though there are a number of sites in the Bicester area where the latest occupation was associated with 'Belgic type' pottery with a total absence of Romanised types. Such assemblages are unlikely to have dated much after the time of the conquest, though the conquest itself is of course not directly represented in the ceramic record. Equally, there is no indication that it was the events of the conquest period which brought activity at these sites to an end, though this is a possibility. There is in any case no sign at any of these sites, of which the possibly high-status enclosure of Bicester Fields Farm is the best known, that their end was sudden or violent. However, the fact that their development history is different from that of most other sites in the region is notable, and it may perhaps be significant that these sites all lay in Catuvellaunian rather than Dobunnic territory.[63]

In contrast to this pattern of development the great majority of sites in existence by the middle of the first century AD, characterised by pottery in the 'Belgic' tradition, continued to be occupied beyond the end of the century. In a large number of cases, however, occupation can be shown to have ceased at about the end of the first quarter of the second century, a situation that seems to apply particularly to sites first established in the late Iron Age. A wide variety of sites were affected in this way, including the relatively high-status 'proto-villas' at Barton Court Farm and Appleford, the enclosure complex at Gravelly Guy and individual enclosure sites such as Old Shifford Farm and Linch Hill Corner, Stanton Harcourt, among a significant number of lower-status rural settlements, and probably the nucleated settlement at Abingdon as well. The pattern can also be detected in older excavations, such as that at Hinksey Hill of a site of slightly uncertain character.[64] Nor was it confined to the Thames valley: at Hatford in the Vale of the White Horse a site with both middle and late Iron Age settlement came to an end early in the second century, while an unenclosed site at Oxford Road, Bicester, just over 1km north of Alchester, also had the late Iron Age to early second-century date range typical of sites in this group.[65] In fact so common is this trend that in the Upper Thames valley at least, sites terminating in the first half of the second century were probably more numerous than sites occupied throughout the Roman period.

The corollary of this is that a substantial number of rural settlements sites were newly established in the second century, most of which then seem to have survived into the late Roman period. In many cases these will have been the direct successors of earlier sites and were situated close to them, but in other instances there is no clear evidence of predecessors in the near vicinity. At the upper end of the Thames valley there is again a local variation in that several sites established in the second century were occupied into the third century but not, apparently, into the fourth. This phenomenon, encountered around Lechlade, for example, appears to have been a feature of some Gloucestershire rather than Oxfordshire sites.[66]

In terms of the overall development of the rural settlement pattern, therefore, it is the period at about the end of the first quarter of the second century that sees the most radical dislocation of sites. The dating evidence, consisting almost entirely of pottery, does not allow us to judge if this was a sudden change or whether it took place over a generation or so centred around a date of *c.* AD 130, but the evidence is remarkably consistent from a number of sites, which might suggest that the period of change was shorter rather than longer. On present evidence this dislocation is most marked in the Thames valley itself, but occurs elsewhere, as we have seen.

Such a major change in the settlement pattern demands explanation, but this is not straightforward, as a few examples will show. It is clearly not the case that those sites which 'failed' were all established early in the Iron Age and that conversely the sites which developed through the Roman period all originated in the later Iron Age.[67] Both Gravelly Guy and Yarnton were occupied throughout the Iron Age and both saw a degree of settlement shift in the late Iron Age – rather more clear cut at Gravelly Guy – but while the latter then ceased to be occupied at a date estimated to be around AD 125 Yarnton continued to develop through the Roman period and even beyond. While there are some distinctions in their respective layouts there are no really significant discernible differences between the character of the sites in their early Roman phases. Gravelly Guy is one of a group of sites in the vicinity of the Windrush/Thames confluence that shows this dislocation, others being Linch Hill, also in Stanton Harcourt parish and one of the 'type sites' for the late Iron Age of the Upper Thames, Old Shifford Farm (Shifford) and Smith's Field (Hardwick). In the same area, however, second-century activity at Watkins Farm (Northmoor) and Eagle Farm (Standlake) probably continued at least to the middle of the century if not beyond, and there was low-level late Roman activity at Watkins Farm. Here and at Eagle Farm late Iron Age activity appears to have been lacking, in contrast to the situation at the other sites just mentioned.[68]

Further down the Thames, sites in the Abingdon area were also affected by the hiatus. These included the probable high-status/nucleated site in the centre of Abingdon itself, where the character of settlement activity seems to have undergone a marked change, and the site of Barton Court Farm as already mentioned, but the settlement at Ashville was also affected. Here reassessment of the pottery makes it clear that the late Iron Age period (period 3) extended well beyond the Roman conquest and was probably continuous with the development of ditch systems into the first half of the second century AD, a situation paralleled in excavation at the nearby Abingdon Business Park in 1994. Late Roman activity was essentially confined to the excavation of wells and graves, both of these activities following after an apparent break in occupation of at least a century.[69]

Overall, therefore, a majority of the excavated rural sites which have adequate evidence reflect this period of settlement dislocation, with occupation either terminating in the first half of the second century or commencing at some time within the second century. In the latter cases the earliest settlement is often difficult to date precisely, but generally seems not to belong to the early part of the century. It appears most likely that these sites reflect the appearance of a new settlement pattern after the early second century. As far as can be seen, however, most of the major nucleated settlements and the early North Oxfordshire villa sites were not affected by this dislocation, but other continuously occupied rural sites are unusual, though some clearly existed, such as Yarnton.

The potentially early Cotswold villas are of considerable interest. North Leigh, Ditchley, Shakenoak, Bury Close (Fawler) and Callow Hill, all lying within the North Oxfordshire Grim's Ditch, have all produced evidence indicating late first or (at the latest) very early second-century origins.[70] While it cannot be absolutely certain that the earliest structures at all these sites were of villa character this seems very likely. It may simply be the case that evidence of comparably early origins has not been sought in other Oxfordshire villa sites, but the concentration of early evidence in this area is still striking, as is the association of a number of these sites with evidence, in the form of 'carrot' amphorae, a relatively rare amphora type more usually encountered on military sites, for their precocious connection to a particularly Romanised pattern of trade.[71] Unfortunately the lack of detailed evidence for non-villa sites in this area makes it uncertain if these, like the villas, escaped the early second-century disruption of the regional settlement pattern, which may therefore possibly have been a phenomenon confined to the central and southern parts of the county. This seems unlikely to have been the case, however, and it is more likely that the Grim's Ditch villas had particular characteristics that rendered them resistant to, or set them apart from, the processes of change seen elsewhere.

The appearance of the majority of the known villas in the county follows on from the early second-century period of settlement dislocation, though it is unclear how many developed immediately after it. The limited excavated evidence from sites such as Islip, for example, is consistent with such a date, though other villas may have developed later. Immediately outside the county, the villa at Roughground Farm, Lechlade, certainly seems to have been established in the first half of the second century. Moreover, adjacent and related settlement of non-villa character, arguably the accommodation of estate workers, was also newly established at this time. Pre-existing landscape divisions and trackways were largely retained, however,[72] so while settlement was reorganised or rationalised the broader landscape was less obviously impacted. In the Stanton Harcourt area, however, there are some indications of a more radical change. Here the abandonment of such sites as Gravelly Guy seems to have been followed by the development of a number of settlements situated closer to the boundary between the second gravel terrace and the floodplain, well placed to exploit the resources of both and maximising the use of the gravel terrace soils for arable agriculture. These settlements are characteristically linked by well-defined trackways which, while not a new feature type in the landscape, are certainly more pronounced than their counterparts in the late Iron Age and early Roman periods (Fig. 4.16). A

4.17 Rural settlement: plan of cropmarks around Cote. Several trackways converge on an open space surrounded by settlement components. (RCHME)

similar development may have taken place at Cote, near Bampton, where settlements linked by trackways define the edge of the second/third terrace gravels (Fig. 4.17). These sites appear to date to the second to fourth centuries rather than earlier.[73]

Some important nucleated settlements may also have come into existence in the early to mid-second century, perhaps corresponding to the apparent change in character of sites such as Abingdon. In particular there is no evidence for occupation earlier than this time at Gill Mill, Ducklington, and Bowling Green Farm, Stanford in the Vale, may also have developed at this time rather than earlier, though the exact nature of this site in its earlier phases remains uncertain.

One interpretation of the processes of settlement and landscape replanning in the second century is to see these as 'a further stage in the break up of earlier Iron Age structures, in the context of a more capital intensive system involving a much more complex social, economic and political infrastructure'.[74] This is possible, and interpretation of the specific developments at Roughground Farm and in the Stanton Harcourt area in terms of economic development is plausible, but there must also have been a strong social impetus for such developments. The fact that the early villa sites discussed above were apparently little touched by these processes might suggest that their occupants, who have already been potentially identified as senior members of the Dobunnic tribal élite, were among the prime movers of the process. It is possible that their development represented an earlier phase of rural settlement reorganisation. While there is no direct evidence to link this to the contemporaneous establishment of the first Roman phase of the site at Claydon Pike, Fairford (again just across the county boundary into Gloucestershire), very likely directly concerned with military supply,[75] a connection is possible, but its investigation requires further work.

On present evidence it is only in the north of the county that (some) villas developed to become very substantial and ostentatiously wealthy establishments in the later Roman period and there does seem to be both a quantitative and qualitative distinction in this respect between the Dobunnic area and the Atrebatic and Catuvellaunian parts of the region. The principal difficulty with this line of interpretation would seem to be the evidence which suggests that the major phase of settlement dislocation was relatively short-lived and broadly contemporaneous across the county. This is at variance with the view of what should have been a more gradual and potentially piecemeal trend. Is it possible, therefore, that there was also a specific political initiative to bring about change? This is not to suggest that the observed settlement disruption was the object of any such initiative, but rather a side-effect of it.

Whatever the immediate causes, once new patterns of settlement were established across the region, for the most part by about the middle of the second century, they appear to have remained fairly stable throughout the rest of the Roman period. The pace of change thereafter in such areas as technological development in agriculture, as has been pointed out (by George Lambrick), would not have been uniform and measuring the extent of the general adoption rather than documentation merely of the introduction of new technologies or subsistence strategies (or architectural styles) is still a significant challenge.[76]

ENVIRONMENT

Aspects of the environment within which Roman settlement in Oxfordshire was situated have been referred to above and are also mentioned in relation to agriculture in Chapter six, but some main points can be summarised here. The environment is most easily reconstructed in the Thames valley. Here the combined records of pollen, other plant remains, insects and snails suggest a consistently open landscape. In a few cases it is possible to suggest declining levels of woodland, but for the most part the open landscape was well established by the early Roman period. The range of habitats varies from pasture to arable fields and, in some cases, disturbed or even scrubby ground. Most of these habitats are consistent with an intensively exploited landscape with pasture and arable fields, some of which were certainly hedged. The downland landscape was also open and intensively exploited. For other areas the picture is less clear. There were presumably still some significant areas of woodland, but these were not in locations where extensive environmental sampling has taken place and it has been suggested that 'woodland need not have been much more abundant . . . than during the nineteenth century'.[77] Some indication of the survival of established woodland came from Barton Court Farm, on the Thames gravels, where gaps in the stone lining of a well had been packed with moss. The mosses themselves and associated insects and pollen indicated that they derived from old-established oak and hazel woodland.[78] Comparable woodland still exists today some 3km north of Barton Court Farm at Bagley Wood, and it has been suggested that this might have been the source of the material, though derivation from a more nearly adjacent (and now lost) source would also be possible.

Woodland resources would have been important, where available, not only for domestic fuel but also for industries such as pottery production. It is generally assumed that such resources would have been carefully husbanded and that coppicing would therefore have been widely practised.[79] While this remains likely there is at present little direct evidence for coppicing, however, and recent examination of charcoal from the pottery production site at Blackbird Leys indicates that a range of species was used to fire kilns, which does not particularly suggest systematic woodland management, though the extent to which this situation was typical is unknown.

Useful evidence on the state of woodland comes from a long pollen sequence at Sidlings Copse, less than a kilometre north of the villa at Headington Wick and a similar distance west of the Dorchester-Alchester road, lying within the northern extent of the Oxford pottery industry. Here the principal tree species – oak, alder and hazel – declined to very low levels of representation within the Roman period, so that by about the third century 'no woodland remained around the site'. Woodland regeneration then took place in the medieval period.[80] The reduction in woodland may reflect the impact of the pottery industry on this resource, but it is also accompanied by an increase in cereal pollen, so there may have been several factors at work. Overall, however, the requirement of land for agricultural purposes (whether arable or pastoral), and of timber for domestic and industrial use, particularly for the major pottery industry, would all have had a potentially erosive effect on the surviving woodland resource. The operation of these factors in areas such as the north of the county, where there is much less evidence, is harder to estimate.

One general environmental change observable in the Thames valley was an increase in the deposition of alluvial soils, and hence in the extent of flooding, through the Roman period. This is seen most clearly at sites such as Drayton and Yarnton where early Roman ploughsoils or field boundary ditches were overlain with alluvium. It is likely that the use of some fields for arable was abandoned, but these areas could still have been exploited for grazing in some conditions. A general rise in water-table levels also seems to be characteristic of the Roman period in the region, and is noted at sites such as Alchester away from the Thames valley itself. Here the effects of the rising water-table seem to have been largely mitigated by intensive efforts at maintaining systems of drainage. There may have been resources available at this time for even larger-scale projects. In particular it has been suggested that Otmoor may have been drained in the Roman period. While this remains uncertain, the fact that the Dorchester–Alchester road could be routed straight across Otmoor by about the end of the first century AD does suggest that some improvement in conditions had been achieved there. This kind of proactive involvement with the environment seems to have been characteristic of the period, and the inability to maintain effective features such as large-scale drainage systems at its end may have been a factor in the ultimate abandonment of sites such as Alchester.

NOTES

1. The importance of the aerial photographic evidence was appreciated well before the Second World War. The first synthesis of this evidence was by Benson & Miles (1974), though the plots are superseded by the more recent work of the Royal Commission's Thames Valley survey. The most important field survey includes Hingley's work on the Thames Valley (1983a, partly summarised in Hingley 1989), the Maddle Farm survey at the extreme south-west of the county (Gaffney & Tingle 1989) and the Vale of the White Horse survey centred slightly to the north (Tingle 1991). There has been relatively little systematic field survey in the northern part of the county. The most extensive detailed examinations of the Roman landscape have been at Yarnton (some 20ha) and Appleford (some 14ha). Important overview articles are Miles 1982 and Lambrick 1992a and 1992b.

2. Cf. Millett 1990, 125–6.

3. E.g. Young 1986, 59.

4. E.g. Millett 1990, 56–9.

5. Lambrick 1992a.

6. Allen et al. 1984; Keevill & Booth 1997.

7. Summaries of Yarnton include Hey 1991; 1996a; 1996b.

8. Romanised buildings in other nucleated settlements have also been claimed as villas in the absence of a true understanding of the nature of these sites, so for example buildings at Sansom's Platt are listed by Miles (1982) and Scott (1993) as potential villas, and Scott includes Asthall. These are the only recent lists of Oxfordshire villas. Miles' list of 73 sites (Miles 1982, 69–71) includes 15 which lie outside the county, 8 in 'non-villa' contexts (7 major settlements and 1 shrine), and 2 for which the evidence appears inadequate to justify inclusion. Complete agreement on a definitive list of villa sites is not to be expected.

9. Miles 1986, 9–12, 30.

10. Booth & Hardy 1993. The pottery assemblage is small, however, so the assessment of status should be treated with caution.

11. Shakenoak, Brodribb et al. 1968; 1971; 1972; 1973; 1978. Barton Court Farm, Miles 1986.

12. The (now classic) photographs taken by Major Allen, were so clear that it was even doubted in some quarters if excavation was necessary at all.

13. Radford 1936; the influence of this excavation in Romano-British studies was considerable – Booth forthcoming b.

14. The most convenient recent summary is by Wilson & Sherlock (1980), now supplemented with useful detail in Ellis 1999.

15. Shakenoak, Brodribb et al. 1968, 12–27. For the plan of Harpsden Wood, Rivers-Moore 1951, 24. Goring, Tim Allen pers. comm.

16. E.g. Frere & St Joseph 1983, 195–6.

17. At Shakenoak the round building is demonstrably domestic and this is likely to have been the case at Ditchley, where the excavator's interpretation as a threshing floor is most improbable.

18. For a review, Keevill & Booth 1997; for the Churchill Hospital, Young 1977, 25–8; Faringdon, Saunders & Weaver 1999, 3.

19. *VCH* Berks I, 207–8.

20. Chambers 1989a.

21. Miles 1986, 14.

22. For a short discussion see Miles 1989, 65.

23. Ibid., 70–2; for Roughground Farm in detail, Allen et al. 1993.

24. Ibid., 197. See also Hingley 1989, 102–5.

25. Miles 1989, 66.

26. Old Shifford, Hey 1995, 108; Watkins Farm, Allen 1990a, 82.

27. Hingley 1988, 91.

28. Lambrick & Robinson 1979, 134–5.

29. See for example maps 21 and 22 in Benson & Miles 1974.
30. Hingley 1988, 91.
31. Cf. note 7.
32. Shipton, Ware & Ware 1993; Rollright, Lambrick 1988, 67 and 96.
33. Ware & Ware 1993 – it is of course possible that the site was more extensive than the pottery scatter, but there is no particular reason to believe this; Shawyer 1998, 65–70; 1999, 60.
34. Gray 1977, plan opposite p. 2, discussion of cropmarks in appendix (Miles 1977).
35. Lambrick & Robinson 1979, 121–2.
36. Roden Down, Hood & Walton 1948.
37. Lambrick et al. forthcoming (Gravelly Guy); Barclay et al. 1995, 113 (Devil's Quoits).
38. Hey 1995, 170.
39. Hey 1996, 67.
40. Lambrick & Robinson 1979, 72–6.
41. Lambrick 1992a, 98–9.
42. Hinchliffe & Thomas 1980, 68–9; cf a similar arrangement at Roughground Farm, Lechlade, Gloucestershire (Allen 1993, 187).
43. Several probably at one time contained structures, but these did not survive – see general comment on structures above, also Hinchliffe & Thomas 1980, 69.
44. Booth & Hardy 1993.
45. Booth et al. forthcoming.
46. Rhodes 1950; Fowler (1983, 102) suggests that the emphasis on individual 'field' morphology may be misplaced and that it is more appropriate to see the individual 'fields' as plots within wider units, on the analogy of the furlongs of medieval open field systems.
47. Ford et al. 1988; Bowden et al. 1991–3.
48. Gaffney & Tingle 1989, 93; Mark Robinson pers. comm.
49. Campbell 1994, 13.
50. Rams Hill, Bradley & Ellison 1975, 67–9; Lowbury Hill, Fulford & Rippon 1994, 162.
51. Chris Day pers. comm.
52. Mark Robinson pers. comm.
53. Maddle Farm, Gaffney & Tingle 1989; Alfred's Castle, Gosden & Lock 1999, the exact nature of the enclosure, which many would consider a small hillfort, is debated.
54. Lowbury, Atkinson 1916; Fulford & Rippon 1994. White Horse Hill, Cromarty et al. forthcoming b. For the eastern part of the Downs see also Kendal 1993.
55. Miles 1982, 62–4.
56. Tingle 1991, 58–60.
57. Hatford, excavations by Tempus Reparatum,

unpublished; Faringdon, Saunders & Weaver 1999.
58. Lambrick et al. forthcoming.
59. Hingley 1984, 78–82; Hingley 1988.
60. Hingley 1988, 73. The basic distinction in settlement pattern between the upland and valley areas has of course been observed over a long period, and was drawn by M.V. Taylor in *VCH*, 268–9.
61. Gatehampton Farm, Allen 1995a; Harpsden, *VCH* I 323–4; Rivers-Moore 1951. Bix is unpublished, Roger Kendal kindly provided information.
62. Clarke 1996; 1997. See also further below; for the coin hoards see King 1997.
63. The sites are Slade Farm, Bicester (Hughes & Jones 1997), Bicester Fields Farm (Cromarty et al. forthcoming a), and A421 Site D, just north of Alchester (Booth et al. forthcoming), and the Finmere Bypass site on the Oxon/Northants border (Grundon 1999).
64. Myres 1931.
65. Mould 1996.
66. Such as Stubbs Farm, Kempsford and Whelford Bowmore, unpublished excavations by Oxford Archaeol. Unit.
67. As Fulford (1992, 32) would suggest.
68. Gravelly Guy, Lambrick et al. forthcoming; Linch Hill, Grimes 1943; Old Shifford Farm, Hey 1995; Smith s Field, Allen 1981; Watkins Farm, Allen 1990a; Eagle Farm, Allen & Moore 1987.
69. Timby et al. 1997; Parrington 1979, 22–5.
70. For a summary with references see Booth 1998, 15.
71. Ibid.; Booth forthcoming b. The sites in question are Shakenoak, Bury Close (Fawler) and Ditchley, as well as the nucleated settlement of Wilcote.
72. Allen et al. 1993, 196–7.
73. For a general plan of the Stanton Harcourt area, Lambrick 1992a, 91; for Cote see Hingley 1988, 91–2.
74. Ibid., 105.
75. Allen et al. 1993, 196; Miles 1984, 208–9.
76. Ibid., 103.
77. Robinson & Wilson 1987, 53.
78. Miles 1986, 22–3.
79. E.g. Robinson & Wilson 1987, 53.
80. Day 1991, 467–8. The sequence is dated by radiocarbon and the lowest level of tree pollen representation is put at roughly 1700 BP (before present, i.e. before AD 1950) in uncalibrated radiocarbon years).

CHAPTER FIVE

THE PEOPLE OF ROMAN OXFORDSHIRE

The Roman Empire depended on literacy for the proper ordering of society, and the use of the written word would have underpinned the lives of the inhabitants of what is now Oxfordshire just as it did in the villages and small towns of Egypt.[1] Such an assertion is not a claim that everyone was able to read and write, though as we will see there is evidence that literacy was quite widespread, but trade, taxation and religion all depended on documents. Where Oxfordshire differs from the Fayum is that documentary evidence has not survived. There are no contemporary literary references to the area of modern Oxfordshire in the Roman period and even the ancient names of the two small towns, Dorchester and Alchester, are uncertain. Bede gives the name of the former as *Dorcic*, which has a British root possibly including *derc*, 'eye' and hence 'bright (or splendid) place' or possibly *duro*, 'fort or walled town'. It is possible that Alchester is the *Alauna* cited in the eighth-century Ravenna Cosmography as suggested by a mid-twelfth-century name *Alencestr*, although Rivet & Smith for example think this particular *Alauna* was Alcester in Warwickshire. The name is a very common one whose meaning is uncertain, though it may have the significance of 'good' or 'holy'.[2] Not a single papyrus nor its likely local equivalent, the wooden ink-inscribed *tabula* like those recently excavated at the military station of Vindolanda, remains. Nor, despite the preservation of metal styli, at Wilcote for example, is there any waxed tablet like that from London, recently published by Roger Tomlin, which contained a legal text concerning a dispute about a wood in Kent, though no doubt such legal wrangles took place over the Oxfordshire countryside with cases being heard in the great basilicas of *Corinium Dobunnorum* (Cirencester), *Verulamium* (St Albans) or *Calleva Atrebatum* (Silchester).[3] Lesser disputes were doubtless taken to the gods and examples of the so-called curse tablets scratched on sheets of lead have been found at many temple sites including Bath and Pagans Hill in Somerset and Uley and Lydney Park in Gloucestershire.[4] These are in fact prayers to the gods asking them to restore rights – especially property – and to punish malefactors. It is presumably only a matter of chance that Woodeaton has to date yielded no such complaint couched in legal language that whoever, whether man or woman, slave or free, had stolen some item of property should suffer in his health unless or until he or she returned it.

This means that for the most part we have to learn about life in the region through analogy with other areas (see Chapter two) and from archaeology. Enough inscriptions remain, however, to tell us a little of Oxfordshire's inhabitants and their lives. Roman cities and even smaller towns would have been full of inscriptions cut in capital letters on stone, many of them dedications of buildings, honorific statues and altars to the gods. In the majority of cases allusion was made to the Emperor, a reminder to the reader that he or she was inextricably bound into a vast, divinely protected Empire. Coins, found on every Roman site, are generally used by archaeologists as aids to dating or, if there are enough of them, as indicators of the economy locally or over a wider area, but it needs to be stressed more often than it is that ancient coins with their imperial images, titles and slogans played a vital part in disseminating official propaganda. If they don't always tell us what the people in Roman Oxfordshire thought, they do tell us something of what those in authority wished them to think.

A fragment of a first- or early second-century honorific inscription (Fig. 8.9), carved on a slab of Purbeck marble, was found in a pit 300m north of Alchester, though it almost certainly came from a grand building within the settlement. Only five letters remain but they may contain part of the name of an emperor or a governor. In general one can compare it with a far grander inscription, commemorating the inauguration of the Forum at Verulamium in AD 79.[5] Purbeck marble, the finest native stone for inscriptions, was brought from Dorset and could not have been cheap. Its extraction may originally have been in the hands of or contracted out by the Second Legion and it is tempting to see the hand of officialdom here, perhaps in connection with a *mansio* at a nodal point where the road from the south approaches Akeman Street. There is, incidentally, another official dedication from Alchester, a bronze weight purportedly of one *libra*, but slightly underweight, with the inscription CAES · AUG on the side showing it to be imperial property and possibly indicative of government maintenance of weights and measures.[6]

The other inscription from Oxfordshire whose contents demonstrate the hand of the state is the well-known altar from Dorchester (Fig. 2.3).[7] Although now lost, its lettering with its ligatures and the name of the dedicator shows it to have been set up in the early third century. Marcus Varius Severus was a *beneficiarius consularis*, a legionary seconded from his unit and assigned to serve both as a collector of customs dues and as an officer charged to secure the smooth running of the imperial post. He must have been a figure of some consequence in a small community, administratively a *pagus*, and this is emphasised by the wording on the altar. It is addressed to Jupiter Optimus Maximus and the imperial *numina*. The word *numen* is best translated as the divine spirit which envelops the emperor. The Dorchester inscription names more than one *numen* so two emperors, probably Septimius Severus and his son Caracalla, are implied. If so it is possible that Marcus Varius Severus was helping to marshal supplies in about AD 208 for the imperial expedition to Scotland, in which case it is just possible that members of the imperial entourage, if not the emperors themselves (who presumably set out from London), glanced at the altar with its screens (*ara cum cancellis*) on their way north. In any case this would have been Varius Severus' own contribution to the success of the venture as it was set up from his own funds (*de suo posuit*). The altar is now lost but it was probably of oolitic limestone from the Cotswolds like the altars and reliefs discussed below. These no longer bear any inscription (if they ever did), but are carved with the images of deities.

Other names recorded in the county are predominantly those of native Britons. The only other inscription on stone is a plain limestone grave slab from Woodeaton cut in cursive capitals with the name Dec(i)mus Malus(ius) or more probably of Dec(i)mius son of Malus(ius). Temples were not generally places of burial and this memorial evidently came from the cemetery of the nearby settlement.[8] The text does not preserve the name of the dedicator, by analogy likely to have been a relative, but the fact that he had a permanent monument demonstrates that Decimius had a certain consequence in the community. The absence of other tombstones is not surprising; they are relatively rare in southern Britain and even Cirencester has yielded no more than a handful. Others would certainly have existed. The statue of a stone lion of which the hindpart remains (Fig. 5.1) and a length of coping-stone with part of the

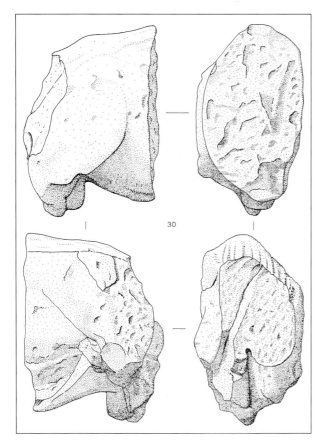

5.1   Hindquarters of a lion from Shakenoak. Height 300mm. After Brodribb et al. 1972, fig. 13.

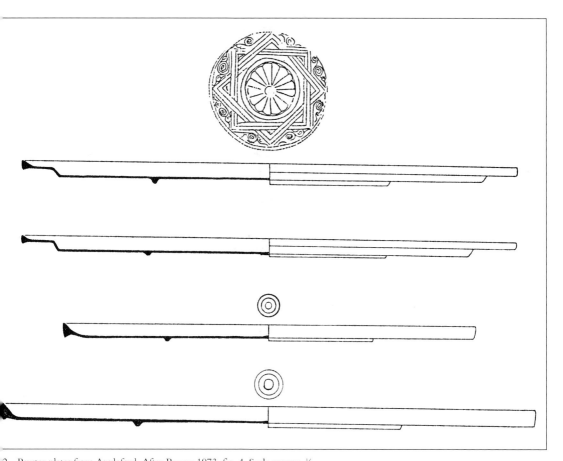

2 Pewter plates from Appleford. After Brown 1973, fig. 4. Scale approx. ⅙.

figure of a smaller lion come from a tomb or tombs near Shakenoak; these demonstrate that at least one villa owner here had a substantial monument, surely inscribed with his name and perhaps also his virtues.[9] Fortunately the practice of epigraphy extended beyond the formal to smaller, generally personal, objects on which owners sometimes recorded their names.

Pewter took the place of silver in farms and small villas. The large Appleford hoard of pewter (Fig. 5.2) comprises a service (*ministerium*) or perhaps a combination of parts of several services. Four plates are inscribed with personal names of women (Fig. 5.3), presumably the wives of farmers: Melluna (or Meliuna) on one, Narina on another and Pacata on two more.[10] The first names are purely Celtic, but the last is ultimately a celebration of the Roman peace. A famous bearer of the name was Julia Pacata, daughter of Julius Indus and wife of the procurator C. Iulius Classicianus.[11] One of the Pacata plates has a longer secondary inscription proclaiming that Lovernianus had presented his own purchased acquisitions.[12] It would seem that the items in the hoard, previously used domestically, were ultimately dedicated to some god or goddess, not alas named. Another dish evidently from north Oxfordshire but now lost carries a graffito wishing long life to Docilinus and his family and was evidently a present from a friend or relative.[13]

The nature of some items demonstrates the existence of craft activities in the populace. An oculist's stamp, a tablet of fine-grained limestone carved retrograde *Mauri collyruum* ('the salve of Maurus') was found at Shakenoak villa near Wilcote. Such tablets are widespread in Britain, many of them from towns and other settlements on roads recorded in the Antonine Itinerary.[14] In this case the stamp was lost very near a roadside station on Akeman Street. Eye-troubles were common in Roman Britain; dust on the roads may have exacerbated some complaints and a *mansio* or *mutatio* may have been the ideal place for a specialist to set up his stall. More important to the wider economy was the pottery industry. In the second century the potter Vossullus stamped white-ware *mortaria* (mixing bowls) at Cowley. In addition two sherds from another *mortarium*, a waster from the kilns on the site of the Churchill Hospital, Headington, were each incised with a graffito in capitals reading *Tamesubugus fecit* ('Tamesubugus made this'), and reveal a potter whose name was derived from the

5.3   Graffiti on pewter from Appleford. After Brown 1973, fig. 9.

5.4 *Mortarium* sherd from Churchill Hospital, Oxford, with *Tamesubugus Fecit* ('Tamesubugus made it') inscriptions. After RIB 2496.4.

nearby river Tamesis (Fig. 5.4). A colour-coated vessel perhaps of the late third century was stamped *Patern(us)*.[15]

One of the most remarkable objects recovered from the villa at Shakenoak is a baked clay *syrinx* (pipes of Pan) with seven or perhaps eight pipes. One side has the name Satavacus cut upon it, the other Bellicia. Few items from Roman Britain bring us so close to the romantic world of young lovers enjoying themselves on a hot afternoon. Such instruments must have been quite common in Roman times; they are frequently shown in art, as upon one of the panels of the *triclinium* mosaic at Chedworth in the Gloucestershire Cotswolds, beside an amorous satyr embracing a maenad, and a few other actual sets of panpipes carved out of boxwood have been found including examples from the London waterfront, Alesia in Gaul and Uitgeest in the Netherlands. It has been calculated that the notes of the Shakenoak panpipes were G, G#, A, B, C, D and D#.[16] The names of other women and men from Oxfordshire are recorded in simple graffiti on pots: Anna and Sentica from Shakenoak, Corilivius from Alchester and Minutus from Lowbury Hill. They were presumably the owners of these vessels.[17]

People also signed votive dedications to the gods. A votive plaque from the temple site at Woodeaton evidently carries a personal name ending in '–edo', such as Macedo or Pedo, while a fragment of bronze sheet is incised with a dedication by someone possibly called Venovius though the exact reading is uncertain. A similar piece of metal bears what may be a woman's name, Mossa. One text appears to be in Celtic though it is too fragmentary to read with confidence and the standard practice was to use Latin. Relevant here are single capital letters which could be nailed to a board, including an M, an A and the ligatured letters TI (Fig. 5.5). The letters TI suggest that such texts included invocations in the dative case, presumably to Mars to whom all dedications would have ended *MARTI* and who is attested here by a votive plaque, a small votive relief and

5.5   Votive bronze letters M, TI and N, from Woodeaton. Height of TI 74mm. Ashmolean Museum.

miniature spears. Evidence from Woodeaton thus suggests that the formal practices of
Roman dedication had been adopted by ordinary members of local society.[18]

Greek would generally have been used by the rare visitors from the east
Mediterranean although a magical invocation on a piece of gold sheet bears the word
'Adonae', transliterated into Latin. Originally the name, which means 'Lord', was
semitic and thus this little text is a wonderful example of cultural blending. Also
suggestive of influence from the other side of the Empire is our one evidently literary
text, a fragment of a bronze plate from the Akeman Street settlement at Wilcote, cut
in Greek with part of a hexameter mentioning battles. This find emphasises the
importance of the road system for the spread of people and ideas across the province.[19]

An impression of quite widespread literacy can be substantiated by the finding of
objects connected with writing such as styli and wooden writing tablets as well as by
intaglios from seal rings (discussed below in the context of art) and seal-boxes.
However, the ability to read and write was not universal and this is best indicated by
the fact that with the exception of the stamps listed above, most of those on
Oxfordshire pottery were illiterate and indicate both the inability of potters to write
their names and also that their clientele did not require them to do so, even if a
semblance of a regular stamp was thought to be important. This provides a warning
not to overestimate the extent of even basic education among the country-dwellers
and artisans of the region. On the other hand the very existence of such stamps
demonstrates an awareness of the Roman habit of advertising a product through the
manufacturer putting his name on it.

RELIGION

The form of temple generally found in southern Britain is usually called 'Romano-Celtic'. Many of its elements derived ultimately from the Iron Age house with the central area as the living quarters for (in this case) the god with a surrounding space to give access to the god's servants. However, this was combined with the structural techniques of Roman building and classical forms of decoration. The result took the architectural form of a central tower (or *cella*) and a veranda or ambulatory. In the *cella* stood the cult image of the deity and perhaps the most important offerings while others would have been placed in the ambulatory. Sacrifices were performed not in the temple but on an altar outside it. Temple, altar and sometimes ancillary buildings and perhaps sacred trees and pits comprised a sacred space, for which we generally borrow the Greek word *temenos*, bounded by an enclosure wall. Ritual was centred on the contractual relationship between votary and god. The former would come to the temple and make a prayer, a *nuncupatio* (literally 'an announcement') saying what he or she wanted; if the request was granted then came the occasion of the pay-off, the *solutio*, generally the sacrifice of an animal and the gift of a small altar or suitable figurine or item of jewellery. In addition to such personal responses to the gods, there were special ceremonies on feast days, including processions and perhaps sacred dramas and entertainments in a theatre.

No temple has yet been found in Dorchester but at Alchester air photographs show at least two temples, one north-west and the other north-east of the central crossroads. If Alchester *is* Alauna and if the name has a sacred significance it is tempting to invoke these buildings as evidence. Almost all the other evidence for shrines and ritual practices in Roman Oxfordshire comes from rural sites even though, at Frilford for example, the surrounding settlement was quite extensive. We know most about Woodeaton, north-west of Oxford, in part because of the actual quality of the evidence, but also because of the distinction of the scholarship on a site which has attracted a number of specialists including M.V. Taylor, Joan Kirk and Richard Goodchild (who conducted an excavation and established the plan of the Romano-Celtic temple) and in the past few years Jean Bagnall Smith who has not only reassembled the evidence derived from the votive finds already known but published many others from a private collection in two magisterial and comprehensive papers. The result is that Woodeaton has become central to our understanding of religion in the countryside of Roman Britain as a whole, a type site to vie with Lydney Park and Uley in Gloucestershire, Nettleton Shrub in Wiltshire and Harlow in Essex. Very significant evidence also comes from other Oxfordshire temples, especially Frilford in the south-west and Lowbury Hill in the south-east, both of which have been the sites of important excavations.[20]

The sanctity of some of these sacred places may have begun in the Iron Age, as suggested by finds, though as yet the quality of the evidence for pre-Roman religious activity does not match that at Wanborough, Surrey; Hayling Island, Hampshire; and Uley, Gloucestershire. A few finds of Iron Age date and one or two Iron Age coins from the hilltop where the Woodeaton temple stands suggest a pre-Roman cult site, and such may have been the position elsewhere: Bradford & Goodchild believed that the sanctuary at Frilford was of Iron Age origin but Professor Harding later reassessed their evidence so that the religious finds at least look later. The siting of temples may be suggestive of their origins. Woodeaton seems to have lain on the border between the Catuvellauni and the Dobunni while Frilford and Lowbury Hill to the south lay near the north-eastern border of the Atrebates towards the Catuvellauni. Perhaps they marked boundaries as they existed in the earlier first century AD? No doubt in pre-Roman times sanctuaries belonging to the gods could have served for the settlement of disputes as well as being advantageous sites for markets; certainly in the Roman period there is evidence for fairs, commercial activity and light manufacture.[21]

It is a commonplace that temples were special, liminal places where the world of men touched that of the gods but we will not understand the pervasiveness of religion in Roman life if we fail to realise that the gods were everywhere. The second-century Greek writer Lucian describes the superstition of P. Mummius Sisenna Rutilianus, who had at one time served as legate of the sixth legion at York who 'if he but saw anywhere a stone smeared with holy oil or adorned with a wreath, would fall on his face forthwith, kiss his hand, and stand beside it for a long time making his vows and craving blessings from it'.[22] The gods were everywhere and several reliefs and altars from the open country and domestic sites depict genii loci or images of Fortune. Nevertheless the temple came to be regarded as the house of the god or goddess.

No full-sized cult statue nor any part of one, such as the gilt bronze head of Minerva from Bath or the limestone head of Minerva from Harlow or the head and feet of the statue of Mercury from Uley, has yet been found at Woodeaton or any other Oxfordshire temple. Presumably such an image or images normally stood within the *cella* of the temple and could be seen by votaries who looked through its doors. In the first instance the worshipper went to the shrine with his or her *nuncupatio*, often recording it in a sealed deposition, couched in legal language; it has been suggested that some of the seal-boxes from Woodeaton and other temples were used to protect these requests from prying eyes. In cases which involved the recovery of stolen property such petitions, which included invocations praying that the malefactor might be punished in life and limb, would be scratched on lead and some day such tablets as have been found at Uley (Glos.) and Bath and Pagans Hill (Somerset) may be found at an Oxfordshire sanctuary. Assuming that the request was fulfilled, there would follow the *solutio*, exemplified by sacrifice and the presentation of gifts such as coins, brooches, figurines, carved reliefs and votive altars. Most votaries were quite humble and as we have seen the partly preserved names of dedicators on plaques from Woodeaton are all those of Britons.

The ubiquitous cult act was the sacrifice of animals, represented most obviously by bones found on site but also by the presentation of model axes, like three from Woodeaton (Fig. 5.6), which perhaps represented such sacrifices at the temple; they would have been cheaper as offerings than a steer or even a ram.[23] Such axes are found at known shrines but also elsewhere, for instance at Asthall. Some may be from temples as yet unrecorded (very probable at Asthall), though it must be remembered that little shrines to the gods were ubiquitous in domestic settings and at the wayside, very much as are Catholic or Orthodox Christian shrines in large parts of Europe today.

Coins were always welcome gifts and some lead tablets, for instance from Bath, specify the size of such monetary gifts. Woodeaton has yielded a great many coins, but of especial interest are pieces of sheet-metal on which coins have been pressed to leave

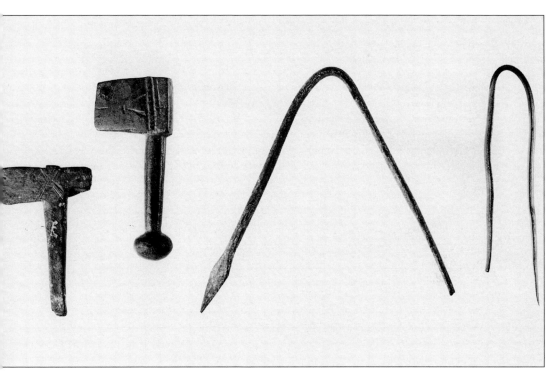

5   Votive bronze axes and spears from Woodeaton. Spears 142mm and 120mm; axes 39mm and 48mm. Ashmolean Museum.

impressions, these pieces of sheet perhaps then serving as temple money, acceptable to the gods if not to men. One of them was in fact an issue of Cunobelin, though the rest are Roman issues.[24] Other metal plaques include Mars standing with spear and shield and Mars as a rider god. The former is paralleled by a fragmentary stone relief from the site and many others from the Cotswold region; the latter by two horse and rider brooches at Woodeaton as well as by a relief from another possible temple site at Gill Mill, Ducklington, and other reliefs from Gloucestershire.[25] That Mars was the major deity at Woodeaton is further implied by a number of votive spears, some of them bent in order to 'kill' them and thus send them beyond this world into that of the gods (Fig. 5.6), who could presumably employ them at any scale they wished. Votive spears at Lowbury Hill as well as miniature swords and shields from Frilford and Woodeaton equally point to a warrior deity. This evidence should not be taken as proof that the people remained warlike; in Roman religion Father Mars was in the first instance a god of the growing crops and he would have used his weapons against the pests and diseases which assailed them each year.[26] In any case, Roman religion was not exclusive and there are quite a number of allusions to other deities among objects from Woodeaton. Another plaque depicts a cupid, possibly alluding to Venus, who is shown on two figurines, one of them of stylised, native form; Mars and Venus, lovers in myth, shared the function of protecting growing things and thus it is not surprising to find them

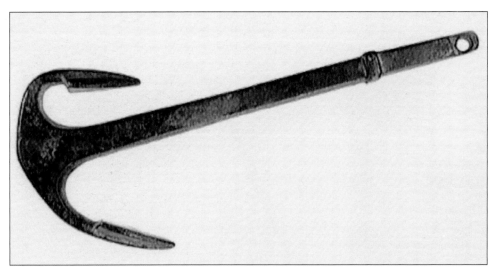

5.7 Miniature bronze anchor from Barton Court Farm, Abingdon. Length 70mm. Oxfordshire Museums.

5.8 Three bronze figurines found 'near Oxford', probably at Woodeaton. Apollo, man-eating monster, and bird, heights 91mm, 63mm and 68mm. In British Museum. Photo: Julian Munby.

5.9 Bronze bird from Ramsden near
Finstock. Length 49mm. Photo: Institute of
Archaeology, Oxford.

venerated together. A plaque displaying a Medusa mask alludes to Minerva, goddess of
craft, and also widely venerated in Britain, for instance at Bath and Harlow.[27] The
Thames, Cherwell and other rivers explain a miniature anchor which alludes to
Neptune (or perhaps to the god of the Thames) who must have been frequently
invoked by those who used the river system; a similar model anchor (Fig. 5.7) comes
from Barton Court Farm, Abingdon, where it may have been dedicated in a household
shrine. The god himself is shown on a glass gem from Woodeaton, presumably worn by
a visitor to the temple and perhaps dedicated there.[28] Figurines thought to come from
Woodeaton (Fig. 5.8) include representations of Apollo (the god of music and light but
also a mighty healer and hunter) and of Fortuna.[29] Both were popular deities
throughout the Empire in Roman times. In addition there is the frightening image of a
wolf-like creature devouring a man, doubtless a power of the underworld. It is the
work of an accomplished Romano-British bronzesmith but also a reminder of the
survival of Celtic religion which prior to AD 43 had, indeed, included human sacrifice.
Hounds were widely regarded as other-worldly creatures among the Greeks and
Romans (note Cerberus, guardian of the underworld) as well as among the Celts.[30]

The commonest category of figurine at Woodeaton is that of birds, some of them
certainly eagles (associated with Jupiter), others probably doves. Such bird models are
found on other religious sites in southern Britain, including Willingham Fen in
Cambridgeshire and Felmingham Hall, Norfolk. A stray bird figurine (Fig. 5.9) was
recorded in fieldwalking at Ramsden, near Finstock, perhaps from another shrine. A
possible explanation for all these birds is that they allude to the practice of augury
whereby priests were able to divine the will of the gods from studying bird flight.[31]

The finds from Woodeaton show that both women and men worshipped here. Pins,
bracelets, beads and other parts of necklaces certainly imply the former; while a spur
and scabbard chapes, possibly the offerings of mounted huntsmen rather than soldiers,
suggest the latter.[32] Lack of inscriptions makes it hard to say much about the cultural

origins of individual votaries. Most were British, as implied by the Celtic-sounding inscriptions on votives, but they probably included a small foreign element of travellers passing through to cities such as Corinium. Orientals are not only attested by the gold 'Adonae' lamella but probably also by a tiny figurine worn as an amulet, evidently showing the Egyptian god Harpocrates, a figurine paralleled in Britain by similar amulets from London and Chester.[33]

Near the temple at Frilford there was an amphitheatre (Fig. 3.9), probably a theatre-amphitheatre, reminding us that processions and spectacles as well as the baiting of wild animals were associated with festivals. In Britain comparison can be made with the theatre beside the temple near the forum at Verulamium and the theatre at Gosbecks outside Colchester but there were surely others. Even if Woodeaton and the other Oxfordshire temples lacked such built structures they must have had theatral areas for cult ceremonies, even if these were no more than cleared areas of ground: the instant theatres created in Oxford college gardens every summer show how such things could be done.[34]

Lowbury Hill in the parish of Aston Upthorpe has yielded a large quantity of material which is probably votive, although no building has yet been found.[35] However, the most interesting object which can be associated with the site was found to the south-east of the site, just over the modern county border in the parish of Aldworth, Berkshire.[36] It is a heavily leaded bronze 'spearhead' with a three-leaf blade, but too thick and blunt to allow it to serve as a spear. Moreover between each of the blades is a draped female bust while the spear-head sits on a calyx of acanthus. This object is an example of the head of a sceptre or tip-staff, carried by a priest or official of the temple in a religious procession. Examples from various parts of Britain depict Mars, Venus and Minerva as well as imperial heads which represent the *numen* (the divine power or spirit) of the reigning Emperor. In the case of the Aldworth sceptre, there is little doubt that it represents the Matres, the three mother-goddesses who were no doubt venerated in our area (as they were in the Gloucestershire Cotswolds, at Chichester, Winchester and London) but were not previously attested. How this sceptre came to be found where it was is not known: was it stolen from the temple or did it fall unnoticed from its staff during a religious procession, plausibly a bound-beating ceremony like those which occur today on Rogation Day? Another sceptre head made of iron, with two piercings for chains from which pieces of jingling metal or even bells could have been hung, has been found on the site. Were other deities venerated here? Mars is a strong possibility to judge from the spears (see above);[37] so too is Mercury because a pipeclay figurine of a cockerel, Mercury's cult bird, was also discovered at Lowbury. At Uley in Gloucestershire where both spears and a range of items including sculpture, figurines and inscriptions dedicated to Mercury were found it has been surmised that in some way a Mars-like god came to be identified as Mercury, which is not all that unlikely when it is recalled that both gods had a protective function.[38]

Very little sculpture has been found on these temple sites, though it probably once existed in quantity to be robbed out in later times for building or the lime-kiln. As stated above no cult image has yet been found but there are a number of smaller images given by votaries. A small relief of a standing Mars from Woodeaton has already been mentioned, as has one of Mars as a rider from Gill Mill, Ducklington.[39] This too

5.10 Relief of a *Genius* from Gill Mill, Ducklington. Height 248mm. Photo: Institute of Archaeology, Oxford.

was probably associated with a shrine and a figure of a *Genius Loci* (a god of the place) has also been found here (Fig. 5.10). A large altar recovered from the Thames at Bablock Hythe (Fig. 2.4) and carved with a Genius could be from a wayside shrine, as might the altar of Fortuna from Knaps Farm, Bampton (Fig. 5.11).[40] The other deities recorded in stone sculpture from the county are Jupiter, Mercury and Vulcan. Jupiter is represented by a noble head from a relief found at Glyme Farm, Chipping Norton (Fig. 5.12). A head of Mercury from a stone statuette comes from Lees Rest near Charlbury (Fig. 5.14) and is thought to be associated with a temple set within a ditched enclosure (Fig. 5.13). A small statuary group from Cowleasure Field, Swalcliffe (Fig. 5.15), depicts Mercury sitting beside his female consort, often known in Gaul as Rosmerta (the cult of the two deities is otherwise attested in Cirencester, Gloucester and Bath). Vulcan, the smith god, is shown holding his tongs and standing beside his anvil on a relief found at the foot of Ilbury Camp, Duns Tew (Fig. 5.16); this may be significant as the site lies in the ironstone district of north-west Oxfordshire and Vulcan would no doubt have been particularly venerated by smiths. Vulcan (or his Celtic equivalent) was worshipped in Britain from the Iron Age – a smith (god?) appears on coins of Cunobelin – and representations from the Roman period include a magnificent head from a figurine of Vulcan found at Cirencester.[41]

5.11   Relief of Fortuna from Knap's Farm, Bampton.
Height 950mm. Photo: Oxfordshire Museums.

5.12   Head of Jupiter from Glyme Farm, Chipping
Norton. Height 265mm.

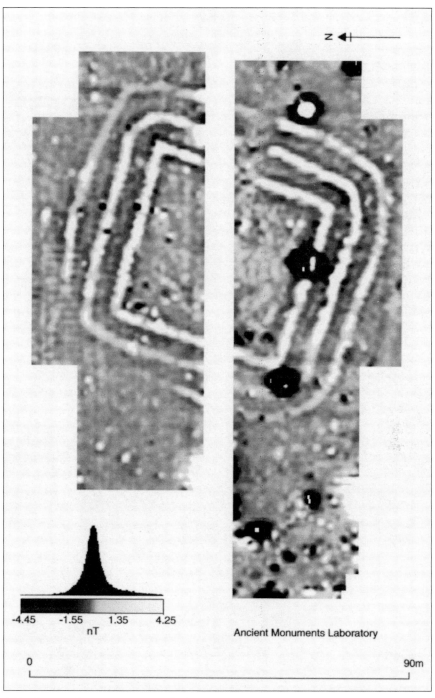

5.13 Shrine enclosure at Lees Rest, Charlbury. The plan, from a magnetometer survey, shows three concentric ditches each with a south–east facing entrance. English Heritage.

5.14   Head of Mercury from Lees Rest, Charlbury. Height 60mm. Photo: Ashmolean Museum.

5.15   Relief of Mercury and Rosmerta from Swalcliffe. Height 280mm. Photo: Oxfordshire Museums.

5.16 Figure of Vulcan from Duns Tew. Height 400mm. Ashmolean Museum.

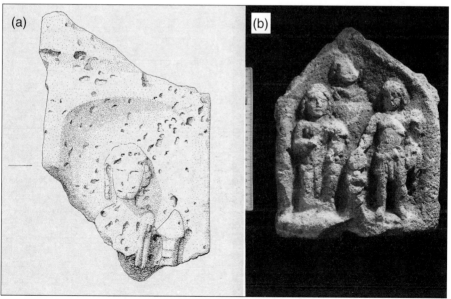

5.17 (a) Altar of Fortuna from Shakenoak. Height 280mm. After Brodribb et al. 1972, fig 12. (b) Domestic deities from Stonesfield villa. Height 310mm. Photo: Institute of Archaeology, Oxford.

Some sculpture was certainly used in the domestic setting of the house shrine, such as the Fortuna altar from Shakenoak (Fig. 5.17a) and most interestingly a relief from the site of the Stonesfield villa depicting a Genius with Fortuna possibly accompanied by the Lar who protected the house (Fig. 5.17b). Perhaps these were associated with *lararia* (shrines to the *Lares*) which might have contained little metal, clay and wooden images of the gods together with other items of sentimental or religious significance to the villa owner.[42]

BURIALS AND RELIGION

Beliefs about what happens to the individual after death varied in the Roman world from scepticism to complex religious beliefs about the salvation of the dead, for example in the mystery religions and Christianity. The dead required protection as much as the living and some of the motifs associated with graves were designed to ensure this. The sculptures of lions from tombs at Shakenoak are characteristic examples of a theme found in Greek, Roman and Etruscan burial cults. As the most powerful of animals they could be interpreted as symbols of ravening death. Here a link can be seen with the wolf-lion figurine from Woodeaton and, indeed, a figure of a lioness from a tomb at Cramond in south Scotland likewise shows a man being devoured head first. However, felines were also regarded as guardians of the tomb from evil demons, and this protective rôle explains the use of lion head attachments on furniture. The same function was also attributed to hounds who were sometimes buried with the deceased (as at Yarnton; see Fig. 7.3). This was presumably more than simply taking a pet with one to the other world; not only did dogs have mythological connections with the underworld, but one of the primary purposes for keeping these animals was for their value as watchdogs.[43]

Grave offerings were frequently placed with the deceased, whether it was thought they needed such gifts in the tomb or for a journey to the otherworld. Several examples may be cited. A late second- or third-century burial from Ardley contained two pots and a vase-like vessel that were presumably originally containers for food and drink. The deceased seems to have been a woman, judging from two jet pins found beside her skull and perhaps suggesting that she was laid out with her hair arranged in an elegant fashion. Although by this period inhumation was the more normal rite in the Roman Empire, cremation continued to be common in Oxfordshire and there was, in fact, a contemporary cremation at Ardley, likewise furnished with pots. Two other cremations of the middle Empire may be cited: one from the Vicarage Garden at Dorchester because the two vessels it contained, a flagon and a two-handled bottle, were rare and quite expensive items, made of clear glass; the other, from Aston Rowant, because although it was found in the late seventeenth century it was meticulously recorded and illustrated (Fig. 8.2). It contained a samian platter and other vessels, one of which is said to have held an 'aromatic liquor'. Two bronze bowls from near Didcot (in the parish of Sutton Courtenay) can probably be associated with a cremation cemetery; they were possibly of local manufacture, though no doubt they were intended both in their material and their form to recall highly prized Campanian bronzes.[44]

The most ubiquitous grave goods were coins, which according to Graeco-Roman tradition were required to pay the ferryman of the dead. Coins, sometimes more than one, have been recovered from graves in fourth-century cemeteries at Stanton Harcourt and at Cold Harbour Farm, Crowmarsh, for example. In a grave at Radley the deceased was accompanied by a cache of nine coins of Constantine and Crispus wrapped in a piece of linen.[45] A possible variant for a coin is the substitution of a flint in the mouth for a coin at Crowmarsh (Fig. 5.18), though one can think of other explanations such as preventing evil spirits entering the orifice. Two other burials at Crowmarsh are examples of a burial practice that was especially widespread in our region and is found in most late Roman cemeteries, comprising some 8 per cent of inhumations. The posthumous decapitation of the body and the placing of the head by the side or more commonly, as at Crowmarsh, between the legs is most plausibly explained by the notion that it helped the spirit to escape from the corpse. The rite suggests that Celtic ideas about the importance of the head continued to be held very strongly through the Roman period. It is recorded at Yarnton (Fig. 7.3), Stanton Harcourt, Wroxton, Barrow Hills Field, Radley, Ashville Trading Estate, Abingdon, and at Curbridge near Witney.[46] Interestingly, the rite seems to continue well beyond the Roman period in Wessex (see

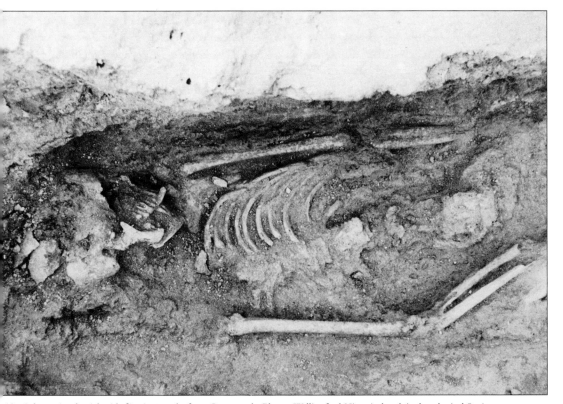

.18   Inhumation burial with flint in mouth, from Crowmarsh. Photo: Wallingford Historical and Archaeological Society.

Chapter seven). Another practice which indicates a journey is the placing of hob-nails (or rather boots) in graves so that the dead could walk to the other world. Hob-nails have been found with burials at Stanton Harcourt and at Curbridge.[47]

Absence of grave goods and orientated burials at Ashville Trading Estate, Abingdon, and notably at Queenford Farm (Queenford Mill), Dorchester, indicate a Christian population in late Roman and post-Roman times. The bodies were placed east–west so that at the Last Trump the resurrected dead would face Jerusalem. With Christianity the boundaries between life and death observable in pagan religious practice were breached. The idea of rebirth was inherent in baptism, so that the lead vessel with its chi-rho monogram from Caversham (now Reading but formerly in Oxfordshire), probably correctly identified as a font, marks the washing away of sin and the rebirth of the Christian to a new life. Baptism, here the Baptism of Christ by St John, is one of the themes depicted on a beaker of fourth- or fifth-century date from what appears to be a Frankish burial at Long Wittenham (Fig. 7.4). The object is very probably Romano-British and may well have been used for the Eucharist. It is one of the most important (but least known) relics of the Church in Roman Britain and will be discussed more fully in a later chapter.[48]

ART

Men and women express themselves through images and abstract patterns as well as through writing. Evidence from Oxfordshire is reasonably varied, substantiating the impression of a native society which came to enjoy the fruits of Romanisation. In describing Pacata's world it seems appropriate to begin with portable art, which has a continuous history from the Iron Age, before turning to those arts by which the wealthiest houses in the region were provided with permanent decor.

Display and ornament is apparent in Iron Age art such as the Celtic-style decoration of the Little Wittenham (Fig. 1.10) and Standlake sword scabbards, as well as in the stylised horses on native coins (Fig. 8.1); even that great hill-figure, the Uffington white horse, has recently been dated by the optically stimulated luminescence technique to the early first millennium BC, though art-historical considerations should bring it down at least to the origins of La Tène art of c. 500 BC. This artistic style did not cease with the arrival of Roman administrators. A native tradition of animal art is, for example, represented by a bull's head bucket escutcheon from Shakenoak. The type goes back to the Iron Age but continues right through the Roman period. Bulls of course had an important place both in a partly pastoral economy and in cult. Presumably the Shakenoak escutcheon and its fellow were intended to protect the bucket and its contents. Most Celtic art was, however, abstract. A terret found at the villa at Ditchley dates from the Roman period but is ornamented with a typically Celtic design of running scrolls, and similar curvilinear designs embellish two brooches of Aesica type (so-named after a fort on Hadrian's Wall where the type example was found), one from Hook Norton and an even more beautiful one from a burial at Yarnton (Fig. 5.19).[49]

Other jewellery was essentially Roman in form. Just within the defences of Alchester was found a jeweller's mould for the manufacture of serpent rings and bracelets

5.19 'Aesica'-type brooch from Yarnton.
Length 44mm.

(Fig. 5.20a). Strips of gold or silver would have been beaten into either a pair of larger or a pair of smaller impressions to make jewellery of a form similar to that produced by the itinerant jewellers whose stock-in-trade was found at Snettisham, Norfolk. The findspot may be significant: did the owner of the mould have a shop in the north of the town in order to attract clients passing along the road, or was he himself travelling either to Cirencester or to Verulamium, or on the southerly road to Silchester? A serpent ring of somewhat different type was found at Barton Court Farm (Fig. 5.20b).[50]

Engraved gems are a much underestimated index of attitudes and interests. A number of those from the county are illustrated here as objects which really bring the past to life. The earliest, from Blackthorn Hill in the Alchester region, shows a cupid with a goose (Fig. 5.21a). It is of Augustan date and was probably brought in by a soldier in the Roman army associated with the likely vexillation fortress at Alchester. Cupids were widely used emblems of prosperity, belonging to the worlds of Venus and of Bacchus, and they frequently appear on parade armour, sword scabbards and other military metalwork. The Alchester site has recently yielded another intaglio showing Jupiter's thunderbolt, a very suitable theme for a soldier.[51]

Among later ring settings pride of place should be given to a nicolo (blue onyx) intaglio set in a third-century gold ring found near Oxford (possibly from Woodeaton)

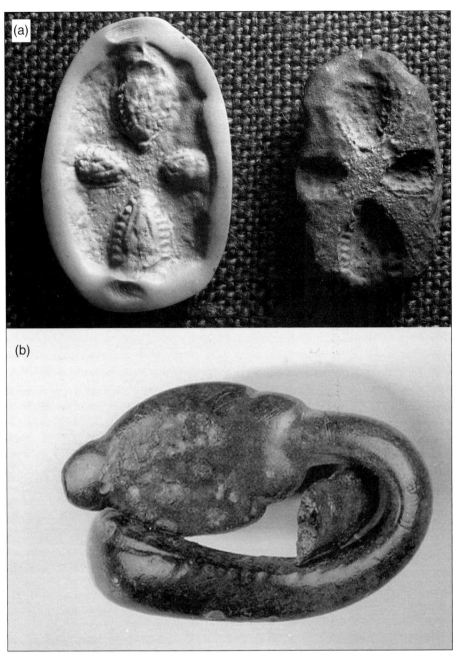

5.20 (a) Mould for making serpent jewellery from Alchester. Length 45mm. Photo: Ashmolean Museum. (b) Serpent ring from Barton Court Farm, Abingdon. Length 20mm. Photo: Oxfordshire Museums.

and depicting the goddess Minerva (Fig. 5.21b). Gold rings, originally the privilege of the Equestrian order in Roman society were by this time worn by soldiers and other highly regarded members of society (*honestiores*) but this is clearly an object of high status, as indeed is a silver ring with a gold bezel from Wendlebury depicting the helmeted head of the goddess Roma (Fig. 5.21c), not in this case a signet as the device is in relief.[52]

Many gems relate directly to agriculture. These include a chalcedony seal depicting the corn-goddess Ceres, from Bridewell Farm near North Leigh, and a fragmentary cornelian from Frilford showing her male consort Bonus Eventus (Fig. 5.21d). The two together may have been based on a statuary group by Praxiteles in Rome but in Oxfordshire the gems express hopes for a fruitful harvest.[53]

The evidence for crafts and craftsmen working in roadside settlements is augmented by a cornelian from Wilcote showing Daedalus making a wing (Fig. 5.21e), a subject also to be seen on a very low-grade glass intaglio from Alchester (Fig. 5.21f).[54] An onyx gem from Bridewell Farm near North Leigh is perhaps the one certain portrayal of a gladiator on jewellery from Britain. An intaglio, now in the Ashmolean Museum, carved in blue onyx and found near Burford (and thus perhaps from Asthall) shows a male figure with a mask, probably a genius of comedy (Fig. 5.21g), and another of the same material from Abingdon shows a satyr likewise holding a theatre mask. Entertainers would doubtless travel to large centres like Cirencester where both a theatre and an amphitheatre existed, or to small ones like Frilford with its combined theatre-amphitheatre.[55]

Animals quite often appear on gems; in general they played a more important part in Roman life than they do in ours, not just economically but as pets and as creatures that generally had symbolic meaning. An onyx from Asthall showing a countryman milking a goat is a copy of a theme common in pastoral art and found on coins of Vespasian, but it is also a reminder that livestock was important to the local economy. A beautiful blue onyx gem from Woodeaton depicts a squirrel eating an acorn (Fig. 5.21h). It may have represented a much-loved pet or perhaps have been a reminder to the wearer to be provident, as squirrels store up their food for winter and were also believed to use their tails as covering in stormy weather.[56]

Engraved gems were no doubt quite expensive and gem-set signet rings would always have been marks of status. The poor would have made do with moulded glass seals, though even these trinket gems reflect higher culture. A glass gem imitating blue onyx from Woodeaton, showing Neptune, is a reminder of the many watercourses in the Thames valley. Another similar glass gem from the same site portrays a hare, dressed as a human, perhaps here evoking some lost fable. The intaglio from Alchester depicting Daedalus may, as mentioned above, have belonged to an artisan, while another nicolo glass from Asthall figures a boar, a reminder of the hunt and of traditions which stretch back to the Iron Age – for example, an issue of King Eppillus of the Atrebates struck at Silchester showed a boar breaking from a covert. From Lowbury Hill comes a glass gem showing the ever-popular Bonus Eventus and another depicting an animal leaping from a nautilus shell, symbolising rebirth. No cameos in relief cut upon hardstone have yet been found in the county but a yellow glass ring from Shakenoak has a bezel which portrays a head, probably a cupid's head, in relief; it may have been intended to imitate a ring carved in amber, which would have been fairly precious.[57]

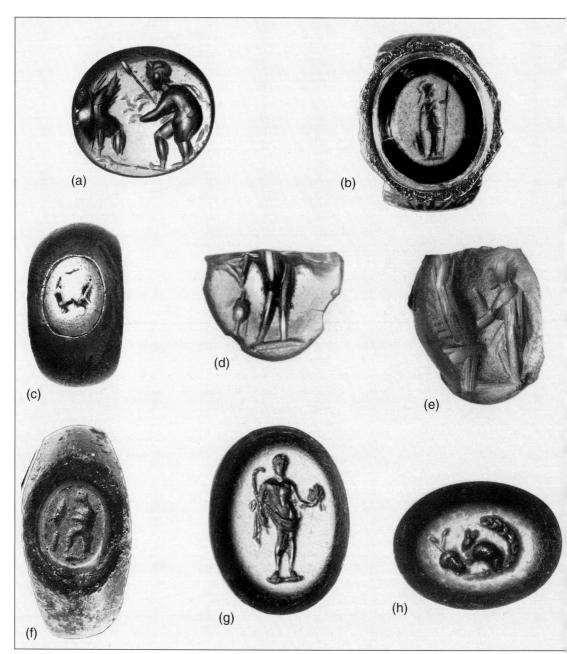

5.21   Intaglios and rings: (a) cornelian, showing Cupid and goose, from Blackthorn Hill near Bicester; (b) nicolo in gold ring showing Minerva, found 'near Oxford' – perhaps at Woodeaton; (c) silver ring with inset gold bezel showing bust of Roma or Minerva, from near Wendlebury; (d) cornelian showing Bonus Eventus from Frilford; (e) cornelian with figure of Daedalus from Wilcote; (f) nicolo-glass in bronze ring showing Daedalus, from Alchester; (g) nicolo showing *Genius* of Comedy, from near Burford (h) nicolo with squirrel from Woodeaton. All at X4 except (c) (X2). Photos: Institute of Archaeology, Oxford, except (b) (author).

Other examples of portable works of art include appliqués from furniture, litters or vehicles, among them a bronze bust of a woman from Adderbury whose head matches another from Aldworth, Berkshire, near Lowbury Hill.[58] Others are recorded from Cockfield, Suffolk, and from Tarrant Hinton, Dorset, the last almost certainly a vehicle fitting. All four have a curious coiffure, with the hair gathered up to a knot on the top of the head. The subject may be intended as the goddess Diana but such images probably reflect what women of the villa-owning class looked like. The pronounced linearity of the castings certainly suggests north-west European, perhaps Romano-British, workmanship. Such women would have owned jewel-boxes, often embellished with protective mounts, like the casket shown on the tombstone of the Catuvellaunian woman called Regina, at South Shields, Co. Durham.[59] These were often embellished with protective mounts in various materials. They might be of bronze like the lion-head from Barton Court Farm or of jet like the plaque from the same site, perhaps carved in Yorkshire, which depicts a seated nude male figure, his legs apart in a somewhat lecherous pose and probably to be identified as a satyr, one of the companions of Bacchus.[60]

Bacchus was above all the god of wine; he was a deity who came into his own at night when his feasts and mystic revels took place and was also a powerful saviour from death – both reasons why he was shown on the famous Stonesfield mosaic. He was connected with wild beasts, especially felines, and it is not surprising that the little tables, generally with three legs, which stood beside dining couches were ornamented with panther heads and claw feet. In Britain these were frequently carved in Dorset from shale; from here they were often exported and the upper part of just such a leg is recorded at Alchester. Other evidence comes from miniatures, for example a leg cast in bronze, possibly part of a lamp stand, from Charlbury, displays both protome and claw, while the elegant claw foot from Shakenoak comes from a three-legged candelabrum. In addition lion-head appliqués, like the example from Barton Court Farm, ornamented and protected chests. These all serve as reminders of the sort of furniture which graced the elegant dining room and evoke the world of the Roman banquet.[61]

Indeed Tacitus lists dining and bathing only slightly behind the use of Latin as features of the Roman way of life. With regard to the former, Roman practice was also no doubt influenced by native traditions of feasting, and certainly the use of cauldrons suspended over the fire on wrought-iron chains goes back to the Iron Age. The superb chain from the Appleford hoard with its decorative central link (Fig. 5.22) is paralleled elsewhere in Britain (including at Cirencester and Winchester), and cauldrons suspended from chains are depicted in sculpture from Gaul and Germany.[62] More Romanised fashions in the service of food are represented by a tripod terminal from Dorchester-on-Thames in the form of a bust of a maenad, one of Bacchus' female followers, an animal skin (*nebris*) draped over one shoulder; such a tripod would have supported a bowl or plate at the table.[63] Flagons and other vessels likewise bearing zoomorphic or figural ornament would have been used for wine and water. An elegant bronze handle from Asthall in the shape of the head and neck of a swan comes from just such a small flagon. Swans, which were associated with the sun-god Apollo, were sometimes incorporated into little lamp stands like one support from London

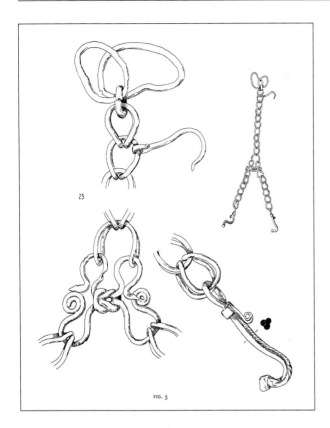

FIG. 5

25

5.22   Iron cauldron chain from Appleford
hoard. Length 1.47mm. Ashmolean Museum.

where a somewhat similar protome terminates in a feline foot, of course alluding to
Bacchus, who can be regarded as Apollo's antetype: both deities were associated with
the feast, an activity which combined the emotions, heightened through the
consumption of alcohol, with culture, good conversation, poetry and music.[64]

Vessels for eating and drinking include some of the most attractive objects to survive
from Roman times They include imported glass such as the thin-walled clear glass
bowls from Ditchley and Shakenoak (not very special villas) dating predominantly
from the second century and compared by Donald Harden to Alexandrian glass from
Karanis in Egypt. One of the treasures of the Ashmolean Museum is a fourth-century
bowl from Wint Hill, Somerset, made in the Rhineland. The owner of the Shakenoak
villa had a similar bowl featuring a bear-hunt, of which only a fragment remains
though it is sufficient to reveal something of the tastes of the owner.[65] British pewter,
as it happens, is mainly of late Roman date and reveals another facet of contemporary
style: a love of pattern, which is well exemplified by the central motif on one of the
Appleford plates, ornamented with a striking pattern of interlocking squares (Figs 5.2,
5.23).[66] Another pewter vessel of square form and embellished with geometric devices
in the corners comes from the University Farm at Wytham. It is a type of plate
matched in silver by a vessel from Mileham, Norfolk, and is perhaps a British form.[67]

The only group of table items made of silver actually from the county is a cache of elegant rat-tailed silver spoons from Dorchester of fourth-century date. No doubt more was originally to be found, at least in such establishments as North Leigh and Stonesfield, but none has been recovered. Such items would have been removed by their owners when the great villas were abandoned. A hint at the use of silver by the very rich is provided by the recovery of a fluted bowl designed for hand-washing from the site of what is very probably a villa at Blunsdon near Swindon in Wiltshire; this is exceptional in apparently being buried on the site but it is quite likely that such bowls were in use in the large villas of western Oxfordshire.[68]

Most people in the Roman world would have used pottery for eating and drinking. In the first and second centuries samian ware from Gaul would have served the purposes of most dinner-tables but thereafter it was largely replaced by pottery from the Rhineland and Britain. That produced in the vicinity of Oxford from the first to the fourth century is of more than local importance, especially in late Roman times

23   Detail of decoration in centre of large pewter dish from Appleford. (See Fig. 5.2 top.)

and was distributed well beyond the boundaries of present-day Oxfordshire by merchants (*negotiatores*).[69] Many vessels from the kilns of Headington, Cowley and Horspath are aesthetically pleasing for their shapes and ornament (Fig. 6.10). Creamy parchment ware, with its fine fabric and red ochre-painted patterns of banding with some curvilinear ornament, is reminiscent of some of the simpler patterns of fresco-painting. Colour-coated vessels are more widespread (Figs 5.24, 5.25) and while some were painted in a variety of patterns others bore trailed barbotine scrolls or running animals (hounds and hares) found in contemporary pottery industries, for instance in the Nene valley. Other vessels were stamped with rosettes and other simple devices. Taken together these exemplify the increasing love of pattern and abstraction in the late Roman period widespread in all media.[70] One small group of Oxfordshire vessels has been the subject of special study: flagons with human masks applied to their necks, generally in the form of beautiful women with elaborate hair-styles (Fig. 5.26).[71] These were evidently ornamented in white and dark slips. Examples reached London in the east and Lydney Park in the west. Although certainly late Roman in date, the

5.24   Oxford colour-coated ware bowl, Barton Court Farm, Abingdon. Diameter 220mm, height 100mm. 1984.194.461 Oxfordshire Museums.

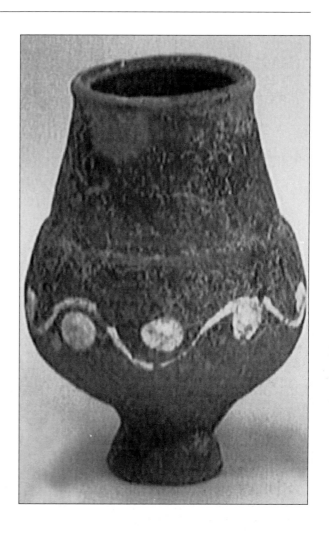

5.25 Oxford colour-coated ware beaker
with white paint decoration, Grave 11,
Ashville Trading Estate, Abingdon. Height
92mm. 1984.26.57, Oxfordshire Museums.

coiffures perpetuate those of the second and third centuries. A unique find was a mould for impressing a face on to a flagon, found at Horspath. In this instance the face appears to have been moulded from a prototype, possibly of metal, and is very finely executed in contrast with a caricature of a head crudely modelled on the outside of the object, produced by a workman in an idle moment.[72]

While portable objects such as jewellery would have been made in small towns and village settlements or imported from the great cantonal capitals such as Cirencester, larger items can seldom have been the product of such speculative sale and were generally specially commissioned by wealthy patrons. The Roman sculpture found in Oxfordshire and discussed above is almost all made of oolitic limestone from the Cotswolds, either quarried from within the area of the modern county or beyond it in what is now Gloucestershire. Most of it comes from the Cotswold region but a few

5.26   Face mask from Oxford colour-coated ware flagon, Toot Baldon. Height 110mm. Ashmolean Museum. Photo: Julian Munby.

5.27   Fresco from Wigginton villa (restored) with architectural perspective. Height 350mm. 1992.54 BM6, Oxfordshire Museums.

pieces from beside the Thames hint at the passage of stone along that great waterway. Indeed much of the sculpture in London is of Cotswold stone and it has been hypothesised that some sculptors went east to make their fortunes. Though no doubt there were village craftsmen who could provide low-quality carvings more locally, for the most part orders would have been made at workshops in Cirencester for the best pieces like the lion tomb (at Shakenoak), the relief depicting household gods (at Stonesfield) and Fortuna (at Bampton). The Dorchester *beneficiarius*, no doubt able to command transport very readily, would have been in a privileged position when it came to getting in a building team to put up his altar with its screens, which may have been embellished with scrollwork or other decoration. Very probably this altar, like others (that from Bablock Hythe for instance), was shipped down the river Thames.[73]

The quantity of Roman painting surviving from Oxfordshire is quite small; it includes simple panel schemes which embellished the walls of the small villa at Shakenoak, presumably imitating marble veneer, and slight evidence for much more ambitious decor at Wigginton ranging from a ceiling painted with roundels containing vegetal motifs to an architectural scheme with Ionic columns, perhaps representing a theatre-stage (Fig. 5.27). The paintings were invariably done on site but the painters themselves are also likely to have been brought in from workshops situated in large centres such as Cirencester, spending a week or two at villas such as the two mentioned. The situation is reminiscent of that which prevailed in Elizabethan and early Stuart England when Oxford (in common with other English cities) seems to have had its own Painters and Stainers guild.[74]

The position has been best studied with regard to mosaics, the most ubiquitous products of Roman culture. While there is a great deal still to learn with regard to organisation, it appears that in the second century there were mosaic studios operating in Colchester and Verulamium in the east and at Cirencester in the west but in rural Oxfordshire the mosaics belong to the fourth century when the villas were at their most prosperous. Cirencester was again a major centre in southern Britain with two 'schools' of mosaicists, and there were others at Dorchester (Dorset), in Hampshire (where Winchester and Silchester could both have been centres of the craft), and in the East Midlands, possibly based on Water Newton.[75]

The great villas towards the north-west of the county are within the ambit of Cirencester and it is very likely indeed that the owners of the large houses at North Leigh, Wigginton and Stonesfield were *curiales*, engaged in cantonal government, and possessed of town houses in Cirencester as well as country estates. In many cases mosaics are known only very partially. That at Fawler is attested simply by the Anglo-Saxon name derived from *fagan floran* ('variegated floor'). Of others only fragments remain or have at least been recorded, such as the white and blue meander border discovered (or rediscovered) recently in a building at Lower Lea, Swalcliffe, which is probably the same as that found in 1926.[76] A detail of a mosaic from Great Tew illustrated by Robert Plot shows a simple scheme of circles (Fig. 8.1) while another fragment (from Beaconsfield Farm), found in 1810 and illustrated by Beesley, depicted a cantharus flanked by dolphins (Fig. 8.6), almost certainly laid by a Cirencester mosaicist. Dolphins were associated with a cantharus on a mosaic from Littlecote, Wiltshire, discussed below, but the theme was quite widespread on mosaics.[77] An intriguing area of mosaic was exposed until recently in the chancel of St Oswald's Church, Widford, not far from Burford, which stands on the site of a villa. Now covered over, this mosaic has a scheme of interlaced octagons, commonest in the East Midlands and so perhaps laid by mosaicists from elsewhere, perhaps again Water Newton.[78]

At North Leigh a number of very fine mosaics, all geometric, were recorded by Hakewill (Fig. 8.5). One is still extant *in situ* (Fig. 5.28) and is deservedly famous as perhaps the finest remaining example of the so-called Corinian 'saltire' school which has been attributed to the second quarter of the fourth century. Its ornament is here based on a scheme of three saltire crosses. Some of the geometric motifs within the mosaic are very distinctive, including what looks like a conflation of a pelta with a chalice. The mosaic was almost exactly paralleled by one excavated in Cirencester. Another mosaic has a design of interlocking squares, quite a common device and again found in Cirencester, but it is worth recalling its similarity to the device in the centre

5.28   Mosaic of Corinian 'saltire school' at North Leigh. Photo: R. Wilkins F.S.A.

of the Appleford pewter plate discussed above. At the Wigginton villa fragments of a number of attractive geometric mosaics possibly related to the same tradition have been recorded. The most attractive and complete of these is that of the apse of a hypocausted room containing a cantharus flanked by ivy-scrolls (Fig. 8.7).[79]

Geometric floors as represented by those of Stonesfield as well as Wigginton and North Leigh provided the normal decor for mosaic floors in Roman Britain and in the fourth century catered for an increasing appreciation for abstract forms – what John Onians terms a 'culture of imagination'.[80] For us, however, figural floors are generally more exciting and provide readier access to the cultural aspirations and thought processes of those who had them laid. This was also true three centuries ago and the Bacchus mosaic at Stonesfield (Fig. 8.4) will be central to our historical chapter; it is attributed by David Smith to the earlier Corinian school, the so-called 'Orpheus school' of *c.* AD 300–320, of which it was surely one of the finest examples. The bi-coloured running scroll associates it closely with the frieze around the Woodchester pavement (Glos), a fragment from which is now displayed in the British Museum, while a length of scroll with the same motif forms an element in a floor at the villa (or temple/guest-house) site at Yanworth (Chedworth) in Gloucestershire and sprays of similar leaves occupy the spandrels of the Orpheus mosaic from Barton Farm, Cirencester. In addition it should be noted that the geometric panel in the Bacchus and panther mosaic at Stonesfield is very closely matched among the geometric elements at Woodchester. The major figural theme of Bacchus on his panther is, of course, an entirely appropriate one for a dining room floor, and should be compared with the central devices of mosaics from Gloucester and London as well as from a villa at Thruxton (Hampshire). Bacchus was the god of wine who presided over the feast. The device on the Stonesfield mosaic can be found throughout the Roman Empire even if stylistically it belongs to a specific Romano-British group. The other figural motif, a mask of Neptune in the scroll, is likewise widespread. The juxtaposition of Bacchus and Neptune is not fortuitous and can be observed, for example, on the great silver dish in the Mildenhall Treasure as well as in the Orpheus mosaic at Woodchester which belongs to the same local workshop tradition as the Stonesfield mosaic. The Corinian mosaicists had a somewhat limited iconographic repertory which was centred on Bacchus and Orpheus because these were what the patron wanted. This suggests that a key factor was not merely the provision of an appropriate motif for fashionable dining but allusions to salvation. Bacchus was a saviour god and Orpheus, his prophet, had visited the underworld. Neptune represented the sea over which, it was believed, the souls of the dead must pass to the Blessed Isles.[81]

It is presumably merely chance that no other figured pavement has yet been recorded in Oxfordshire (save the Beaconsfield Farm, Great Tew, dolphins) but there are mosaics from neighbouring counties which show what was available. The mosaic at Littlecote just over the Wiltshire border from Berkshire is an Orpheus pavement which alludes both to Bacchus (with panthers) and to Neptune with sea panthers and dolphins. It has plausibly been assigned to a private chapel devoted to cult purposes. At Croughton, in Northamptonshire, just beyond the county boundary in the region of Banbury there is a mosaic which shows Bellerophon slaying the Chimaera, a mythological theme of a hero who destroys a monster, very probably symbolising the defeat of death. It has reasonably been associated with Christianity at Hinton St Mary and Frampton in Dorset where other panels display the chi-rho and at Lullingstone in Kent with possibly a cryptic Christian inscription and certainly later Christian frescoes, and it may have been given the same gloss here. A corridor mosaic from the villa at Thenford, likewise just into Northamptonshire, incorporated a bust of Venus. As the goddess of gardens and growing things this may be no more than an evocation of prosperity, but Venus too can be interpreted as a renewer of life.[82]

Such mosaics demonstrate that by the fourth century the upper classes of provincial society living within our area were not only enjoying the comforts associated with Roman life but were also educated enough to understand and take over its cultural assumptions and myths. Almost every find suggests analogies not only elsewhere in Roman Britain (and, it should be added, for the most part within a journey of a day or two from Oxfordshire — we are, after all, concerned with the heartland of the province) but also with the wider Empire, notably with nearby provinces such as Gaul. Nevertheless there is nothing in the evidence to suggest that these 'Romans' were anything more than native Britons whose forebears had long ago enthusiastically adopted Roman ways.

NOTES

1. Bowman 1986.
2. Gelling 1953, 152; Ekwall 1960, 148 and Rivet & Smith 1979, 57 and 513 (Dorchester); Gelling 1953, 241–2; Ekwall 1960, 5 and see Burnham & Wacher 1990, 92 for Alchester; the name is discussed by Rivet & Smith 1979, 243–4.
3. Hands 1998, 65, fig. 23, nos 35–7 (styli); Tomlin 1996 (London tablet).
4. Henig 1984, 142–5. One addressed to Mars has recently been recorded from the Marlborough Downs, not many miles south-west of the county (Tomlin & Hassall 1999, 378–9, no. 3)
5. Hassall & Tomlin 1992, 312, no. 7 (Alchester inscription); cf Frere 1983, 69–72, fig. 28, pl. ix (Verulamium forum inscription).
6. RIB 2412.99; see Burnham & Wacher 1990, 103.
7. RIB 235.
8. RIB 240.
9. J.M.C. Toynbee in Brodribb et al. 1972, 49–51, nos 30–3, figs 13 and 14; Henig 1993, nos 163, 164.
10. RIB 2417.25–8.
11. RIB 12.
12. RIB 2417.28.
13. RIB 2417.34.
14. RIB 2446.17.

15. Young 1977, 57–60, 128, 176–81; cf RIB 2496.4 for Tamesubugus.
16. Brodribb et al. 1973, 44–6, fig. 23; Woltering 1999, 180–1; and RIB 2457.1; 2505.4; for other panpipes see Clare 1993; Woltering 1999.
17. RIB 2503.186; 2503.412 (Shakenoak); RIB 2501.143 (Alchester); RIB 2501.394 (Lowbury Hill).
18. RIB 236; 2504.16; Bagnall Smith 1998, 152, no. 3.1 (votive plaques); Bagnall Smith 1995, 186 and fig. 11 for example in Celtic; RIB 238; 239; Bagnall Smith 1998, 152, nos 3.2; 3.3 (letters) and cf. Bagnall Smith 1995, 185.
19. RIB 2430.2; see Hassall & Tomlin 1996, 457d (Woodeaton); RIB 241 (Wilcote).
20. Burnham & Wacher 1990, 100–2, fig. 26 (Alchester); Kirk 1949; Goodchild & Kirk 1954; Bagnall Smith 1995; Bagnall Smith 1998 (Woodeaton).
21. Pre-Roman finds see Plot 1705, 315–16, Tab. XV, 19 and 20; Kirk 1949, 7.
22. Lucian, *Alexander*, 30.
23. Kirk 1949, 40, nos 1–4.
24. Kirk 1949, 44, nos 21–3; Bagnall Smith 1998, 177–8.
25. Goodchild & Kirk 1954, 29, no. 6 and Bagnall Smith 1995, 186 and 188, fig. 12 (standing Mars); 187 and 190, fig. 14 (as rider god). See

Henig 1993, no. 61 and Bagnall Smith 1995, 189–90, fig. 15 (stone plaque of standing Mars); Henig 1993, no. 124 and Bagnall Smith 1995, 201 and 197, fig. 26 (Gill Mill relief of rider); Bagnall Smith 1995, 192 and 190, fig. 17 (horse and rider brooches).

26. Kirk 1949, 40–1, nos 6–12; Bagnall Smith 1995, 183–5, fig. 8; 1998, 152, nos 2.3–2.10.

27. Bagnall Smith 1995, 187–8, fig. 13 (Cupid); 1998, 150, no. 1.2 (Medusa). For Venus figurines see Bagnall Smith 1995, 179–80, figs 2 and 3.

28. Bagnall Smith 1995, 185 and 183, fig. 9; Miles 1986, 47, fig. 29.

29. Henig 1971; Henig & Munby 1973.

30. Henig & Munby 1973; Henig 1984, 65, ill. 22.

31. Kirk 1949, 31; Henig & Munby 1973 (Woodeaton); Henig & Chambers 1984 (Ramsden).

32. E.g. Bagnall Smith 1998, 162–74 for female jewellery; 153–4 for scabbard chapes, spur and mail.

33. Bagnall Smith 1995, 182–3, fig.7.

34. Bradford & Goodchild 1939, 13–14; Bagnall Smith 1995, 199 and 196–7, figs 21, 22 (sword and shield); Hingley 1985 (amphitheatre).

35. Fulford & Rippon 1994, 178–9; Bagnall Smith 1995, 193–6.

36. Henig & Cannon, forthcoming.

37. See note 35. Bagnall Smith 1995, 196, fig. 18 for pierced spearhead.

38. Bagnall Smith 1995, 196, fig. 19. See Woodward & Leach 1993 for Uley.

39. See note 25. For the *Genius loci*, Henig 1993, no. 36 and Bagnall Smith 1995, 201 and 197, fig. 25.

40. Henig 1993, no. 67; Bagnall Smith 1995, 200 and 197, fig. 23 (Lees Rest Mercury); Henig 1993, nos 35 (Bablock Hythe, Genius loci) and 28 (Bampton, Fortuna).

41. Henig 1993, nos 46 (Chipping Norton, Jupiter), 82 (Swalcliffe, Mercury and Rosmerta) and 90 (Duns Tew, Vulcan).

42. Henig 1993, nos 27 (Shakenoak, Fortuna) and 42 (Stonesfield, domestic deities).

43. Henig 1993, nos 163 and 164 (Shakenoak lions) and see Keppie 1998, 380 and frontispiece for the Cramond sculpture; Hey 1996, 8 (dog burial at Yarnton).

44. Benson & Brown 1969 (Ardley); Ashmolean Museum 1886, 28–30 (Vicarage garden, Dorchester); Kennett 1695, 22–3 and Tab. 1 (Aston Rowant); Miles 1976 (Didcot).

45. McGavin 1980 (Stanton Harcourt); for Crowmarsh see Wallingford Historical and Archaeological Society interim report; Atkinson 1952/3, 34–5, burial no. 9 (Radley).

46. McGavin 1980 (Stanton Harcourt); Chambers 1986 (Wroxton); Atkinson 1952/3, 32–4 (Radley); Parrington 1978, 25, burial 3 (Abingdon); Chambers 1976 (Curbridge).

47. McGavin 1980; Chambers 1976.

48. Parrington 1978, 25 (Abingdon); Chambers 1987 (Queenford Mill cemetery, Dorchester); Hassall & Tomlin 1989, 333–4, no. 13 (Caversham tank); Akerman 1860, 350, pl. xvii (original publication of Long Wittenham beaker).

49. Radford 1936, 55, fig. 10 and pl. x, A and B (Ditchley terret); Hey 1996, 8 and *VCH*, 338–9, fig. 42 ('Aesica' brooches).

50. Henig 1999.

51. Henig & Hornby 1991; I am indebted to Eberhard Sauer for information about the new gem.

52. Henig 1974; Henig 1990.

53. *VCH*, 341 and pl. xvii A = Henig 1978, no. 262; Goodburn & Henig 1998.

54. Henig in Hands 1998, 76 cf. Henig 1975 and 1978, no. App. 88.

55. Gladiator gem, *VCH*, 341 and pl. xvii A = Henig 1978, no. 492; actor, Henig & Wilkins 1982; Bacchus or satyr with mask, unpublished, British Museum acc. no. 1995, 11–1, 1. For the Cirencester theatre see Holbrook 1998, 142–5; amphitheatre, 145–75.

56. Henig in Booth 1997, 99–100; Bagnall Smith 1998, 159, 161, fig. 5, no. 6.1. For ancient sources on squirrels see Martial, *Epigrams*, v, 37, 13; Pliny, *Naturalis Historia*, viii, 138.

57. Henig 1970a = Henig 1978, nos 18 and 389 (Woodeaton); Henig 1975 and 1978, no. App. 88 (Alchester); Henig 1978, no. 621 (Asthall); Henig 1978, nos 192 and 394 (Lowbury Hill); Henig 1977= Henig 1978, no. App. 206 (glass ring-cameo from Shakenoak).

58. Brown 1973; Henig & Cannon forthcoming.

59. For Regina see Henig 1995, 67, ill. 38.

60. Henig in Miles 1986, m/f 5, G6–8.

61. H. Syer Cumming in *J. Brit. Archaeol. Assoc.* xii (1856), 168 (Alchester, shale leg); Oxfordshire Museums 1974.8.28. Kibble collection (Charlbury, lamp stand); Brodribb et al. 1968, fig. 28, 9 and 10; (Shakenoak candelabrum); Miles 1986, 31, fig. 21 (Barton Court Farm, lion mount).

62. For banquets in Roman Britain see Tacitus, *Agricola*, 21; Brown 1973, 193, 195–6, no. 25, fig. 5 (Appleford cauldron chain).

63. Ashmolean Museum 1886.792a (Dorchester tripod mount), cf. Henig 1976 for comparable example from London.

64. *Oxoniensia* 20, 1955, 90, pl. xv, C (Asthall) cf. Henig 1970b, 184–5, pl. xxv, A, B (swan/feline support from London).

65. Harden in Radford 1936, 62–6; in Brodribb et al. 1971, 101–8; 1973, 98–103 cf. no. 213 for fourth-century bowl with bear-hunt.

66. Brown 1973; Henig 1995, 133, ill. 81.

67. Ashmolean Museum 1979.83 (Wytham dish); see Henig 1995, 93–4, ill. 59 for comparable silver dish from Norfolk.

68. *VCH*, 294 and pl. xiii, F (Dorchester spoons); *Current Archaeology* 163 (June 1999), 257 (Blunsdon, bowl).

69. Birley 1979, 125–7 for *negotiatores*.

70. Young 1977; Miles 1986, m/f 7:D4 for a very fine painted necked bowl from Barton Court Farm (Young, fig.62, type C77.1; OXCHS 1984.194.461).

71. Munby 1975.

72. Hassall 1952/53.

73. For transport of freestone from the Cotswold eastwards to London see Henig 1993, xxi–xxii.

74. Brodribb et al. 1968, 74–5; 1971, 93–7; 1973, 91–8 (Shakenoak); Davey & Ling 1981, 191–4, no. 46 (Wigginton). Altar fragments from North Leigh, Ellis 1999, 227–8, fig 13.

75. Smith 1984.

76. Gelling 1953, 421; *VCH* I, 308–9.

77. Plot 1705, 334–5, tab. xv; Beesley 1841, 41, pl. x.

78. Neal 1981, 104, no. 77 (Widford); Hakewill 1826, pls 2 and 3 (North Leigh).

79. Beesley 1841, 41–2, pl. xi; Neal 1981, 105–7, nos 78–80.

80. Henig 1995, 139–40; Onians 1999, 268–73.

81. For Stonesfield see Taylor 1941; Levine 1978/1987. For a discussion of Bacchus in connection with the Thruxton mosaic (Hants) see Henig & Soffe 1993.

82. Walters 1984 (Littlecote); *Current Archaeology* 157 (May 1998), front cover (Croughton) cf. Thomas 1998 for the meaning of the inscription on the Lullingstone mosaic; Neal 1981, 99, no. 72 (Thenford).

CHAPTER SIX

THE ECONOMY: AGRICULTURE, INDUSTRY AND TRADE

The main emphasis of economic activity in Roman Oxfordshire, as for most of Roman Britain, was on agriculture. For many of the inhabitants of the area this may have been carried on at little more than subsistence level, but there must have been a degree of integration into the wider economic framework, even if only at the level of paying taxes, and it is likely that at many sites, not just the villas, agricultural production was a means of generating disposable income as well as just the day-to-day essentials of life. The majority of the detailed evidence for the agriculture of the region in the Roman period comes from the Thames valley, where environmental aspects of settlements have been quite widely studied. Some of the resulting evidence may be specific to this locality rather than applicable to the county as a whole, but it indicates a picture of development and diversity which probably is representative in many ways.

ROMANISATION

The development of Oxfordshire in the Roman period cannot be understood without some consideration of the question of Romanisation, an issue which has been central to Romano-British studies since the early part of the twentieth century.[1] Put very simply it has been thought that the degree to which Roman domination was accepted is reflected in the extent to which Roman habits, customs and thinking were adopted, and that archaeologically this is most clearly measured in terms of material culture – towns, villas and samian ware pottery having one set of meanings, their absence another. In this sense the evidence falls mainly in the economic sphere, though the factors which affected the choices made by individuals or communities could have been political, social or religious as well as economic ones.

This issue raises many questions about the relationship not only of conquerors and conquered but of different strata in the native British population hierarchy. At one level, the position appears reasonably clear – it is likely that at least significant sections of the élites of the three tribes within whose territories Oxfordshire lay were essentially well disposed towards Rome.[2] This need not mean, however, that average members of the rural population felt the same way – they had no particular political benefit to derive from the conquest. Nevertheless it would be grossly simplistic to see reaction to the Roman conquest as either straightforward acceptance or outright opposition, and there is no completely clear evidence for the latter.

A wide range of reactions to the Roman conquest may therefore be anticipated, though distinguishing between these on the basis of archaeological evidence alone may generally be agreed to be impossible. For much of the rural population, however, their most immediate relationships with Roman power would have revolved largely around the payment of taxes, and if, as is likely, collection of these devolved largely to the local élites it might be argued that there was little difference from the situation that had prevailed before the conquest. Much then would depend on the extent to which these taxes involved an increased level of exaction. In turn, such increases might in part have reflected the awareness of the élites that there were profits to be made from the process. At the same time, the relationship between élites and the rural population in the crucially important area of land tenure would have been significant. We know that in the later Roman empire it was possible to buy and sell estates, and that such estates could be held by absentee (and even overseas) landlords. How early in the Roman period this situation prevailed is less certain, but it is likely that consolidation of estates by the local élites and perhaps also outsiders was a process which developed through the Roman period, with potentially profound implications for the status of those who farmed the land. In Oxfordshire, for example, it has been suggested that changes in the scale and quality of domestic accommodation at the small to medium-sized villas of Shakenoak and Ditchley in the third century reflects their absorption into the large adjacent estate of North Leigh.[3] Whether or not this actually happened, such developments were certainly possible.

The rural population would have become aware of other developments, such as the appearance of Roman roads, of large settlements and of the villas which their social superiors were building. Up to a point such changes could be ignored, but the large settlements became important local market centres of a type which had been at best scarce before the Roman conquest – places where a wide range of goods was readily available because of the increased mobility afforded by the new roads and other factors. Amongst other things the towns provided opportunities for people to move and perhaps establish themselves in craft-based or other service activities. It is generally agreed that the Roman period saw greater social mobility than had been possible previously, and it may also have been the case that, as in the later medieval period, towns were net consumers of people – i.e. that death rates outstripped the capacity of urban populations to sustain themselves, so that their levels could only be maintained by a steady influx of population from the countryside. Whether such a situation would have prevailed in an area where the only 'urban' settlements were the small towns is perhaps debatable, but the possibility that these settlements could have been perceived as offering exciting new opportunities for self-advancement must be admitted, even if it cannot be quantified.

One of the most characteristic manifestations of the gradual process of change was a major transformation of pottery styles. The dominant types of pottery locally available at the time of the conquest were gradually transformed in the second half of the first century AD into the typical 'grey wares' found almost universally in Roman Britain, and at the same time were supplemented by a diversity of imported vessels, offering a variety of shape, finish, function and (in some important cases) contents, such as olive oil and wine, which hitherto had been available only to a select few within the region, if at all.

This process was almost universal across lowland Roman Britain, at least. Some of the changes have important implications for quite fundamental aspects of daily life such as food preparation and diet – always assuming that the specialist vessels found on rural sites were used in the generally accepted fashion. The *mortarium*, or gritted mixing bowl, for example, is found almost universally even on low-status sites across the region. The driving mechanisms behind these changes, and much more overt ones such as the replacement of timber buildings with substantial stone ones, may have been diverse, however. In the case of pottery, the development of locally produced coarse wares may indicate nothing more than a technological innovation: the rapid spread of the pottery kiln. The adoption of this material was thus a question of using what was available, rather than making a conscious choice between old and new styles of what were essentially still the same vessel types. The appearance of imported pottery, however, was presumably affected more by personal choice, though the distribution of what in the Iron Age would have been seen as prestige goods may still have been controlled in part by local élites, without the full operation of simple market forces. In the case of villa building, the desire of individuals to demonstrate their wealth and status in new ways was most probably the primary motivating factor. Here, and in the development of towns (though more so in the provision of facilities in the tribal capitals which lay outside our area), a reaction to positive Roman encouragement in these directions may be seen, though the much-discussed words of Tacitus on the subject cannot be taken entirely at face value.

By the later Roman period, with the growth of a more fully monetarised economy (see below) it can be argued that the adoption of pottery, building types and their interior decoration and the construction of temples and town walls were conditioned more by choice and less by social factors. Essentially, however, economics probably lay behind many of the decisions made – the absence of villas in certain areas reflecting the economic as well as the social status of the inhabitants. At a lower level of material culture, such as in the choice of pottery used, differences were largely of degree rather than kind – similar sorts of pottery were available to all, but on lower-status rural settlements they were simply less numerous, and much less likely to be supplemented by vessels of glass and metal. The implication of the Oxfordshire evidence is that the process of acculturation, the use of buildings and objects which are considered as characteristically Roman (though in most cases disseminated through the filter of the continental north-western provinces), was pursued by the inhabitants of the region as a matter of course, with little or no conscious opposition but equally, in many cases, with perhaps little awareness on the part of the rural population that they were 'becoming Roman', the principal limiting factors of basic social and economic status being largely (if to a lesser degree than previously) beyond their control.

AGRICULTURE

Many of the basic characteristics of the Romano-British agricultural regime were already established by the late Iron Age, though there were important developments which can be assigned to the Roman period. These included a new emphasis on the development of hay meadows, possibly the introduction of new crops (though the principal cereal grains were the same as in the Iron Age), and certainly other horticultural plant species (and weeds), and some improvements in livestock, particularly with regard to size. There were also improvements in agricultural implements such as the development of the mould-board plough with an iron coulter to cut the sod and the use of long-bladed scythes for reaping. New technologies for storing and processing grain were also developed. An important question with regard to these developments is whether they should be seen as responses to the need to produce more in order to meet the requirements of taxation and respond to the other pressures outlined in the chapter above, or whether there was a stimulus to provide a surplus which could be invested or spent on non-essential items (such as building structures of Romanised form and decoration). Alternatively, did agricultural practice simply evolve 'naturally' because the improved techniques, tools and expertise in developing plant and animal species were there to be taken advantage of?

The essentials of agricultural production were typical of much of southern Britain. The principal cereal crop across the region was spelt wheat, which had been common in the Iron Age. Emmer wheat, which, like spelt, required special processing to release the grains from the husks, was much less common. Bread wheat was also relatively rare, but its occurrence is of interest. At Barton Court Farm, where it was apparently introduced early, its appearance was seen as a sign of a 'progressive' agricultural regime which was contrasted with that of the supposedly more conservative farmers of the nearby Ashville site.[4] Even here, however, spelt wheat seems to have been the dominant cereal in most of the samples examined. The occurrence of bread wheat has also been taken as an indicator of particularly intensive agriculture. It may have become more widely used in the late Roman period, as at Mount Farm, Berinsfield,[5] but was still not found at all on many sites. In fact it occurs so infrequently that it is hard to judge the true importance of this crop. Its absence from features associated with probable villa sites, such as that at Gatehampton Farm, Goring,[6] suggests that it was not widely produced even in higher-status rural sites, but it was found at the villa site at Roughground Farm, Lechlade (just outside the county), which may support the suggestion that there was some association between such sites and bread wheat production.[7]

The cereal species which occur consistently across the region are spelt and barley, with a low-level representation of oats at a number of sites. In at least some cases the oats may have been the wild species occurring as weeds and they rarely appear in sufficient quantity to suggest that they formed a major part of arable production.

The principal cereals were supplemented by a range of other vegetable and herb plants, the diversity of which is in marked contrast to the situation in the Iron Age, though this may have been a situation which developed gradually. Legumes are found quite widely, and may indicate nitrogen depletion of overworked soils as has been suggested at Ashville,[8] and perhaps corresponding attempts to improve this. Elsewhere this problem may have been addressed by manuring.[9] Celtic bean was cultivated at Barton Court Farm and peas were certainly grown for consumption.[10] The use and in some cases cultivation of new species is indicated at several sites, an example being the early Roman occurrence of coriander at Alchester, but coriander has also been found in lower-status rural contexts as at Farmoor and dill also occurred there.[11] The occurrence of a range of horticultural crops is a general characteristic of the Roman period which contrasts with the preceding Iron Age. It has been suggested that sites such as Mount Farm, where the identified plant species included celery, may have had a specific function in supplying the larger nucleated settlements – in this case the adjacent small town of Dorchester – with such produce.[12]

Flax or linseed, a crop that is known before the Roman period in the region, became more common and is found quite widely. Its seeds could have been eaten or used for oil, but the clearest indications of its use relate to retting – the breaking down of the stems to produce fibres. This activity has been tentatively identified at Old Shifford,[13] but is less clearly evidenced elsewhere.

Animal husbandry, like arable agriculture, also saw developments in the Roman period, though again the principal species exploited were the same as those found in the Iron Age. Cattle were generally dominant and sheep were also important, although generally less so than earlier. Pigs were consistently present but always in far smaller numbers than the two main species. There is some evidence for species improvement in relation to animal size during the Roman period, particularly in cattle. At Alchester, for example, there was marked diversity in size in the later Roman cattle bones, suggesting that two different strains, one substantially larger than any seen in the region before the Roman period, were bred. There is, however, relatively little indication of specialist exploitation of animals, though this may reflect the relative lack of evidence from large-scale marketing and butchery sites, which can be presumed to have existed at least in most of the major settlements. The general balance of age and species data therefore indicate the use of cattle for meat, hides and perhaps milk. They also served as draught animals, and a considerable amount of pathological evidence, again from Alchester and from other sites including Barton Court Farm, suggests that some cattle were overused in this way.[14]

Sheep were also widely used for meat as well as for their wool. In fact there are few clear indications of the keeping of the older sheep which would be consistent with a particular emphasis on wool production. While there is relatively little evidence from both the northern and southern upland areas of the county, where sheep breeding is most likely to have been important, what little information we do have, for example from the villa at Shakenoak and the small town at Asthall, does not suggest any particular emphasis on wool production in the Cotswold area.[15] One less usual aspect of the economy of the Shakenoak villa was demonstrated by the presence of three fishponds, suggesting fish-farming on a considerable scale. This may have been of coarse fish rather than the trout suggested by the excavators, but could still have generated a fairly substantial income.[16] Such a development has to be seen as a commercial venture on the part of the owners of the site, as the quantities of fish which could have been held in the Shakenoak ponds are far beyond what might have been required for consumption on site. Comparable evidence of specialist economic diversification elsewhere in the region is lacking, however.

Evidence for the chronological development of the whole range of agricultural practices in the region comes mostly from the Thames valley, where the most detailed work on the appropriate evidence has been carried out. The rate of development, with regard to the uptake of technological advances, will not necessarily have been uniform, however. This can be seen in relation to the occurrence of particular cereal crops, discussed above, but also in straightforward aspects such as plough technology. The plough-marks in the early Roman fields at Drayton were mostly made by a

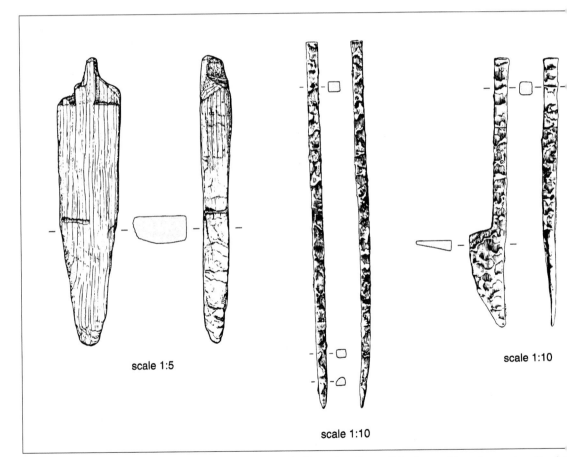

scale 1:5

scale 1:10

scale 1:10

6.1   Old and new plough technology: wooden share from Ashville Trading Estate, Abingdon, and iron share and coulter fr[o] Dorchester. After Parrington 1978, fig. 62, and Frere 1984, fig. 32.

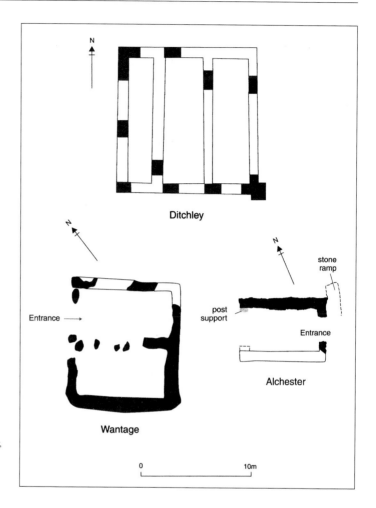

6.2 Barns and granaries: Ditchley, Wantage and Alchester. Excavated foundations are shown solid and restored elements in outline.

simple ard plough of Iron Age type which did not turn over the soil. A wooden share from exactly such a plough (Fig. 6.1) came from a third-century well fill at Ashville Trading Estate, Abingdon.[17] In contrast, physical remains of more advanced plough types include the coulter(s) from a late Roman iron hoard at Dorchester.[18] Environmental evidence also sheds light on developments, hinting at a general increase in the level of arable agriculture – for example in the pollen record at Sidlings Copse, near Oxford, where an increase in cereal pollen in the Roman period was matched by a decrease in woodland – and also at the use of more marginal land, as demonstrated by the frequent inclusion among charred cereal remains of weeds and other plants characteristic of damp ground, a feature not typically seen in the Iron Age.[19]

The use of damper ground for arable may indicate that the amount of land under cultivation was on the increase in the Roman period. However, at about the same time there is fairly consistent evidence from the Thames valley for a general rise in water-table levels and an increase in the amount of soils deposited by alluvial (flood) action. The two occurrences are not necessarily directly related, nor does either necessarily indicate a significant increase in rainfall at the time, and there is no compelling evidence for such an increase owing to climatic deterioration at this time.[20] More frequent deposition of alluvium may, however, be evidence for a greater emphasis on autumn ploughing, resulting in increased run-off of soil into streams during the winter months. Aspects of the weed assemblage from Ashville, for example, suggest that quite a considerable proportion of the cereals grown there were probably autumn sown even in the Iron Age and the same distinctive weeds (principally goosegrass) have been identified at Old Shifford in the early Roman period.[21]

The Roman period also saw developments in techniques of crop processing. Corresponding evidence for storage is not as clear, however, and in the absence of fully excavated villa complexes some of the best evidence for barns comes from the major settlements of Alchester and Wantage (Fig. 6.2). The use of probable raised-floor granaries, an Iron Age technology producing characteristic 'four-post' or larger structures, survives in the early Roman period at Barton Court Farm and at Eagle Farm, Standlake.[22] With regard to crop processing the most obvious and widespread innovation was the introduction of so-called corn drying ovens. These are a regular feature on a whole range of rural sites, from villas such as Barton Court Farm and probably Goring, and low-status sites like Farmoor and Yarnton (Fig. 6.3).[23] Both the well-known T-shaped type and other, simpler, forms are known. The latter include one of the two driers from Farmoor and possible or probable examples at Crowmarsh and Knighton Bushes, both in the southern part of the county.[24] Corn driers also occur in suburban contexts, as at Alchester, and perhaps at Abingdon, and even on industrial sites like the pottery production complex at the Churchill Hospital, Oxford.[25] These corn driers could have been used in a variety of ways,[26] which included straightforward drying of wet grain. Parching of the most common cereal crop of the Roman period, spelt wheat, which required special treatment to facilitate threshing and winnowing, is another likely function, and roasting of germinated grain to halt the germination process, as a stage in beer production, is another. These and other operations can leave distinct residues of charred material which allow (in some cases) identification of the specific processes practised. In many cases a multifunctional use is likely, but both use before winnowing and in the malting process are attested in Oxfordshire examples. It is possible that at the Churchill Hospital, where no fewer than nine driers (four T-shaped and five of simple forms) were found, some were also used in an agricultural context (a suggestion supported by the presence of cereal chaff)[27] but the occurrence of such numbers, and of similar structures on pottery production sites elsewhere, indicates that they were considered suitable for use for drying pots prior to firing. This is likely to have been the primary function of most of the 'corn driers' here.

The expansion of arable production would not only have resulted in the possible utilisation of increasingly marginal soils, but presumably also have had an effect on the pastoral economy by reducing the amount of land potentially available for grazing. It may have been partly in response to this that the Roman period saw the probable introduction and then increasing emphasis on haymaking as a means of increasing provision for animals. As with evidence for developments in cereal production this can

6.3 T-shaped corn-drying oven, Yarnton. The fire was lit at the far end of the long flue. The floor carrying the grain and other traces of superstructure are lost.

be seen in several aspects of the archaeological record – in the plant remains which indicate a range of species typical of hay meadows from several sites, in the physical survival of hay itself at sites such as Farmoor, and in the appearance of tools suitable for harvesting hay. Blades of the characteristic very long scythes used for this purpose (but also suitable for other crops) are known from Hardwick and from Farmoor and a further fragment of such a blade comes from Appleford.[28] These and comparable tools from elsewhere in the country all come from late Roman contexts.

The development of hay cropping is very important. It provided a means of maintaining stock in or near the farmyard over winter when the alternative, keeping them out in the fields, might have had serious adverse effects on the pasture, particularly in the increasingly wet conditions that prevailed in some low-lying areas in the later Roman period. A further advantage of keeping stock in the farmyard is that manure can then be collected and distributed over arable fields. This, however, was clearly also done in the early Roman period, probably without the benefit of stocks of hay, so the availability of this resource was not essential to an effective regime of manuring.

INDUSTRY

For the most part, 'industrial' activity was on a relatively small scale and was concerned principally with the production of the goods and other commodities required by the agricultural community. Much of this production would have been carried on at local market centres, particularly the nucleated settlements located on the major road network, though lesser sites could also have housed craftsmen of various kinds, and a number of the smaller agricultural settlements may have had their own blacksmith, for example. In addition, some specialist craftsmen could have been itinerant, taking their skills where they were needed.

Metalworking can be quite readily detected archaeologically, and evidence for iron working in particular is fairly widespread. There is little indication of basic iron production in the region, and while possible smelting sites have been suggested in the vicinity of Woodeaton and at Camp Corner, Milton Common, on the M40 in the south-east of the county, the evidence is not completely convincing for either.[29] It is possible that the ironstone of the north-eastern part of the county was exploited, perhaps at sites such as Swalcliffe Lea, but the present evidence from there is more consistent with smithing than smelting. For the most part, therefore, the iron used in the smithies of the region is likely to have been imported, either from Northamptonshire or from the Forest of Dean, both major centres of production. A rare example of an iron billet, the form in which the raw material was traded, comes from a hearth at Asthall, lying within the only structure from the county which can be confidently interpreted as a smithy (Fig. 6.4) (individual rooms within some buildings, clearly seen at Swalcliffe (Fig. 6.5), also had this function, rather than whole structures).[30] This was a building of relatively slight construction located at the margin

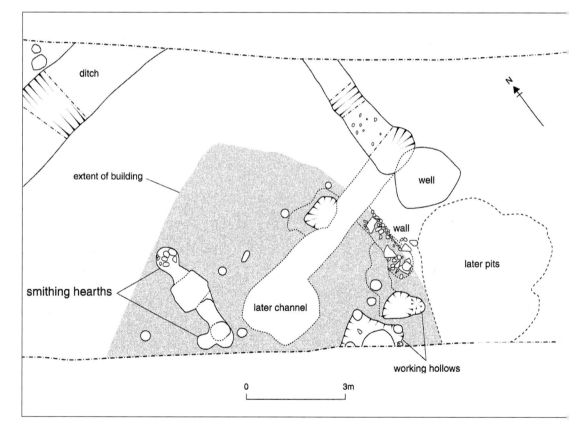

6.4 Asthall, smithy building located at the edge of the settlement in the second and third centuries. The well contained a large boulder which had almost certainly been used as an anvil. After Booth 1997, fig. 3.4.

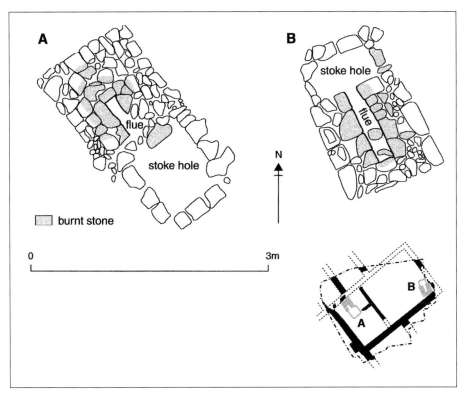

6.5   Hearths or iron-working furnaces from Swalcliffe Lea. The inset shows their location within a partly excavated building. After Shawyer 1999, fig. 20.

of the roadside settlement and was in use principally in the second and third centuries. Analysis of the slag and other debris makes it clear that only smithing, and not smelting, was carried out here. Generally, smithing can be identified from the type of slag recovered in excavation, even if this is not associated with other evidence. Such material occurs quite widely on settlement sites of different types. In some cases smiths may have been peripatetic and well-defined smithy buildings may not always have existed. Collections of ironwork probably gathered for reworking, such as the hoards recovered from Dorchester, also indicate the presence of smiths.[31]

Direct evidence for large-scale working of metals other than iron is quite scarce, perhaps owing to the relative lack of excavation in the larger settlements where such activity may have been concentrated. Working of copper alloys – bronze and brass – is likely to have been quite widespread, albeit usually most likely on a small scale, but is relatively little known beyond the occasional recovery of slag and crucible fragments. It is indicated by objects such as a mould (Fig. 5.20a) and an imperfect brooch casting from Alchester and by small quantities of slag from a number of sites including Asthall. More unusually, the latter site has also produced a crucible which had been used for refining silver.[32] It was found in a building facing on to the main road through the settlement, presumably the location of this activity (Fig. 3.6 inset, middle building). Copper alloy working in a rural context is known both at Old Shifford Farm and at Gravelly Guy in the early Roman period and a crucible from Alfred's Castle, probably of Roman date, may perhaps suggest the presence of more than just an itinerant craftsman.[33]

Other manufacturing industries may have left even less clear traces. So for example there is almost no clear evidence for the production of textiles (beyond the occurrence of objects associated with spinning), though this would have been widespread and by no means confined to the larger settlements. Possible evidence for flax retting at Old Shifford may indicate the production of linen there.[34] On recent evidence, however, there is no indication that any textile production occurred other than at a domestic level.

One potentially important extractive industry in the county must have been stone quarrying. Substantial quantities of stone would have been needed at the Akeman Street settlements of Asthall, Sansom's Platt and Alchester, where stone buildings were common, as well as at Dorchester (these last two, of course, also having been surrounded with stone walls); the villas, again particularly in the north of the county, would also have been significant consumers. A particular feature of the archaeology of Wilcote is the number of quarry pits, in some cases quite substantial, located adjacent to Akeman Street and presumably dug to provide material for the construction of that road. Much quarrying would have been carried out on a small scale, and this is reflected in part in the use of local stone types where available – again particularly in the north of the county, where Ironstone (in the Banbury area), Cornbrash and Forest Marble as well as higher-quality oolitic limestones were widely exploited. Further south the villa at Barton Court Farm, Abingdon, used ragstone from the nearby Corallian ridge, and in the south-east of the county, for example in villas near Henley (such as Bix and Harpsden Wood), local materials, in this case flint, were again used, while at the villa at West Challow, near Wantage, local chalk was employed.

Some of the higher-quality Cotswold stones may have been extracted on a more systematic basis, but by its nature evidence for ancient quarrying and mining is frequently hard to detect as it tends to be destroyed by later exploitation of the same resources. Thus there is little certain evidence for Roman period quarrying in the county. There is equally little clear evidence for the distribution of Oxfordshire Cotswold stone to south-east England, though Taynton stone has been reported at Colchester. It is widely assumed that such stone would have been commonly used in places like London, to which it could have been transported quite easily by river, but while Cotswold limestones are quite common there these are most usually attributed to sources in Gloucestershire and the Bath area.[35] Transport of the former, however, might very likely have been routed through the county along the Thames. A slightly less likely stone export from the county is ragstone from the Corallian ridge south of the Thames, but this material (or less probably, Forest Marble) was identified at Silchester in the amphitheatre.[36]

The extent of Roman, as opposed to later, exploitation of Stonesfield Slate, a well-known roofing material, is also uncertain. This material has been found at Ditchley and at Shakenoak,[37] for example, but is very poorly represented (on present evidence) at Alchester and was absent in recent excavations at Asthall, only 12km from the source. Some identifications of Stonesfield Slate in Roman contexts may be unreliable; its use may only have been small scale compared with the post-medieval period,[38] but it has been claimed recently, for example at the villa at Bancroft in Milton Keynes.[39] Stonesfield was also a source of ordinary building stone, which was certainly used at the nearby villa of North Leigh, and presumably in the villa buildings at Stonesfield itself, though unsurprisingly this is not recorded in the antiquarian accounts of these sites.

While more work is needed to establish the scale of stone export outside the county the willingness of the Romano-British community to move stone and other building materials over considerable distances is also demonstrated in reverse. One roofing material which did occur at Asthall, for example, was an Old Red Sandstone which most probably came from the Forest of Dean, perhaps traded with quernstones from the same source.[40] There is almost no evidence for the production of ceramic building material (brick and tile) within the county, though debris from a possible tile kiln has been found recently at Wilcote. If this lack of evidence reflects the true position (and tile kilns might reasonably be expected in the vicinity of Alchester in the second century AD, for example) tile and brick must have been imported from surrounding areas. Such sources probably include the Minety kilns in North Wiltshire which supplied sites in the Upper Thames valley, and industries operating in the vicinity of Towcester and in North Bedfordshire, whose products are found at Alchester and were probably routed, along with related pottery, through Towcester.

Much the most archaeologically visible Romano-British industry in Oxfordshire was pottery production. Even small-scale local production in the Roman period tended to be in kilns which are readily recognisable, in contrast to the situation in the late Iron Age, when (presumably) comparable local production, without such installations, remains obstinately invisible. In the early post-conquest years much of the pottery in use continued to be made in the so-called 'Belgic' tradition established in the later Iron Age, with gradual developments both of fabrics – the clay and its tempering agents – and of the repertoire of vessel types. Kilns of later first and second-century date, all essentially working in the developed form of this tradition and producing mainly utilitarian vessels such as jars, have been found to the west of Oxford at Long Hanborough, Cassington and more recently at Yarnton, where two kilns of a relatively unusual type with two flues (also seen at Long Hanborough) have been found (Fig. 6.6).[41] Early Roman coarse ware kilns have also been found on Boars Hill, and two more occur at the Churchill Hospital in Oxford itself.[42]

A completely different potting tradition is suggested by a range of vessels including beakers and flagons in fine white, grey and orange fabrics which appear quite widely across the county in small numbers but concentrate particularly at Abingdon and Dorchester in mid first-century AD contexts.[43] These vessels have affinities with similar material from Chichester and Silchester, but were probably produced somewhere in the Abingdon/Dorchester area and may possibly reflect a military interest in fine ware production. Probably the most important form represented was the butt beaker, a drinking vessel type which was first imported to Britain before the Roman conquest, though there are no certain pre-conquest fine ware butt beakers from our area (the

6.6   Early Roman pottery kiln at Yarnton. This example has a flue on each side of the central firing-chamber. The pots to be fired probably rested on bars laid between the sides of the kiln and the central oval pedestal.

vessels from a well-known burial at Watlington,[44] for example, are probably of relatively local manufacture and are perhaps post-conquest in date).

   These two distinct traditions may have united in the Oxford area, perhaps by the AD 60s as there is little evidence that the fine wares continued in their original form into the Flavian period (AD 70–96), to constitute the origins of what was eventually to become one of the three or four largest pottery industries in the whole of Roman Britain. An element of continuity with the early fine ware tradition is suggested by the continued appearance of butt beakers, possibly even into the second-century. Roughly around AD 100 this industry was supplemented by the arrival of potters from the Verulamium (St Albans) region, who specialised in the production of flagons and *mortaria* (gritted mixing bowls) in sandy white fabrics, and added these types, particularly *mortaria*, to the Oxford repertoire for the first time. The shapes of early Oxford examples of these types are very close to those of their Verulamium ancestors, but by the later second century AD distinctive *mortarium* shapes had evolved. These and other products of the industry were distributed quite widely across the region from the mid-second to the mid-third century. At this point there was a significant development

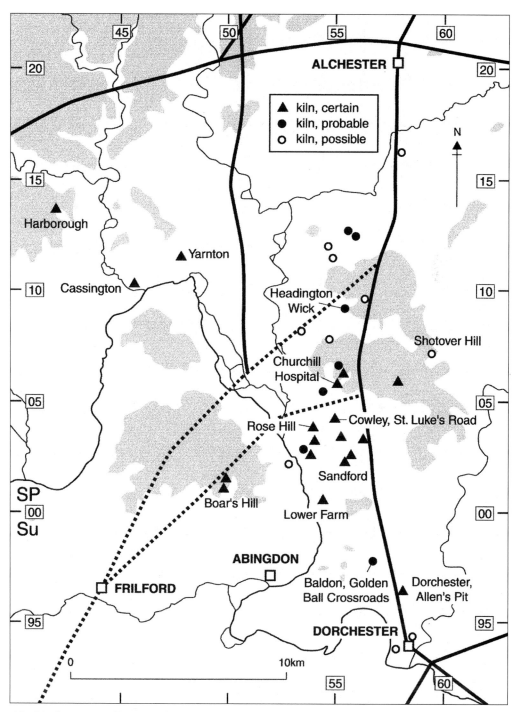

6.7   Distribution map of known Oxford pottery production sites.

in the industry, with major expansion of *mortarium* production and the development of new lines, including so-called parchment ware (white or cream-coloured vessels, mostly bowls, with red-painted decoration) and red-brown colour-coated ware. The latter attempted to imitate the surface appearance and a number of the vessel shapes of late samian ware, the import of which (from Germany, in far smaller quantities than from France in the previous centuries) was now in terminal decline. These Oxford products developed rapidly and were distributed across the whole of southern Britain and even to the continent in the fourth century.

The Oxford potteries extended across an area from Dorchester in the south to Noke and Woodeaton in the north, lying mostly between the Thames and the Dorchester–Alchester road (Fig. 6.7).[45] Parts of this area, perhaps particularly in the south-eastern part of Oxford itself, may legitimately be described as a semi-industrial landscape, in which were sited groups of kilns, often within enclosures defined by ditches, together with workshop buildings and a range of ancillary structures and features related to preparation of the potting clay. Some of this clay would have been dug close to the kiln sites. The iron-free white-firing clay used for *mortaria* and parchment wares, however, was only obtainable from the vicinity of Shotover Hill, and the distinctive grits used in the *mortaria* came from the greensand deposits on Boars Hill, so there would have been considerable traffic in these commodities (and also of large supplies of timber for firing the kilns) between their sources and the many component production sites of the industry.

Recent work has greatly expanded our conception of the scale of these individual component sites. When the first major review of the industry was published by Young in 1977, only about forty kiln structures were known, from twelve of some twenty-six identified locations within the spread of the industry. A further seventeen or so kilns have been excavated since, all in south or east Oxford – four at The Churchill Hospital, four at Cowley and nine at Blackbird Leys and Minchery Farm.[46] The main advances in understanding, however, have come about through a combination of geophysical survey, fieldwalking and excavation on individual sites. At Lower Farm, Nuneham Courtenay, the chance discovery of a previously unknown production site in the course of pipeline construction in 1991 led to a programme of work which shows that the site covers more than 10ha and contains at least forty to fifty kilns, though as yet these are only known from the geophysical survey (Fig. 6.8).[47] The kilns are grouped in enclosures on either side of a trackway which runs eastwards, presumably to link with the Dorchester–Alchester road. The nine kilns lying between Blackbird Leys and Minchery Farm revealed in 1995–6 were concentrated less densely than at Lower Farm but occurred in small clusters in ditched enclosures spread across an only partly examined area of almost 25ha. This sort of scale of operation is what would be expected of a nationally important industry, and we may imagine that over the 300 or more years of its existence there must have been many hundreds of kilns constructed and used, even if it is assumed that an individual kiln may have remained in use for a number of years – a matter on which there is considerable uncertainty.

Elsewhere within the Oxford area, other recently discovered sites, including several in the vicinity of Noke,[48] are identified only from surface material, the principal

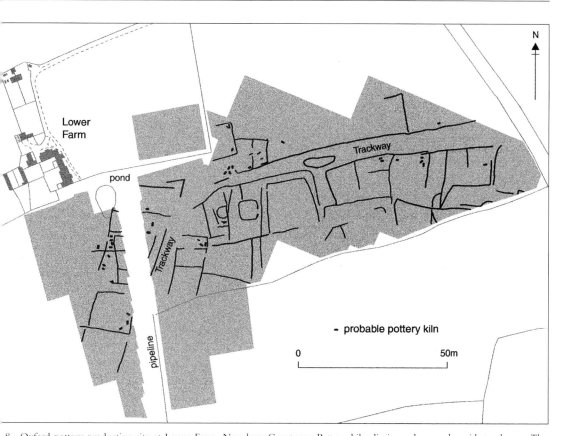

.8   Oxford pottery production site at Lower Farm, Nuneham Courtenay. Pottery kilns lie in enclosures alongside trackways. The
ᴴain east–west trackway probably ran to the Alchester–Dorchester road to the east. Outline plan based on geophysical survey by the
ₙcient Monuments Laboratory, English Heritage. The extent of the survey area is shaded.

indicators of such sites being abnormal concentrations of mortaria, and the presence of
kiln debris. Again one of the important aspects of these sites is to indicate the scale of
the individual production centres within the industry.

    If anything, however, much of the recent work on the Oxford industry serves to
demonstrate the lack of detailed knowledge of many of its component parts and of their
potential diversity. Nevertheless it is becoming increasingly clear that even some of the
major centres within the industry had different histories of development and different
emphases in terms of production. This can be seen by contrasting the excavated material
from the Churchill Hospital (Fig. 6.9) – until very recently much the best excavated and
understood production site, though probably only partly examined – and Lower Farm.
After a short-lived phase late in the first century, there was no known production at the
Churchill site until perhaps the mid-third century and the site was most intensively
active in the fourth century, specialising mainly in *mortaria*, parchment ware and colour-
coated wares (Fig. 6.10). At Lower Farm the excavated sample, which is admittedly

6.9   Late Roman Oxford pottery kiln at the
Churchill Hospital, Oxford. The vent holes
which allow the passage of hot air can be
clearly seen round the edge of the raised,
circular firing-chamber floor. The middle of
this floor has collapsed, leaving a hole.

localised but seems on the basis of surface material to be reasonably representative, shows production probably commencing in the early second century. Second-century products here included a range of fine ware fabrics which had not previously been known within the industry, the most important of these being brown colour-coated beakers dating to the second half of the century which have now been recognised at a number of consumer sites in the county.[49] In terms of fabric and finish these vessels are very similar to the widely distributed late Roman products, but the vessel forms are quite distinct from the later repertoire and at present there is no indication that their production led directly to the development of the later colour-coated wares. Overall production at Lower Farm continued to about the mid-fourth century, but with a substantial peak of activity in the later third century, indicated both by *mortaria* of that date and by the new colour-coated wares – parchment ware being very rare. The later third-century peak also seems to be identified in the recent excavations at Blackbird Leys, and in a sample of the surface material from Noke. However, another site known only from surface material, at

Baldon, seems like the Churchill site to have a heavy fourth-century emphasis, particularly on colour-coated wares.

Many questions thus remain to be answered about the dynamics of the industry's development. Although there was considerable, and in some cases quite remarkable, consistency of products across the industry as a whole, such consistency was not absolute. The industry was therefore not a monolithic entity, except possibly with regard to *mortarium* and colour-coated ware production from the mid to late third century onwards. It is possible that individual producers or groups of producers within the industry had their own distribution networks and relationships with particular markets. At present, however, this cannot be demonstrated because it is not possible to distinguish systematically the products of the individual kiln sites. This could perhaps be done through the study of potters' stamps, as has been documented in studies of the distribution of Spanish olive oil amphorae, for example, in which some correlations between particular production and market areas can be observed.[50] Unfortunately, unlike many of their contemporaries, the second-century Oxford *mortarium* potters rarely stamped their products (the practice of stamping *mortaria* disappeared universally in the later second century) and the only other significant instance of the use of potters' stamps in the industry is in the later third century when the imitation of the samian ware prototype of one particular colour-coated ware bowl type extended to the use of a maker's stamp in the inside of the vessel.[51] These stamps are not common on production sites, however, a few examples being known from Allen's Pit (Dorchester) and Cowley, and rather larger numbers from Lower Farm and Blackbird Leys, the latter complex including for present purposes the immediately adjacent site at Sandford.[52] Moreover, the great majority are illiterate and use a common repertoire of lines and crosses, which hinders confident identification of specific stamps. Nevertheless it may be possible in time to assign particular stamps (and hence the associated vessels when they occur on consumer sites) to particular production centres.

There is thus still room for differences of opinion on the ownership and spatial organisation of the land within which the industry operated, and the economic basis and nature of control of both production and distribution. The considerable degree of

6.10   Late Roman pottery from the Churchill Hospital, Oxford. A white ware *mortarium* (centre rear) is flanked by bowls and a small jar in parchment ware, white with red-painted decoration.

consistency of the later Roman products has suggested to a number of commentators a significant measure of centralised control, probably by a small number of landowners. In this respect the relationship between the industry and the villa at Headington Wick, where there seems to have been some production, is very important and it is unfortunate that the only significant evidence for this site comes from excavations published in 1851, well though this was done by the standards of the day.[53] Such sites could hold the key to determining the extent to which pottery production was integrated with agriculture. The fact that there is little direct indication of the latter in the east Oxford area may support the view that the primary economic emphasis here was industrial, but it may more simply reflect a lack of relevant evidence. It is quite likely that there was systematic exploitation of sustainable timber supplies, involving woodland management through coppicing, but the scale of this is quite unknown at present. Where charcoal from production sites has been examined, however, as at Blackbird Leys, a variety of material appears which does not seem likely to have derived from carefully managed woodland. Pollen evidence from Sidlings Copse which indicates the complete disappearance of woodland in the Roman period could also be taken to indicate that this resource was not carefully nurtured.

One further factor which has been remarked on is the broader location of the industry, which is both rural and also close to probable tribal territorial boundaries, in this case not only that between the Catuvellauni and the Dobunni, but also the boundaries between these tribes and the Atrebates. Comparable rural and (in several cases) tribal boundary locations are characteristic of all the really large-scale late Roman pottery producers.[54] This might suggest that these industries were located to take advantage of several different but adjacent market areas.

The distribution of Oxford pottery in the later third and fourth centuries has been quite extensively studied, and interpretations of its significance vary. Although these products reached sites across most of central and southern England there was still, as might be expected, a heavy concentration of them in the core area around the industry. This can be seen, however, not simply as a reflection of 'normal' market forces but as supporting the view that aspects of trade were still subject to social control in the late Roman period and that the distribution of Oxford products was particularly concentrated within the territory of the Dobunni. This suggestion appears to be supported, for example, by evidence from the neighbouring county of Warwickshire. In the southern part of that county, which lay in Dobunnic territory, Oxford products are common, but their representation declines markedly in the northern part, assignable to the Corieltauvi. The extensive distribution of Oxford products down the Thames, plotted by Fulford and Hodder[55] in an important study, is consistent with the use of river transport, potentially in a situation governed by market forces, but the corresponding concentration of Oxford wares in the lower Severn valley, noted in the same study, cannot be interpreted so easily since it relies on land transport to take the pottery beyond the Upper Thames and over the Cotswold scarp. Such a distribution can again be seen in the context of a market at least partly controlled by the hierarchy of the civitas.

As well as the *mortaria*, parchment and colour-coated wares which were very widely traded, the Oxford industry was a major source of 'coarse' wares, which were distributed more locally. In many respects, however, these vessels are not particularly distinctive, particularly in terms of their fabrics, and at least some of the pottery recovered from settlement sites in the region may come from (mostly unknown) kilns outside Oxford producing vessels in a similar tradition using similar clays. One clear example of this can be seen at Compton, in northern Berkshire, where many vessels from a fourth-century kiln mainly producing grey wares are effectively indistinguishable from Oxford products. In this instance there are hints that the potter was directly copying some aspects of the Oxford repertoire, such as stamped and indented beakers, and may even have worked in the industry. Other Oxford potters moved away from the area in the late Roman period and established themselves in new locations. Examples are found at Hartshill, North Warwickshire, Harston, Cambridgeshire and in East Sussex, probably in the Pevensey area.[56]

Pottery production west of Oxford in the early Roman period has already been mentioned. For the most part this was on a small scale and had a localised distribution. From the mid-first to the third century, however, an industry located at an as yet unknown site or sites probably north-west of Oxford and working in a slightly different tradition was a major supplier both to Thames valley sites such as Yarnton and to the Akeman Street settlements of Wilcote and Asthall in particular, though its products reached as far east as Alchester. A wide range of oxidised and reduced coarse ware vessels was produced by this industry, which has some affinities – both in the nature of the fabric and in the occurrence of vessel types such as tankards which are unknown in the Oxford kilns – with potteries located in the Swindon area. In the south-east of the county recently collected surface evidence suggests the presence of a more local pottery industry at Sonning Common, perhaps dating from the mid-second to third century.

Pottery has always been one of the clearest indicators of trade in Roman Britain because of its relative indestructibility and the possibility that much of it can be assigned to known sources. Oxfordshire is no exception, and its sites produce a wide variety of traded material, though in most cases this is consistent with commonly observed trends. In the first and second centuries continental imported material consists principally of the glossy red samian ware, mostly bowls, dishes and cups, coming first from southern and then from central France and eventually from Germany. This was supplemented by small quantities of vessels such as colour-coated ware beakers from various sites in France and Germany, and an assortment of amphorae, of which only the globular olive oil containers from southern Spain are at all numerous. Apart from the locally produced pottery discussed above, vessels from sources in surrounding areas are found in varying quantities. White wares and *mortaria* from Verulamium; north Wiltshire products, both from the Swindon area already mentioned and from Savernake Forest, and small quantities of Severn valley ware all occur in the early Roman period and Dorset black-burnished ware appears from the early second century. *Mortaria* and flagons perhaps from the Cirencester area occur in the western part of the county in the second and third centuries. In the later Roman period, and particularly from the mid-third century onwards, continental imports were effectively absent. Nene valley (Peterborough area) and New Forest colour-coated wares supplemented Oxford products in small quantities, black-burnished ware continued to be traded and grey wares from Alice Holt (near Farnham in Surrey) are found occasionally. Late Roman shell-tempered ware from northern Bedfordshire was widely, if thinly, distributed. More common were vessels in so-called 'pink grogged ware', a distinctive product from an industry now known to have at least one source at Stowe Park, adjacent to the Roman road between Alchester and Towcester. Although present in the second century, these vessels, particularly large jars, were more common in the third and fourth centuries. It is possible that the large jars, which were very widely distributed, were traded as a commodity container, but if so it is not known what this was. A good example of one of these vessels, with a hole in its lower body plugged with lead, was used for a well-known cremation burial from Dorchester (now in the Ashmolean Museum).[57]

A very wide range of other materials would have been traded alongside pottery. These would have included vessels with complementary uses, for example in glass and also in bronze and pewter. Vessels in the former material are known from Sutton Courtenay, probably from a cemetery, and an impressive collection of pewter vessels was recovered from a well at nearby Appleford.[58] Such vessels, however, remain rare finds since unless specially deposited their metal was always likely to be recycled. The same was also true for glass vessels, though there is no evidence for such working from the county.[59]

Stone objects have the advantage that, like pottery, they can increasingly be assigned to sources and patterns of trade established, some of which mark continuity from earlier times.[60] The commonest items were querns and millstones for grinding grain, and whetstones. Some of the former, imported from the Rhineland, are found at military and urban sites such as Alchester and Wilcote, though they occur at other locations as well. The main sources of supply of querns, however, were the Forest of Dean to the west, the Peak District of Derbyshire to the north and Lodsworth in Sussex to the south, all some distance from the county, though more local oolitic limestone was occasionally used, for example at Shakenoak,[61] but this would generally have been considered too soft a stone for grinding with. Whetstones also came from the Forest of Dean area, but one of the most common stone types used for these was Kentish Ragstone, which was very widely distributed. Northampton Sandstone, used for a variety of objects, is also found in the east of the county, particularly at Alchester. A relatively much more exotic find from Alchester was a fragment of a high-quality monumental inscription in Purbeck Marble (Fig. 8.9). This material also occurred at Shakenoak where several fragments included a pestle which might have been used with a stone mortar rather than a ceramic one.[62]

The occurrence of certain types of pottery and other goods, while generally indicative of trade, does not necessarily illuminate the mechanisms of that trade. In most cases it is assumed that the distribution of non-local and indeed much locally produced material took place in markets established in the larger nucleated settlements, with the rarer types of material perhaps only available in the largest of these. Some materials could equally have been distributed by their producers or by itinerant merchants travelling to individual settlement sites, though this would be very difficult to demonstrate archaeologically. As far as pottery is concerned, however, it is possible to show very clear differences in the scale of use of broad categories from one type of settlement to another. This may reflect marketing patterns, but it has also been argued that these differences can be a useful indicator of socio-economic status.[63]

Differences in pottery assemblages from broadly contemporary sites can be summarised by looking at the quantities of 'fine and specialist wares' (including types such as samian ware, colour-coated wares, *mortaria* and amphorae) compared with the more common vessels in everyday use for cooking and storage, which were mostly in the more locally produced 'coarse ware' fabrics (though products such as black-burnished ware and late shell-tempered ware are good examples of utilitarian wares which were traded over very large distances) (Fig. 6.11). In the late Iron Age and early Roman periods fine and specialist ware representation could be minimal, particularly on some rural sites. Most sites whose perceived status on the basis of structural and other evidence is low had less than 5 per cent fine and specialist wares, and in a number of cases less than 1 per cent. Fine and specialist ware values above the 0–5 per cent range, however, did not only occur at sites with easy access to higher-status ceramics, i.e. where a market factor alone rather than a potential status-related factor might have been responsible for the higher representation. Fine and specialist ware levels above about 5 per cent are therefore potentially indicative of a different range of status from that of the lowest grouping of rural sites. This 'higher-status' group consists

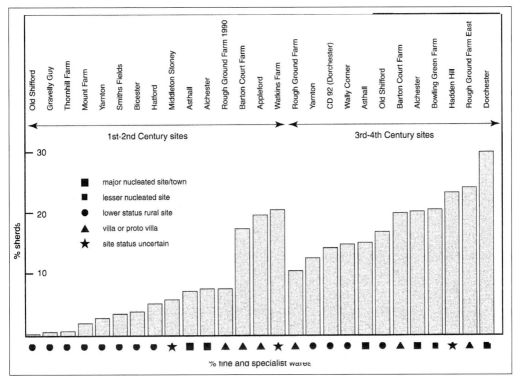

6.11   Bar charts showing relative status of selected sites based on the proportion of fine and specialist wares in their pottery assemblages.

of villas or proto-villas, the major ('urban/suburban') settlements at Alchester and Asthall and probably sites such as Abingdon. A site at Watkins Farm had a very high fine and specialist ware representation which is not yet explained. Despite the problems with the data this assemblage seems to rank with those of contemporary 'villas', while not displaying any comparable architectural development. In the early Roman period distinctions in social or economic status (if the evidence is correctly understood) were thus not necessarily always expressed using the full spectrum of facets of what is generally regarded as Romanisation.

The development of the Oxford potteries in the late Roman period, with their substantial fine ware output, means that the base level of fine and specialist wares in this period was significantly higher than earlier – all sites were receiving at least some fine wares from this industry. None of the later Roman assemblages examined had less than 11 per cent of fine and specialist wares (the range was between 11 and 30 per cent). Variations in the fine and specialist ware representation were perhaps not always as clearly related to socio-economic status as in the earlier period, however. Low levels of representation at potentially 'higher-status' sites such as the villa at Roughground Farm, Lechlade (just over the county boundary in Gloucestershire) and the small town at Asthall, suggest a possible fall-off in the regional distribution pattern of Oxford products north-west of the focus of the industry.

The rural settlements about whose low late Roman status there is relatively little doubt had fine and specialist ware representations in a reasonably restricted range from 13 to 18 per cent. The upper end of the range of late Roman values (above 20 per cent) is occupied by the (possibly unrepresentative) group from the nucleated settlement at Bowling Green Farm, the two urban assemblages (Alchester and Dorchester), the villa-related eastern settlement at Roughground Farm, the Barton Court Farm villa and a site at Hadden Hill, near Didcot. On the basis of these figures Hadden Hill might be suggested as a possible villa site, which may be supported by evidence for tile and building material there.[64]

Ready availability of late fine wares thus resulted in their universal use at least at a moderate level. Nevertheless the contrasting data from Dorchester Beech House Hotel and two nearby rural sites (CD92 and Wally Corner) indicate that there was a significant difference between urban and rural assemblages which was not simply a result of different accessibility to sources of supply – all these sites potentially had equal access to the Oxford potteries. It is less clear if there was any significant difference between late Roman rural assemblages, and it is possible that there was one pattern of distribution/acquisition for all late Roman rural sites regardless of status and another for the larger nucleated settlements. Apparent differences between the assemblages from the two different areas of Roughground Farm, and the possible villa status of Hadden Hill, however, might suggest that some villas continued to have late Roman fine and specialist ware representation significantly above that of contemporary lower-status settlements.

One change that is noticeable across the Roman period is in the relationship between urban and 'high status' rural assemblages. In the first and second centuries the highest-ranking assemblages were from rural sites. The urban groups (Alchester and Asthall), while consistently distinct from the low-status rural sites, were not greatly different from them in terms of fine and specialist ware representation. In the third and

6.12   The Didcot hoard of second-century gold *aurei*. British Museum.

fourth centuries the urban assemblages of Alchester and Dorchester topped the fine and specialist ware scale. The interpretation of this change is uncertain, but may indicate the increasing importance of distributional criteria in determining assemblage composition, though not to the total exclusion of potential status-related factors reflected in the exercise of choice in assemblage composition, as the evidence from the Dorchester area and some of the villa sites indicates.

These analyses suggest that in the later Roman period what might be described as free market forces were more apparent than in the earlier period, but that they were not necessarily dominant in defining distribution patterns of pottery and other materials. Increasing monetarisation of the economy could also be seen as part of the same broad trend. Certainly coins are found far more widely from the mid-third century onwards, in line with national trends. The fact that the individual value of these coins was considerably less than that of first- and second-century issues merely underlines the point that the use of money had become much more a part of everyday life, to the extent that in the fourth century it could be encountered on almost any low-status rural site in the region, whereas on most such sites coins are often never found in first- and second-century contexts.

Coin was of course widely used in the first and second centuries, but its uses were rather more restricted than in later periods. It occurs on military sites, in the major settlements and at villas, all of which were more readily integrated into a market system dealing in more than just day-to-day necessities of life. For many peasant farmers the most likely context in which they would have handled coin was in relation to tax payments. For this section of the population coinage would rarely have been a medium by which wealth or savings were represented, and this was particularly the case in the early Roman period. This did not hold true for all the population, however. The second-largest hoard of gold aurei from the whole of Roman Britain was discovered in 1995 near Didcot (Fig. 6.12), consisting of 126 coins of first- and second-century date deposited around or shortly after AD 160.[65] This was a substantial sum, the equivalent of ten and a half years' pay for a legionary soldier, but we know almost nothing of its owner or the circumstances of its deposition, though there are very slight hints on both of these subjects. One of the coins carried a graffito in Greek on the reverse, indicating at least familiarity with that language, though whether on the part of a previous possessor or the depositor is not known. As regards the deposition, the close similarity of date with that of the Corbridge hoard – the largest second-century gold hoard from Britain and similar to the Didcot hoard in many respects – and of a number of other silver hoards across the country has suggested that these might have been 'emergency hoards', deposited at a time of stress or danger.

By the time coin hoards in the region become relatively common, in the later third century, the unit value of the coins deposited was relatively low, so there are no late Roman hoards from the county to compare with Didcot in terms of monetary value. From the mid to late third century, coins, all of low denominations (generally of copper alloy with at most a notional silver content), become common as site finds for the first time. Even so, there were variations in the supply of coin to Britain and coins of some issue periods, such as the early fourth century, are relatively uncommon compared to the large numbers of coins of the 330s and 340s, and of the period 364–378. In these respects Oxfordshire is no different from most of the rest of southern Britain. A number of Oxfordshire sites, however, have unusually high numbers of coins of the last main issue period found in Britain, dating from AD 388–402 (coins were rarely minted in Britain, and were not struck here officially after AD 324, though there were periods of large-scale production of irregular coinage, one represented by important evidence of irregular minting at North Leigh in the late third century)[66] and several hoards of bronze coins of this period are also known. These are discussed further in Chapter seven.

NOTES

1. Recent work on the subject starts with Millett (1990). The subsequent literature is extensive, but particularly significant contributions include the papers in Webster & Cooper 1996 and Mattingly 1997.
2. This is less certain in the case of the Catuvellauni.
3. Brodribb et al. 1978, 202–4.
4. Jones 1986; Lambrick 1992a, 97.
5. Lambrick 1992a.
6. Letts 1995.
7. Letts & Robinson 1993, 176.
8. Jones 1978, 109.
9. Jones 1986, 41.
10. Barton Court Farm, Jones 1986, 41. Peas have been found recently in a late Roman

settlement at Mansfield College, Oxford (Booth 1999).

11. Alchester, Robinson 1975; Giorgi & Robinson 1984, for Farmoor, Lambrick & Robinson 1979, 120.

12. Robinson 1992, 58.

13. Hey 1995, 167.

14. Alchester, Booth et al. forthcoming; for Barton Court Farm, Robinson & Wilson 1987, 58.

15. Cf. King 1989, 58–9.

16. Brodribb et al. 1978, 15–20. The identification of trout as the species concerned is discussed on p. 17. For the contrary view, Branigan 1989, 46–7.

17. Drayton, Lambrick 1992a, 98–9, Ashville ard, Fowler 1978.

18. Manning 1984, 142–4 for ploughshare and coulter.

19. Lambrick 1992a, 99.

20. Robinson & Wilson 1987, 73.

21. Ashville, Jones 1978, 106; Old Shifford, Hey 1995, 165.

22. Barton Court Farm, Miles 1986, 9; Eagle Farm, Allen & Moore 1987, 96.

23. Barton Court Farm, two examples, Miles 1986, 14–16; Goring, Allen 1995, 39–44; Farmoor, Lambrick & Robinson 1979, 34; Yarnton unpublished.

24. Knighton Bushes, Gaffney & Tingle 1989, 138; the other examples are unpublished.

25. Alchester, Booth et al. forthcoming; Abingdon Old Gaol, Parrington 1975, though this may be post-Roman (Wilson & Wallis 1991, 13). An unusual circular example with two flues comes from the Vineyard site, Abingdon (Allen 1990b). Churchill Hospital, Young 1977, 20–2.

26. Van der Veen 1989.

27. Robinson & Wilson 1987, 53.

28. Rees 1979. For Appleford, Brown 1973, 197–8.

29. Camp Corner, Gray 1973. Salter's map (1997, 99) shows no smelting sites within the confines of the county.

30. Asthall, Booth 1997, 49–55 for the structures and Salter 1997 for the metallurgical evidence. Swalcliffe Lea, Shawyer 1999, 58.

31. Dorchester hoards, Manning 1984.

32. Salter 1997, 91.

33. Hey 1995, 170; Lambrick et al. forthcoming. Gary Lock pers. comm. for Alfred's Castle, where the context is not entirely secure.

34. Ibid., 172.

35. See Williams (1971) and Young (1986, 61) – analysis of oolitic limestones from a monumental complex by the river at London,

for example, suggests that these were all Lincolnshire limestones (perhaps from Northamptonshire) (Dimes 1980). Oolitic limestone pieces (including sculpture) from the Mithraeum are assigned to Gloucestershire (Ellis 1986), while oolitic limestones from other sites in south-east England are assigned to the area around Bath. For Taynton stone at Colchester, Morris 1955.

36. Sellwood 1989, 139–41.

37. Brodribb et al. 1968, 36–8.

38. Cf. Aston 1974a, 21–2.

39. Williams & Zeepvat 1994, 225.

40. Booth 1997, 102.

41. Long Hanborough, Sturdy & Young 1976, Cassington, Case 1982, 134–6, Yarnton unpublished.

42. Boars Hill, Willett 1948; Harris & Young 1974, Churchill Hospital, Young 1977, 31.

43. Timby et al. 1997.

44. Harding 1972, pl. 72.

45. The fundamental study of the Oxford pottery industry is Young 1977.

46. Cowley, Green 1983. The Blackbird Leys sites are unpublished.

47. Booth et al. 1993.

48. Cheetham 1995, 422.

49. Including as far away as Wilcote (Hands 1993, 137, no. 1018).

50. Funari 1996, 76–82.

51. Dragendorff form 31, Young (1977), type C45.

52. For Sandford see May 1922.

53. Jewitt 1951.

54. Millett 1990, 168–74.

55. Fulford & Hodder 1974.

56. Bird & Young 1981.

57. *VCH* I, pl. XIIID. For a distribution of pink grogged ware across the region (now somewhat out of date) see Booth & Green 1989, 83.

58. Sutton Courtenay, Miles 1977; Appleford, Brown 1973, incidentally this site also produced an iron pan, rare as a site find.

59. For a brief summary of glass-working sites nationally see Cool & Price 1995, 226.

60. The following section of stone types and distributions relies heavily on the work of Fiona Roe.

61. Brodribb et al. 1973, 43.

62. Pestle, Brodribb et al. 1971, 50 and 53, no. 27; see also Brodribb et al. 1968, 38.

63. Booth forthcoming.

64. Booth et al. 1993, 100.

65. Bland & Orna-Ornstein 1997.

66. Esmonde Cleary, 1999.

CHAPTER SEVEN

THE END OF ROMAN OXFORDSHIRE

CHRONOLOGY

What happened in Oxfordshire at the end of the Roman period? In some respects the transition to Anglo-Saxon England followed fairly well-established lines, but there are aspects of this transition for which there is particularly interesting, and in part controversial, evidence. This has been examined by John Blair from an Anglo-Saxon viewpoint, but other perspectives emerge when the period is viewed in the context of late Roman Britain.

Before the evidence can be discussed, however, it is necessary to establish the character of the latest Roman settlement in the county. One of the major problems encountered on most Roman sites is that of dating the latest part of the sequence, but it is essential to do this before changes at the end of the period can be understood. The principal categories of finds used for dating – coins and pottery – are of use up to the end of the fourth century but not significantly beyond this point. Supply of coinage to Britain was no more consistent through the fourth century than it had been earlier, although fourth-century coinage was much more common overall than that of preceding centuries, particularly on rural sites, on many of which it appeared for the first time. Some issue periods are almost always better represented than others and variations in quantities of coin between these periods therefore do not generally indicate fluctuations in the level of occupation of the sites on which these coins occur. Coins of the periods AD 330–348 and 364–378 (and, to an extent, irregular issues of the intervening period) are the most commonly found on fourth-century sites across lowland Britain. Coinage of the period AD 378–388 is always rare, and the final minting period represented in Britain is that from AD 388 to 402. With insignificant exceptions no new coin entered Britain after about AD 402, and it remains unclear how long coins of the end of the fourth century remained in circulation. Moreover, such coins are not common as well-stratified site finds, though there are exceptions to this, as will be seen.

As a dating medium pottery is a blunter tool than coinage, and so the difficulties of using it to provide close dating for the latest Roman deposits are even more pronounced. The main features of the late Roman Oxford pottery industry, which produced much of the material found in the region at this time, were largely established by the early fourth century, so definition of developing ceramic phases within the fourth-century Oxford assemblage is difficult. The principal *mortarium* fabrics and parchment ware and colour-coated wares had most, if not all, of their repertoire of forms established by the beginning of the century. A number of colour-coated forms are thought to have been introduced around AD 350, but there are no significant new additions to the range of forms thereafter and the exclusively very late date suggested for at least one type can be questioned.[1] Some characteristics of the colour-coated ware repertoire, such as the widespread use of painted and stamped decoration, seem to have been more common in the second half of the fourth century than earlier, but there is still relatively little hard evidence to demonstrate this, and the amounts of such material in most assemblages are such that quantitative analysis cannot be used to identify the increasing importance of these types. There is effectively no meaningful way of distinguishing between early and late fourth-century coarse wares from the Oxford industry.

A typical late fourth-century assemblage from the region, uncontaminated by residual (earlier) material (a situation that rarely prevails, adding to the difficulties already outlined), is likely to contain a relatively high proportion of Oxford colour-coated ware and other products (often at least 10–15 per cent of sherds, even on low-status rural sites). The latter would include white *mortaria*, supplemented by their white-slipped equivalents, which seem to be more common at this date and may have begun to supplant the standard fourth-century white *mortarium* type, particularly in the last quarter of the century. Nene valley colour-coated wares in utilitarian forms – jars, flanged bowls and dishes – might also be expected. The coarse wares would consist of hard-fired moderately sandy reduced (grey) wares, often with burnished decoration, plus a range of types in late shell-tempered fabrics, some perhaps from the production centre at Harrold, Bedfordshire.[2] Jars of this type were probably present in the region by the late third century, but flanged bowls and dishes seem to have arrived later, and their presence is taken to be indicative at least of a date after AD 350. Oxidised wares, if present, would include some Oxford products, and probably pink grogged ware, though at present there are few typological criteria to distinguish early and late fourth-century versions of forms in that fabric. South of Oxford there are occasional occurrences of reduced wares from Alice Holt, near Farnham in Surrey, but these do not seem to occur north of the city. By the last quarter of the fourth-century occurrences of black-burnished ware are likely to have been residual.

The terminal date of the Oxford pottery industry is not known for certain. As already indicated, it may be that one of its principal fourth-century products, the white *mortarium* type M22, was in decline before the end of the century, and the state of coarse ware production at the very end of the fourth century is unclear. Some component sites of the industry are likely to have been out of production before the end of the fourth century[3] but since, for the most part, products of individual sites cannot be distinguished, this process is identified only at those sites and not at the consumer end of the market. Colour-coated ware, at least, is likely to have been produced right up to the end of the life of the industry. Its demise may be dated in line with the collapse of other major late Roman producers, certainly in the first half and quite possibly in the first decade or two of the fifth century. The collapse is arguably a consequence of the cessation of the monetary market economy, into which the industry is likely to have been closely tied by the later fourth century. The failure of that economy to be sustained by continued importation of coin to Britain after around AD 402 signalled the end for these centralised industries, which were unable to survive in totally changed economic conditions. While the continuation of some small-scale pottery production well into the fifth century is theoretically possible, there is no conclusive evidence from our region that this happened, and no evidence at all to indicate the survival of any part of the Oxford industry in this way.[4] It remains to be seen what were the wider consequences of this and other changes at the end of the Roman period.

THE LATE ROMAN SETTLEMENT PATTERN

Late Roman Oxfordshire lay at the eastern side of Britannia Prima, one of four provinces making up the Diocese of the Britains in the fourth century, and having its capital probably at Cirencester. It is presumed that the basic structure of the settlement pattern at the end of the fourth century was relatively little changed from that at the beginning of the century, although this is often impossible to demonstrate conclusively because of the imprecision of the dating evidence, discussed above. Most if not all of the major settlements continued to be occupied through the fourth century and evidence for very late Roman activity is unusually clear at Dorchester (see below). Elsewhere the level of later fourth-century occupation is, for many sites, less certain. The occupied area at Asthall, for example, had certainly contracted by the second half of the fourth century. At Alchester the extent of intramural activity is uncertain, but in the northern extramural area agricultural activity was maintained and several new buildings, albeit mostly of timber construction, are assigned to a phase dated after *c.* AD 350. Generally, however, it is difficult to identify clear evidence of new late Roman construction at these sites and the extent to which they were still functioning as market centres is unclear. Such functions may have been in decline by the end of the fourth century, if not before.[5] The extent of late Roman activity at Frilford is unclear, but the temple site at least produced a number of coins of the House of Theodosius, and the same is true of the rural sanctuaries of Woodeaton and Lowbury Hill, both of which were evidently patronised at least up to the very end of the fourth century.[6]

In the countryside there is no *a priori* reason to suppose that farming did not continue as it had done, particularly in the lower-status settlements which were arguably less affected by economic or political instability. Here, however, the lack of clearly definable late fourth-century dating material is a problem, though coins of the period 388–402 do occur at a number of sites such as Old Shifford, Yarnton and Farmoor, even though the total quantity of coin of all periods from these sites is small (fewer than fifty in each case). In such cases these coins stand as a useful marker for the likely presence of other contemporary material which cannot be so readily distinguished. The situation in the villas as a whole is also unclear, principally because of the lack of good excavated evidence, but occupation at Barton Court Farm, Ditchley Park and Shakenoak is indicated by relatively plentiful late Roman material including coins of the House of Theodosius. A large hoard of such coins was found quite close to the Ditchley villa.[7]

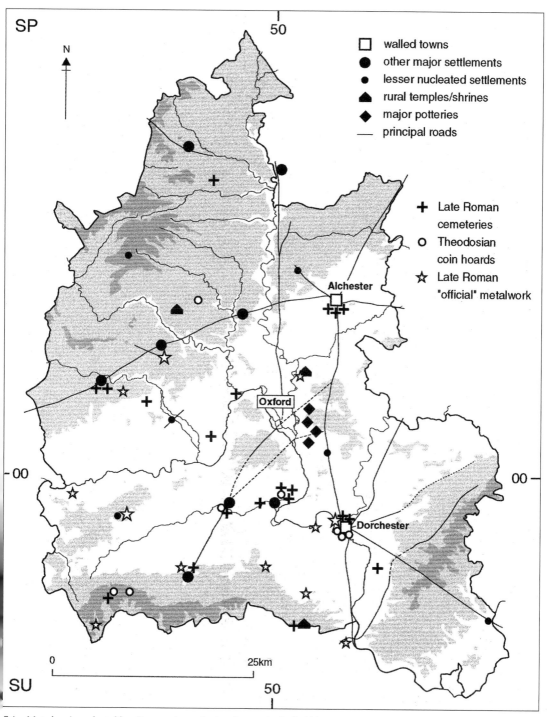

7.1   Map showing selected late Roman sites and other features in Oxfordshire.

The nature of occupation at these sites was variable. At Shakenoak only a small part of the principal house was still in use in the later Roman period, but Building A was clearly occupied through the second half of the fourth century, reaching a peak of prosperity at that time. At Ditchley the latest occupation was seen as indicating 'base uses' and it is possible that the main house there had gone out of use about AD 200.[8] At North Leigh, Stonesfield and Wigginton, for example, there were major developments in the early fourth century, the period to which the principal known mosaic pavements belong, but generally except at Wigginton the nature of the early excavations means that the chronology of the latest developments is very unclear. At North Leigh, however, it can now be shown that the baths at the north-west corner of the villa were out of use by the mid-fourth century, when one room was used by a coin counterfeiter for a dump of waste material. Butchery waste was also dumped here, and pottery and other finds indicate activity probably into the fifth century, though whether in these rooms or immediately adjacent is less clear. At Barton Court Farm both stone buildings were standing and probably in use at the end of the fourth century, though the main building may have been demolished shortly thereafter, while the smaller structure survived rather longer.[9]

This evidence suggests that while there may have been a reduction in the circumstances of some of the larger villas rural life generally continued without significant archaeologically detectable disruption up to the end of the fourth century – as late as the dating evidence can be expected to take us – and perhaps beyond. The effects on rural settlement of a more widespread population decline, either in the late Roman or early post-Roman period, such as has been suggested by some scholars[10] would be very difficult to detect, however, particularly as rural cemeteries are generally rare throughout the Roman period (but especially before the fourth century) and therefore cannot be used as a reliable guide to relative variations in rural population. We cannot of course be certain that continued occupation of villa buildings necessarily meant that the style of life associated with such buildings was maintained, and in a number of cases it is likely that it was not. Nor is it clear that occupation of the 'small towns' at this time was in any way urban in character. In the case of the latter, indeed, it is arguable whether the term urban was ever really appropriate in the way that it was for the large cities, the tribal capitals of the region, but the decline of market functions would have altered the character of these sites, reducing them to little more than agricultural villages. Nevertheless the consistent occurrence of coinage of the period AD 388–402 at Dorchester, Alchester, Asthall, Swalcliffe Lea and other sites suggests that some market functions were maintained at least to the end of the fourth century, and the occurrence of such coinage at a range of rural sites also suggests at least a low level of continued integration of these sites with the local centres.

LATE ROMAN CEMETERIES AND RELIGION

While many scattered burials of various dates are known in Roman Oxfordshire it is only in the late Roman period (broadly the later third and fourth centuries) that cemeteries are clearly identified in the archaeological record.[11] Even so the evidence is quite limited, and for present purposes any group of ten or more burials has been defined as a cemetery. On this criterion some eighteen late Roman cemeteries are known in the county (Fig. 7.1). These are divided evenly between cemeteries associated with known major settlements and those associated with rural sites. Cemeteries are known at the nucleated settlements of Alchester, Asthall, Dorchester, Frilford and Wantage and a number of fairly scattered burials are known at Gill Mill.[12] Of these the evidence from Dorchester, and to a lesser extent from Alchester and Frilford, is particularly important for understanding the very latest phases of the occupation of Roman Britain and are discussed further below. Even at Alchester, however, the largest Roman settlement in the county, the known late Roman burials are few in number and occur in three locations, only one of which has been excavated under modern conditions (in 1991). Comprising some thirty inhumation burials, this lay immediately outside the boundary of the northern extramural settlement area, a typical cemetery location (Fig. 7.2). Few of these graves were closely dated, but most if not all were probably fourth century.[13] The principal late Roman cemeteries of Alchester and many of the other small towns clearly still have to be located.

The late Roman rural cemeteries in the county comprise two at Barrow Hills, Radley, and sites at Ashville, Bloxham, Cassington, Crowmarsh, Curbridge, Stanton Harcourt and White Horse Hill, Uffington.[14] The 'urban' and rural cemeteries share

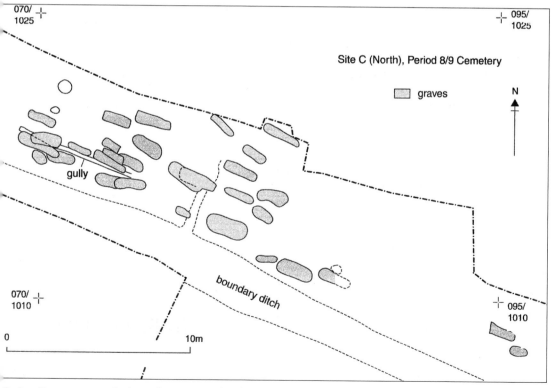

2   Late Roman cemetery in the northern extramural settlement, Alchester.

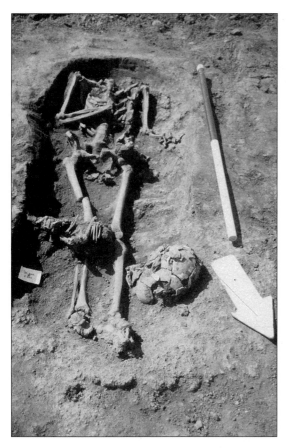

7.3   Late Roman decapitated inhumation from Yarnton. The head has been placed by the feet and a dog lies over the knees.

some characteristics, but there are also important differences. A marked feature of many of the rural cemeteries is considerable variation in grave alignment. While there is a tendency for the burials in the urban cemeteries to be aligned roughly east–west there is much less uniformity in rural sites. A number have north–south alignments which in most cases can be shown to relate to existing boundaries, and other alignments are also known. Burial rites which are more common in the rural cemeteries (though not necessarily exclusive to them) include the continued use of cremation (particularly at Radley and Uffington)[15] and instances of prone (face down) and decapitated burials. Decapitation is encountered in all the rural late Roman cemeteries in the county (Fig. 7.3), and at Cassington a remarkable 15 instances were recorded from a cemetery population of about 110.[16] While not unknown in an 'urban' context, as for example at Alchester, the rite did not occur at sites such as Queenford Mill, Dorchester, which has been taken to indicate that it was absent from the major late Roman, potentially Christian, urban cemeteries.[17]

There is also a tendency for higher numbers of grave goods to occur in rural cemeteries, though the proportion of burials with grave goods is variable and can be quite low. An exception is a small cemetery at Roden Down, 850m south-west of Lowbury Hill just over the county boundary into Berkshire, where seven of the ten burials contained coins and, most unusually, there was clear evidence that all the individuals were buried in wooden coffins (one with a lead lining).[18] Elsewhere, unequivocal evidence for wooden coffins is usually found in rather less than 50 per cent of burials. Lead-lined coffins occur at a number of sites, such as Crowmarsh and Abingdon as well as Frilford and Dorchester, but are always rare, while in the northern part of the county stone coffins are occasionally found.[19]

The cemetery at Uffington Castle, which appears to have consisted of some 49 inhumations and 9 cremations cut into a Neolithic long barrow just north of the hill fort, is also noteworthy for the very close juxtaposition of late Roman and early Saxon burials, the latter occurring in a reused Bronze Age barrow less than 100m from the former. Unfortunately the date of the coins associated with at least five or six of the late Roman burials at Uffington is unknown, but other grave goods included late Roman composite combs and an Oxfordshire colour-coated ware vessel of a type dated after AD 340 and described as 'worn'.[20]

The Uffington finds are typical of those associated with the cemeteries of this group. All produce mid to late fourth-century coins from some graves, and late Roman combs are also a recurrent feature, as at Crowmarsh and Roden Down as well as the 'urban' cemeteries of Frilford (in a lead-lined coffin) and Queenford Mill, Dorchester. This is one of the few artefact types in which there are marked similarities between late Roman and Anglo-Saxon examples.[21] Confident ascription of graves to the very end of the fourth century relies on coinage, however, with only Roden Down of these particular cemeteries certainly producing material of the House of Theodosius.

We should expect late Roman burial practices to persist into the fifth century and even beyond. In this most traditional aspect of human behaviour, material culture touches the metaphysical. Particular populations should be identifiable by physical type and DNA while rituals of interment suggest the nature of religious beliefs. The scientific examination of skeletal remains is still in its early days and for the most part we do not yet have conclusive evidence to say that certain skeletons are those of the Roman or post-Roman population while others are those of Anglo-Saxon incomers, though Heinrich Härke has noted differences in height between individuals as being one possible marker, as well as the presence or absence of weapons.[22]

One late Roman pagan rite which has already been noted is that of decapitation after death, a practice very widespread in Oxfordshire and surrounding counties. The theory behind it probably had something to do with liberating the soul from the body so that it could travel to the other world. There are 'Anglo-Saxon' examples of the practice from Oxfordshire at Chadlington and Wheatley.[23] Other rites are admittedly less diagnostic as both pagan Roman Britons and people of Germanic origin placed jewellery and coins in graves, though it would be a mistake to make a hard and fast rule and assume, for instance, that the presence of an 'Anglo-Saxon' brooch means that the wearer was of necessity of Germanic origin.

The grave of a child at Long Wittenham contained among other objects a little wooden beaker about 15cm in height placed to the right of his head (Fig. 7.4). It was

7.4   Bronze-sheeted wooden vessel with cross and biblical scenes from Long Wittenham. Height 150mm. M. and LA.75.3–10.1, British Museum.

covered in bronze sheet ornamented in repoussée, showing on one side a cross flanked by an alpha and omega and on the other three biblical scenes. The central scene shows the baptism of Christ, identified by the name of St John (*Iohannes*) above (cf Matthew 3: 13–17) and it is flanked by representations of the Miracle of the Marriage at Cana (John 2: 1–10) and of the tax-collector Zacchaeus standing in the tree to get a better view of Jesus (Luke 19: 1–10). The imagery of the vessel is concerned with the saving power of faith and the cup would have been suitable for the Eucharist. It has previously been published as north Gaulish, although now much more is known about late Roman art in Britain, there is no reason to see the attractive linear figures with their patterned clothing as anything other than Romano-British, in which case, in view of its iconography, this is one of the most important early Christian items from late Roman Britain. Metalwork such as this, often from caskets and reliquaries, was quite widespread, and sheeting from such a casket – though of earlier (fourth-century) date – has been found at Uley in Gloucestershire. The grave in which it was found, and others, have been attributed to Franks though there are other possibilities including a much more local origin for some of the members of these élite groups. Even if these burials are taken to be those of Germanic incomers, the presence of late fifth-century provincial Roman objects such as the beaker points to a continuing aspiration to *Romanitas*. The presence of grave goods has generally been taken to indicate that their owners were pagan, but the iconography of the Long Wittenham vessel implies that the owner was a Christian and shared a close alignment in outlook with local Christians. Zacchaeus was a tax-collector, an 'outsider' despite his Hebrew name, and the scene would have been appropriate for a foreign mercenary accepting the religion of the Roman people. The British presence in the vicinity is still recalled by the name Wallingford, meaning 'the ford of the Welshmen' (i.e. the British).[24]

In the fifth and sixth centuries Roman objects such as coins and bracelets, even if old, continued to be placed in graves though the degree to which this was a continuity of practice – or on the contrary masks discontinuity, these items being regarded as exotic trinkets – is uncertain. The British style of workmanship displayed in the sheath of the Brighthampton knife from a sixth-century grave suggests cultural fusion as does the even more unusual enamelled spear-head and the hanging bowl with its enamelled escutcheons from the late seventh-century warrior burial at Lowbury Hill. These have traditionally been seen as the burials of Germanic chieftains who had patronised British craftsmen. However, they could equally be interpreted as the graves of warriors of British, or partly British, descent such as some of the *Gewisse*, whose names attest a British pedigree.[25]

Christianity was probably a minority cult in most places in Roman Britain even in the late fourth century. Indeed, it has been suggested both by Professor Frend and by Dorothy Watts that the influence of the Church was actually in recession at the time. However, there is evidence for large populations of Christians in some places in western Britain such as at Dorchester (Dorset) and in our area at Dorchester-on-Thames where the most dramatic instance of Christian continuity is the east–west oriented cemetery at Queenford Mill. Radiocarbon dating demonstrates the persistence of a large Romano-British population here well after the traditional end of Roman rule. In the very different conditions of the fifth century the Church with its efficient organisation would have provided reassurance and certainty in a changing world, just as the career of Sidonius Apollinaris shows it did in Gaul.[26]

Christian resurgence of a most spirited kind is certainly attested by writings and numerous stone inscriptions found throughout western Britain. These documents are far from being the dying productions of an outworn culture but preserve a style of latinity which has been judged superior to that anywhere else in the former Roman Empire. To what extent did the Church survive in the east, where there are no stone inscriptions and where paganism in both post-Roman and Anglo-Saxon form preserved more of a hold? There are suggestive pointers such as the persistence of the memory of St Alban's shrine outside Verulamium, indeed eventually to replace it as a site of settlement. Although Bede – writing well over a century later, partisan and in this matter not an entirely reliable witness – says that when Birinus came to the lands of the *Gewissae* from Italy he found them completely pagan, this is not likely to be true in the case of the city of Dorcic given him by the kings Cynegils and Oswald. While John Blair finds the suggestion of continuity of Romano-British Christian practice well into the sixth century and beyond 'a large one to accept', we have to envisage such persistence if the choice of Dorchester for Birinus' see and the placing of a church outside the east gate of the Roman town are more than chance. In fact the pages of Bede are full of hints that the Augustinian mission was not faced by a simple matter of converting the heathen. The British (Celtic) Church was active in the east as well as in the west and may have had a continuous presence; hence the need Augustine felt to get rulings on aspects of Levitical law, for example on sexual purity.[27]

If archaeological proof for surviving Roman Christian witness in Oxfordshire remains somewhat elusive, the sort of dramatic evidence for the continuity of a sub-Roman population which may turn up has recently been uncovered by careful excavations in Insula ix at Silchester, Hampshire. As we shall see it has a particular relevance to south Oxfordshire. House i has been identified as very late and as incorporating the remains of two earlier houses.[28] Of particular interest are the pits cut into it, one of which contained the famous ogham stone which has been confirmed as of the fifth or sixth century and read by Dr Mark Handley as that of an Irishman called Tebicatos. Other pits contained earlier complete or near-complete pots and a whole dog skeleton.[29] The excavators have seen these as a 'ritual of termination' presumably by former inhabitants. The tombstone and what were presumably grave goods would effectively hand over the site to the realm of the dead and the hound was certainly regarded as an otherworldly animal.[30] What happened to the former population? The suppression of the Roman town does not necessarily conflict with the notion that the inhabitants were impelled in part by economic pressures to move north to the Thames; in this case the real successor of Silchester should be regarded as Dorchester at or just before the time of Birinus. This is not surprising; Silchester was not really a well-chosen site. It had been an Iron Age oppidum to which its Atrebatic inhabitants were fiercely attached but Dorchester was a far better site with regard to communications and the wonder is that it was not developed earlier. It is very likely that the local ruler of Dorcic was a Briton and the change of residence would not have entailed any major cultural shift. If this hypothesis is accepted the pagan-looking rituals at Silchester at this late date demonstrate that even after the see was founded Dorchester was still a place of mixed religious traditions where evangelism would still have been needed.

Pagan sacred sites are likely to have remained numinous places well after the formal end of Roman rule. The relative remoteness of Britain from the centres of power and the active survival of paganism in the later fourth century meant that sanctuaries such as Woodeaton and Lowbury Hill continued to receive coin offerings down to the end of the fourth century when the money supply ceased. Excavation would probably show a continuing structural sequence as at Uley, Gloucestershire (where the excavators believe the temple was replaced by a church, though in my opinion there is no real evidence for this). Blair points to the name *Harowdonehul* at Woodeaton as suggestive of sanctity being continued from Roman times. The sequence at Lowbury Hill down to the placing of the seventh-century barrow burial mentioned above is suggestive too, even though the exact nature of the use of the hill after *c.* AD 400 is uncertain. Here, as at Silchester, the end is possibly marked by another deliberate 'ritual of termination' though in this case at a rather later date, at a time when the conversion of the ruling classes to Christianity was beginning to make headway. Alternatively, of course, such a burial could be seen as an attempt by new people to invent connections with places used much earlier, a practice which can be seen in the contemporary great barrow of Asthall with its Byzantine bowl and silver cup and the presence of Saxon graves on the sites of Roman villas or Bronze Age ring ditches.[31]

DORCHESTER-ON-THAMES

The centre where sustained activity at the very end of the fourth century and beyond is seen most clearly is Dorchester. Here two of the small number of excavated buildings can be shown not to have been built before the final decade or so of the century at the earliest. The town is also notable for producing abnormally high levels of the latest coins found in Roman Britain, those of the House of Theodosius dated 388–402, and in addition to their occurrence as site finds three hoards of such coins have also been found. This represents unusually clear evidence for very late Roman activity, evidence which is supplemented by that from the adjacent cemeteries of Queenford Mill and Church Piece, Warborough (Fig. 7.5).[32] Both of these are classic late Roman 'managed' cemeteries (i.e. with carefully ordered – generally east–west –

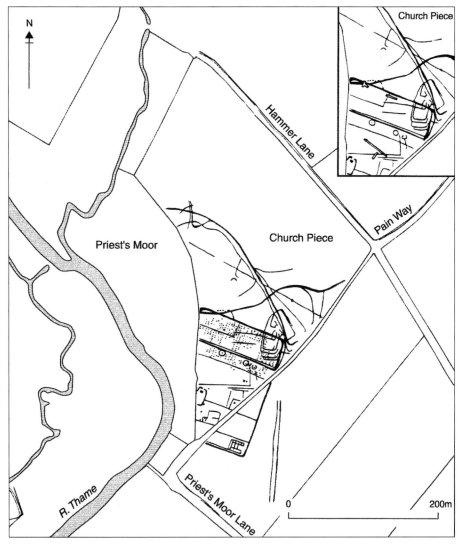

7.5   Late Roman cemetery at Church Piece, Warborough, near Dorchester-on-Thames. After Harman et al. 1978, fig. 2.

layout)[33] and may have originated in the early fourth century, though dating evidence is extremely sparse, a characteristic typical of such cemeteries. For example, the only grave goods from 164 excavated burials at Queenford Mill were a single colour-coated ware dish and a composite bone comb of very late Roman type, as mentioned above. A large number of the burials were contained in wooden coffins, however, some with iron fittings.

Remarkably, radiocarbon dating of selected burials from Queenford Mill has shown that this cemetery certainly remained in use well past the conventional 'end' date for Roman Britain, in the early fifth century, and may have lasted well into the sixth century. Indeed all the dated burials were arguably of post-Roman date (i.e. after AD 410), which therefore suggests a date for at least a significant proportion of the cemetery population. Recent recalibration of the radiocarbon determinations if anything emphasises the post-Roman weight of the dates; two have ranges of 340–650 cal AD at 95 per cent confidence, one is at 420–670 cal AD and one at 430–720 cal AD.[34] These dates thus suggest very strongly the continuation of at least one major Roman-type cemetery into the post-Roman period, and therefore imply the survival of a fairly substantial Romanised population in and perhaps immediately around Dorchester itself, at least as late as the end of the fifth century.

The situation at Dorchester in the fifth century is, however, complicated by the presence of evidence for burials (and settlement) in a very different tradition. There are three such burials from two different locations: a male and a female from a site some 500m south of the town at the east end of the Dyke Hills earthworks (Fig. 7.6) and close to the location of other late Roman burials, found in 1874; and a female found before 1914 at the Minchin recreation ground about 400m north of the walled town.[35] These are probably the most discussed burials in early Anglo-Saxon archaeology, reflecting their great importance for understanding some aspects of the change from Roman Britain to Anglo-Saxon England.[36]

The Dyke Hills male burial contained a range of copper alloy belt fittings of fairly standard late Roman type and also, unusually for a late Roman burial, iron weapons. The female burial likewise contained a belt plate and buckle of a well-known late Roman form with animal heads on the bow of the buckle. Also associated with this burial, however, were a brooch of 'early cruciform type' and the circular back-plate of a brooch which would have had a decorated plate applied to the front. Two such composite saucer brooches and the back-plate of another came from the third burial, at the Minchin recreation ground. They were associated with a key and an assortment of rings and bracelets, most of late Roman types, as well as a very worn coin of AD 364–378. The particular interest of these burials lies in the unusually clear association of objects of late Roman type and date with characteristic continental Germanic brooch types.

The principal points of discussion relating to these burials have centred on their exact date, which depends entirely on that of the associated metalwork, and the ethnicity and status of the individuals concerned. The belt fittings of the Dyke Hills male burial are not of the earliest types of such objects and are best assigned to the first half of the fifth century.[37] The early cruciform brooch with the nearby female burial and the saucer brooches from the Minchin recreation ground burial are also dated to

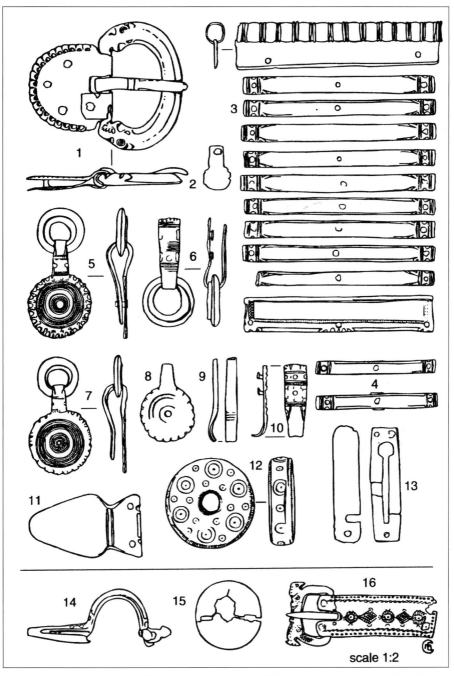

7.6   Grave goods from the early fifth-century burials at Dyke Hills, Dorchester-on-Thames. After Kirk and Leeds 1953, fig. 27.

the first half of the fifth century.[38] All these pieces are likely to have been of continental origin and while the belt fittings are of a type which is found on both sides of the Rhine the brooches originated from areas of north Germany outside the Roman empire. In both the female graves, however, these objects were associated with metalwork of late Roman date and British manufacture, which provide links with an earlier generation of military and other metalwork. While the continental pieces are official (and almost certainly military) issue, the British pieces were probably not military equipment, though an 'official' function is still very likely.[39]

The earliest continental military metalwork from the region is in fact datable to the later fourth century and comes not from Dorchester but from a number of other sites; Shakenoak, Minster Lovell and Woodeaton, the last of which has also produced a crossbow brooch, another late Roman 'official' object type.[40] At Shakenoak, as with the later material from Dorchester, this is associated with belt buckle plate pieces of British manufacture and similar date in a style that has a strong and widespread western British distribution. Related material comes from Ducklington, Streatley and other sites, with a significant number of pieces from the Faringdon area (Fig. 7.1).[41]

The continental belt-fittings from Shakenoak and Dorchester have been interpreted as indicative of the presence of Germanic military personnel, though this association is now widely disputed. The presence of such people at Shakenoak requires explanation, and is seen by Hawkes as originating with a retired veteran of the late Roman army.[42] The Dorchester burials, and in particular the female dress accessories rather than the fifth-century belt set, also suggest Germanic elements, though whether Frankish or of some other people is uncertain. Equally uncertain is the question of whether they were perhaps associated initially with the late Roman army. The dating could suggest, however, that they remained after 'official' Roman military involvement with Britain had ceased and even that these particular individuals did not arrive in Dorchester until this time.

EARLY ANGLO-SAXON CEMETERIES

Whatever the precise significance of the Dorchester burials the region is also notable for a remarkable (though not in total large) number of early Anglo-Saxon graves.[43] These burials are typical enough, but are of a character that might be more readily expected in early Saxon cemeteries further east in England. Generally they are distinguished from the Dorchester burials by being slightly later in date, but there are exceptions, such as at Saxton Road, Abingdon, where three burials were assigned to the early fifth century and West Hendred, where early fifth-century brooches also occur.[44] At Saxton Road there was a fairly substantial mid to late fifth-century phase, and other Saxon burials of this date are found in important cemeteries for example at Wally Corner, Berinsfield, and Frilford. These and other burials indicate, as has been known for a long time, an unusual concentration of fifth-century activity compared with adjacent regions. This may simply reflect the accessibility of the area via the Thames, but is as likely to be the consequence of deliberate policy which resulted in the establishment of small communities of people, probably of Germanic origin, within the region. It is not too fanciful to see at least some of the earliest stages of this process – and perhaps particularly those represented by the initial Dorchester burials – as carried out at the behest of British authorities. In local terms, at least, Dorchester seems to have been a centre of such authority. The late structural evidence there is not in itself conclusive, but the numismatic argument is perhaps more important. In the Dorchester region there were unusual concentrations of the latest coinage found in Roman Britain, and it is quite likely that this reflects in part the presence of troops who required payment.[45] These could have been Germanic, either *foederati* (serving under a treaty agreement) or simply mercenaries, both within the context of the late Roman Empire or in the confused political and military conditions of the early decades of the fifth century.[46] Despite the doubts mentioned above, to see the Dorchester burials as representing military personnel (and their associates) does not seem unreasonable. Either way, it is likely that only small numbers of such people were involved, and it is widely accepted that they were at least initially under the control of locally or regionally important British leaders.[47]

While opinions on the scale of Germanic immigration to Britain have varied widely it has been argued recently both that the logistics of migration preclude en masse movement of very large populations into Britain in the fifth century, and that such a scale of movement is quite inconsistent with the literary evidence for the period.[48] Even if there was substantial population decline among the British in the first half of the fifth century[49] it is unlikely that the Germanic presence in the region at that time and a little later would have been sufficient to constitute one or more powerful polities. One thing is certain, the newcomers did not obviously bring about population decline by fire and the sword – there is no evidence in this region to suggest that British settlements, whether nucleated or rural, came to a violent end.

THE DORCHESTER REGION AND BEYOND

It is arguable that the use of Dorchester as a local power base, with unusual concentrations of resources, helps to make the latest Roman archaeology of the immediately surrounding area more visible than would generally be the case. The occurrence of hoards of Theodosian coinage in Dorchester itself has already been mentioned. Further probable hoards of this coinage are found at Barton Court Farm and further west at Uffington Castle, where there was some limited very late Roman settlement, and a probably contemporary cemetery. A little to the east, at Rams Hill, a burial contained eight clipped silver coins (*siliquae*) and a single bronze coin indicating a date into the fifth century, and another burial with coins of the House of Theodosius occurs at Roden Down.[50] Despite the occurrence of the Rams Hill and Uffington burials, the latter associated with settlement, at hillfort locations, there is little clear indication of widespread reuse of hillforts in the very late Roman period, as is seen further south-west in England. There was some late Roman activity at Madmarston Camp, next to the major settlement at Swalcliffe Lea in the north of the county, but the extent and significance of this is unclear. Elsewhere, occupation of defended sites such as that at Alfred's Castle may well have ceased before the end of the Roman period.

To the west of Dorchester Frilford, like Dorchester, has a high representation of Theodosian coinage, and is particularly notable for the very close association of late Roman and early Anglo-Saxon cemeteries. Unfortunately, however, the circumstances of the discovery mean that some details of the relationship between them are uncertain.[51] However, it seems that of some 180 recorded graves the majority may have been Roman, of which most were probably aligned approximately east-north-east/west-south-west. These included five burials in lead-lined coffins, and others with partial stone or tile lining or packing, the latter a characteristic also thought to apply to some of the Saxon graves. These last included both cremations and inhumations, at least some of which apparently overlay late Roman burials directly, though there was also some evidence for spatial distinction between burials of the two periods, particularly in the later excavations of the site, which appear to have been close to its northern and eastern margins.[52] The exact character of the late Roman cemetery remains an interesting question: was it 'urban', like the main Dorchester ones, or was it 'rural', belonging to the class of sites discussed above?

There is other cemetery evidence from Alchester. Here the small cemetery excavated in 1991 was superseded by a further group of ten burials, mostly located within the former settlement area and with several of the graves cutting the infilled boundary ditch which contained early Anglo-Saxon pottery. There were notable points of similarity between some aspects of burial practice in both the fourth century and later cemeteries. With regard to body position, the placing of the hands together was quite common, being observed in seven late Roman burials and four of the ten later inhumations. An additional feature in common was the use of stones in the graves, particularly around the head and shoulders, found in four late Roman examples (two others had more extensive stone lining) and three of the subsequent burials. It is at least arguable that the second group marked continuity of burial tradition, and therefore potentially of population, with the first.[53]

This type of evidence, and perhaps that from Frilford where a similar situation may have existed, is not unparalleled in the wider region. One of the best cases for continuity of cemetery use from late Roman Britain into the Saxon period comes from Dobunnic territory, at Wasperton in Warwickshire.[54] As at Alchester, successive phases of burials have a number of significant aspects of burial rite in common. The evidence is controversial and has been widely discussed,[55] but a similar situation has been claimed to exist at Stretton on Fosse, also in Warwickshire.[56] In both cases the potential period of overlap from 'late Roman' to 'Anglo-Saxon' is likely to have been in the late fifth/early sixth century.

Another important aspect of the Alchester site was the evidence which it produced for continuity of agricultural practice. One of the deposits cut by the burials just discussed contained carbonised cereal remains of distinctive Romano-British character, also clearly stratified above a deposit containing Anglo-Saxon pottery. The stratigraphic position of this deposit is secure, and the character of the carbonised material suggests that it is unlikely that it can have been either redeposited or significantly contaminated. The simplest interpretation of this material therefore is that some continuity of Romano-British agricultural practice is indicated. This could have involved continued use of an adjacent corn drying oven, since there is evidence which hints at the survival of that structure at this time, but such survival is not essential to the argument. At Gatehampton Farm, Goring, however, Saxon pottery was recovered from the primary destruction deposit in a Roman corn drier, from which possible post-Roman use was also inferred.[57]

No post-Roman structural remains were definitely identified at Alchester, so the evidence for 'early Saxon' activity consists of agricultural practices and burials, both apparently of Romano-British character, but broadly associated with Saxon pottery. Elsewhere within the region where there is close juxtaposition of Roman and early Saxon settlement the principal settlement features are of Saxon character. These include sunken featured and other later structures within the walled town of Dorchester, and sunken-featured and post-hole buildings at Barton Court Farm villa and at Yarnton.[58] It may be significant that at Dorchester the earliest Saxon building was dated by the excavator no earlier than the sixth century, though some pottery of mid to late fifth-century date was identified.[59] Even in the sixth century the building was clearly positioned in relation to one of the Roman streets of the town. Likewise at Alchester the early Saxon site layout reflects the pre-existing Roman pattern, as is seen at Barton Court Farm where, despite the perceived character of the site mentioned above, all the boundary ditches containing Saxon material were of Roman origin. A similar situation also prevails at Yarnton, where early Saxon features respected Roman alignments. Important environmental evidence here indicates the unbroken use of the 'Romano-British' landscape through the fifth century at a time when there is no archaeologically datable evidence for settlement. Equally the pollen sequence from Sidlings Copse near Shotover shows that an open landscape was maintained.[60] At Berinsfield, Wally Corner just north of Dorchester some of the late fifth- to early seventh-century Anglo-Saxon graves cut Roman features but the principal Roman ditch alignments were again respected and there were no significant linear features of Saxon date.[61] At Bishops Court, Dorchester, ditches produced very late Roman pottery directly associated with early Saxon sherds.[62] While technically the Roman material may have been redeposited its quantity and condition is not particularly consistent with such an explanation and it must be possible that the association is genuine, even if the Roman material had been in use for some time before deposition. Continuity of at least some elements of the Romano-British landscape, and in some cases of agricultural practice, as at Alchester, Yarnton and perhaps Goring, thus seems to be a feature of a number of sites in the region.

THE END OF ROMAN ART IN OXFORDSHIRE

The changes manifested in settlement, economy and religion are also apparent in art. The end of a monetary economy meant that enterprises requiring high capital expenditure either by the entrepreneur or by his or her patron were no longer viable. Examples of the former would have included the Oxford potteries and the pewter industry, and of the latter mosaic and wall-painting workshops based in Cirencester or elsewhere. What remained of artistic production was largely confined to what was portable or what could be worn, in other words marking a return to the values of pre-Roman Iron Age society. Finds from Oxfordshire mirror those found elsewhere in southern Britain. Representational art with the exception of the Long Wittenham stoup almost ceased to exist, and the values appreciated were those of abstraction.

Bracelets, finger-rings and belt-fittings should be viewed both as manifestations of continuity and as pointers to new directions in the development of ornament. On the whole this has not been done; and for the most part the rings have been studied from a Roman perspective while the belts have often been classed as belonging to Germanic settlers. It is instructive to consider them together: the sign of being Roman might still be the wearing of a seal-ring even if the owner seldom if ever used it to seal letters. Splendid belts, jewel-encrusted or with gold or silver buckles, would have been regarded as un-Roman in the early Empire but in the late Empire (and by barbarian kings who aspired to behave like Romans) they were often awarded as badges of rank. Equally crossbow brooches were universally worn to define status as well as to hold clothing in place. Both could, of course, be copied and worn by men and women lower down in society and devolved forms of belts and brooches were worn by Germanic peoples and by the inhabitants of early 'Anglo-Saxon' England. Very little of the late metalwork from Oxfordshire is of precious metal; none of gold and only the Dorchester spoons (made within the fourth century) and a ring from Wantage, of silver.[63]

Many of these items still have a representational, Roman aspect to their designs like the confronted sea creatures on the bezel of the (unfortunately lost) Wantage ring (Fig. 7.7). This ring can be compared with three other sub-Roman silver rings with similarly stylised devices found at Amesbury, Wiltshire, with a hoard of coins down to the early fifth century and another ring with an even more devolved device from Corsham in the same county.[64] The same style is to be seen on a frieze of stylised animals around a ring of copper alloy excavated at Barton Court Farm, Abingdon (Fig. 7.8), though this was originally part of a bracelet. Stylised animals are especially associated with brooches mainly from Kent and Sussex (the quoit brooch type) and belt-fittings. However, the Roman source of this animal art is indicated by comparison with late Roman objects of high status including items from the Hoxne Treasure, Suffolk, and locally the zoomorphic brackets of the five late fourth-century silver spoons from Dorchester-on-Thames are not dissimilar.[65]

One of the most characteristic forms of late Roman belt buckle has a loop ornamented with stylised horse protomes. An example with a plate embellished with three circles separated by two lozenges and with ring and dot embellishment was found in a woman's grave at Dyke Hills near Dorchester (see Fig. 7.6, no. 16). The deceased has been thought to be of continental origin because she wore an early cruciform brooch of Germanic type, but her belt was Romano-British. There are several belt-fittings from Shakenoak Farm

7.7   Silver ring with sea-creatures on bezel, from Wantage. Lost.

7.8 Bronze ring with animal frieze from Barton Court Farm, Abingdon. Diameter 25mm. 1984.194.97, Oxfordshire Museums.

near Wilcote. Two rectangular plates, both now broken, come from buckles of identical type. One has a similar lozenge with ring and dot flanking the sides and at the remaining apex of one of the long sides a large open circle with zig-zag border; the other has a border of hatched triangles. Even more attractive is a strap-tag which clearly belongs to the same artistic tradition as the belt-buckles, incorporating two opposed heads of ducks (rather than horses) at the neck and geometric devices, a hatched lozenge with a ring and dot at each angle and a triangular motif composed of three rings and dots on the body. It can be compared with a finer example from Tortworth, Gloucestershire, and it is possible that this series of belt-buckles and tags with its attractive linear ornament and sometimes (though not so far in Oxfordshire) Christian content, peacocks, trees of life, fish or even a chi-rho, originated in the province of Britannia Prima.[66]

Other geometric ornament from belts has a chip-carved appearance, like a circular fitting with zig-zag surround and part of a strap-slide from Shakenoak. These are paralleled in 'Saxon Shore' forts on both sides of the Channel where it is indeed possible that those who wore them were soldiers. The most complete late Roman belt set from the county, however, comes from the male grave at Dyke Hills (Fig. 7.6, nos 1–11). It has circular fittings like one recovered from Shakenoak Farm and a zoomorphic buckle. The dating of the belt is controversial; it has been placed at the beginning of the fifth century or rather later towards the middle of the century. It has been compared with belts from the Vermand cemetery in northern France. Another buckle from Long Wittenham is somewhat similar to that from Dyke Hills, differing in that the plate is cast solid with the loop. Both buckles incorporate debased animal heads at the base of the loop.[67]

The difficulty in classifying metalwork along racial lines, as generally seems to be done, can be seen in the ornament of a small lug brooch from Shakenoak, assuredly of continental form but with the notches and chip-carved embellishment characteristic of Roman crossbow brooches, especially those of the most massive late forms, not to date apparently represented in the county.[68] It is clear that the influences coming from the nearer continent into south-eastern Britain tended to be less Roman and to have a more Germanic character, but that does not always answer the question of who wore them. The owners may well have included Britons whose material culture was shifting in an Anglo-Saxon direction, who were intermarrying and often using the language of the new arrivals, just as their forebears had taken to Latin and to Roman culture after AD 43. They gladly embraced an art tending towards abstraction because that was increasingly a characteristic of the art of late antiquity everywhere. Some items, like the knife scabbard from Brighthampton Grave 22, are hybrids where late Romano-British craftsmanship has been applied to the sort of object normally associated with Anglo-Saxons, though in such cases there is no way (in the absence of DNA tests) of telling the origins of the warrior buried with it (see above). However, the further development of this art including, with the Augustinian mission, the reinvigoration of insular art with the art of a seventh-century, still essentially Roman, Italy lies beyond the appointed end of this book.[69]

CONCLUSION

Whether viewed from an artistic or a socio-economic perspective this evidence raises the important question of the meanings of material culture. Traditionally, Germanic material and other attributes, whether building types, pottery or metalwork, have been seen as inevitably indicating the presence of German immigrants. We have already seen that there are different interpretations even of the standardised late Roman metal equipment types such as belt fittings, which are not necessarily a reliable guide to the ethnicity or even status (military or civilian) of their wearer. Recent work is important in distinguishing between British and continental sources, but still does not necessarily elucidate other problems. With regard to other, more specifically Anglo-Saxon metalwork and pottery it would be invidious to argue that much of it does not reflect a Germanic presence, but one must question whether this can be assumed for all such material. There are clear hints of the survival of at least some of the British population into the period at which some newcomers can be detected in the region. Blair's invisible post-Roman British are perhaps not entirely invisible.[70] His suggestion of essentially peaceful coexistence of native British and German settlers seems reasonable, particularly if it is accepted that political control of the region for much of the fifth century still rested with the former, who were served, and perhaps protected, by a (probably small) number of the latter.

As we have also seen, however, much of the system of material culture enjoyed by the British population through the Roman period had vanished, probably relatively rapidly, at the beginning of the fifth century with the collapse of the economic system which sustained the relevant industries. Into the vacuum created by the demise of the Oxford pottery industry, for example, alternative sources of supply were bound to move eventually. The fact that the pottery ultimately found across the region in the later fifth and sixth centuries was for the most part relatively crude hand-made material strongly reminiscent of what had been in use in the middle Iron Age is neither here nor there. If the material was available it would be used, and it need be no surprise if typically Saxon pottery found its way into surviving British communities, as could be suggested at Alchester, for example. The argument must be used with caution, certainly, but Saxon pottery must eventually have been adopted by surviving British populations unless these remained entirely aceramic. The presence of typical early Saxon pottery will therefore not always indicate the presence of immigrants, though the extent to which this may have been the case must remain uncertain, as will the possibility that other aspects of Saxon material culture were also adopted by the surviving British population.

NOTES

1. Young 1977, 240. Young (ibid., 174) dates his type C102 after AD 390 but such precision cannot be sustained. See also Booth et al. 1993, 160–4.
2. Brown 1994.
3. Young 1977, 240; cf Booth et al. 1993, 168.
4. This was essentially the view of Young twenty years ago (Young 1977, 241), and as yet there seems no good reason to change it. Attempts such as that by Dark (1996, 58–60) to argue for continued pottery production on a wider scale than hitherto believed are unconvincing. The specific argument that a late Oxford beaker from Barrow Hills carries an 'Anglo-Saxon' stamp simply puts the cart before the horse.
5. See Reece 1980 for an extreme statement of the view that towns had effectively ceased to exist as such by the early fourth century.
6. The coin evidence for these temple sites is usefully summarised by Boon 1994, 176.
7. Sutherland 1936.
8. Shakenoak, Brodribb et al. 1968, 16; Ditchley, Radford 1936, 44.
9. North Leigh, Ellis 1999, 242–3; Barton Court Farm, Miles 1986, 16.
10. For balanced views of this question see Esmonde Cleary 1989, 174–5, and Salway 1981, 544–9.
11. The problem in the early period is an absence of evidence, rather than an absence of cemeteries. These would certainly have existed, at least in association with the larger settlements.
12. For these sites see Chapter three above.
13. Booth et al. forthcoming.
14. Barrow Hills, Atkinson 1952–3, 33–4; Boyle & Chambers in prep. Ashville, Parrington 1978, 23–5. Bloxham, Knight 1938. Cassington, *Oxoniensia* 3, 165 (Notes and News) and *VCH* I, 334, for the plan, see Harding 1972, pl. 27. Crowmarsh, Clarke 1996; 1997. Curbridge, Chambers 1976, 43–9. Stanton Harcourt, McGavin 1981. Uffington, Thurnam & Davis 1865; Cromarty et al. forthcoming b. For the purposes of this discussion the Barton Court Farm cemetery consisting exclusively of infant burials (Miles 1986, 15–16) is omitted from the overall total of eighteen sites.
15. Inhumation was the characteristic fourth-century burial rite across the region.
16. *VCH*, 334.
17. Chambers 1987, 41; Harman et al. 1978, 16. See also further below.
18. Hood & Walton 1948.
19. Abingdon, Allen 1990, 74, where three such burials were grouped together. At Frilford there were five lead-lined coffins out of at least a hundred burials. Elsewhere only single examples are known. Individual stone coffins occur, e.g. at Churchill near Chipping Norton (*Britannia* 13 (1982), 367), and three are noted from the vicinity of Swalcliffe Lea (*VCH*, 309).
20. Young 1977 type C38. The description is in the British Museum inventory for 1862.
21. Fragments of a comb of this type have also been found in the villa at North Leigh (Ellis 1999, 226, fig. 12, no. 1).
22. Härke in Fulford & Rippon 1994, 205.
23. Wilson 1992, 92–5.
24. Akerman 1860, 350, pl. xvii; Evison 1965, 23, fig. 13c; Blair 1994, 9. For the Uley sheeting see Henig in Woodward & Leach 1993, 107–11. On the tradition in general see Buschhausen 1971. On Wallingford see Härke in Fulford & Rippon 1994, 204, citing Gelling 1974, 535.
25. Blair 1994, 13, fig. 15 (Brighthampton); Härke in Fulford & Rippon 1994, 203–4, with illus. 17 for spear-head and Atkinson 1916, 21–2, pl. v for hanging bowl (both from Lowbury Hill); Blair 1994, 34, for British element in the *Gewisse*.
26. Frend 1992; Watts 1998; Farwell & Molleson 1993 (Poundbury, Dorchester, Dorset). See Chambers 1987 for Queenford Farm, Dorchester-on-Thames.
27. Thomas 1998; Howlett 1994, 1995 and 1997; further evidence of inscriptions on stone in Howlett 1998, 17–32, 159–61. For continuity in the west see Dark 1994; Bede, *H.E.* 3, 7, for Birinus and Dorchester; Blair 1994, 3 (on possible Christian continuity at Dorchester); Bede, *H.E.* 1, 27 (Augustine's letter to Pope Gregory and replies received).
28. Clarke & Fulford 1998.
29. Handley in ibid., 42; K. Clarke in ibid., 43–5.
30. Clarke & Fulford 1998, 29–32. Green 1989, 144–6 on the chthonic role of dogs.
31. Woodward & Leach 1993, 316–27, for the later phases: they may not have been Christian but

something was going on; Blair 1994, 18, for Woodeaton; Fulford & Rippon 1994, 201; Blair 1994, 46, for Asthall; 32–4 for other cases of the use of ancient monuments.

32. Chambers 1987; Harman et al. 1978.
33. Philpott 1991, 226–8.
34. Chambers 1987, 58, for the original dates. Recalibration of the dates was done by Alistair Barclay and Paul Booth, using OxCal v2. There is no particular reason to doubt the validity of the original dates, but they are strikingly at variance with the evidence from other late Roman cemeteries. Some caution is therefore necessary in accepting them.
35. Kirk & Leeds 1954.
36. See particularly Hawkes 1986, 69–75, and most recently Blair 1994, 1–6, etc. Michael Jones, however, manages a whole book on the end of Roman Britain (1996) without mentioning them once. Publication of the Dyke Hills burials prompted a wider study of comparanda for the metalwork, resulting in a classic exposition of its origins and context (Hawkes & Dunning 1961). Much new material has been added since, and the continental background has been examined in detail, transforming understanding of the sources, sequence and dating of the main groups of material. The most extensive account is Böhme 1986.
37. The case has been argued in detail by Hawkes (1986, 69–70), who suggests that the burial could date as late as the 440s. Böhme (1986, 492–5) simply assigns it to the first half of the fifth century. The artistic aspects of this and related material are discussed further below.
38. Böhme 1986, 533–4 and 531 respectively; for the recreation ground burial see also Hawkes 1986, 70–1.
39. Corney & Griffiths forthcoming.
40. Böhme 1986, 474–6 and 562–3. A further piece in the Ashmolean Museum is not certainly from Oxford. Some of the Shakenoak pieces are discussed by Hawkes in Brodribb et al. 1968, 96–101, and ibid. 1972, 74–7. For a crossbow brooch from Woodeaton see Kirk 1951, 12–13.
41. For Ducklington, Böhme 1986, 566. Most of the other pieces are unpublished and not precisely provenanced. The overall distribution of this material is particularly strong in north Wiltshire and Gloucestershire and manufacture of at least some of these pieces in Cirencester seems very likely (Corney & Griffiths forthcoming).

42. Hawkes 1986, 68.
43. Hawkes 1986; Blair 1994, for the most detailed study Dickinson 1976.
44. Hawkes 1986, 78–9: Hamerow 1993.
45. Cf. Hawkes 1986, 70.
46. For *foederati* see e.g. Esmonde Cleary 1989, 6–7, but he has reservations about the use of this term in relation to the Dorchester burials (ibid., 55–6).
47. Cf. Blair 1994, 5–6; Hawkes 1986, 75, etc.
48. Jones 1996, 39–71. See also the summary of developing archaeological views on this by Hamerow (1994, 166).
49. Cf. Blair 1994, 9: 'a population collapse remains hard to doubt'.
50. Rams Hill, Sutherland 1940; Kent (1994, clxxvii) says there are three bronzes. Roden Down, Hood & Walton 1948, 43.
51. Bradford & Goodchild 1939, 54–66.
52. Most of the excavation took place in the 1860s and the site was subsequently largely destroyed by quarrying. Ascription to period of many of the burials without grave goods was on the (then fashionable) basis of the racial characteristics of skull types. The main sources are *Proc. Soc. Antiqs.* 2nd Ser. 3 (1865), 136–41; Rolleston 1869 and 1880; Buxton 1921; Bradford & Goodchild 1939, 54–8 and 65–6.
53. Booth et al. forthcoming.
54. Crawford 1983, 25–6.
55. E.g. Esmonde Cleary 1989, 201; Hamerow 1994, 168.
56. Ford 1996, 66–73.
57. Allen 1995a, 125.
58. Dorchester, Frere 1962, 123–8; Barton Court Farm, Miles 1986, 16–19; Yarnton, Hey forthcoming.
59. Frere 1962, 130.
60. Yarnton, Hey forthcoming; Sidlings Copse, Day 1991, 467.
61. Boyle et al. 1995, 9. The cemetery includes several fifth-century graves (ibid., 126).
62. May 1977.
63. Janes 1996 for the ceremonial crossbow brooch and see Henig 1995, 168, illus. 97; for the *cingulum militare*, the official belt, see for example Heurgon 1958, 31–2, pl. iii, 1 and 2 and see pl. xxiii, 3.
64. Henig 1995, 172–3, illus. 103 (Wantage), 101 (Amesbury Rings); Henig 1999b (Corsham).
65. Miles 1986, mf 5, D13, D14, fig. 105, no. 2 for Barton Court Farm ring/bracelet; for the Hoxne gold bracelets with running animals see Bland & Johns 1993, illus. on p. 20 (right side);

for the style in general Henig 1995, 170–3. See *VCH* I, 294, pl. xiii, F, for the Dorchester spoons.

66. S. Hawkes in Brodribb et al. 1968, 92–3, fig. 32, no. 58 and p. 96; Hawkes in Brodribb et al. 1972, 69, 71, fig. 30, no. 137 and pp. 75–6 (Shakenoak); Kirk & Leeds 1952–3, 67 and 69, fig. 27, no. 16 and pl. iv B, and Hawkes & Dunning 1961, 2, fig. 1, no. 16 and p. 47, no. 5 (Dorchester, Dyke Hills); Brodribb et al. 1978, 98–9, no. 242, fig. 41 (Shakenoak tag) compare with Hawkes & Dunning 1961, 24, fig. 8 for the Tortworth specimen; Mawer 1995, 61–5, and illus. on pp. 124 and 125 for Christian examples.

67. Kirk and Leeds 1952–3, 64–7, fig. 27; see p. 70 for Vermand; Blair 1994, 5, ill. 10 (Dorchester, Dyke Hills); see also note 36 above for the dating. Akerman 1860, 352, pl. xix, Hawkes & Dunning 1961, 58 and fig. 209 and p. 60 and Evison 1965, 27 and 79, fig. 12a (Long Wittenham).

68. Hawkes in Brodribb et al. 1972, 78ff. On the crossbow brooches see note 31 and Hattatt 1987, 285–8, nos 1265–9.

69. Onians 1999, 268–73, on the late Roman 'Culture of Imagination' as for example applied to veined marble; Dodwell 1982 for later developments in 'Anglo-Saxon' art.

70. Blair 1994, 9.

CHAPTER EIGHT

THE RECOVERY OF OXFORDSHIRE'S ROMAN PAST

Awareness of the presence of Rome was never completely lost after the end of Roman political control. The names Dorchester and Alchester contain the *ceaster* element, in the second case transferred to nearby Bicester. Although J.H. Parker was almost certainly right that the establishment of Birinus' bishopric at Dorchester largely depended on documentation in Rome surviving from late imperial times, local memory and perhaps even the continuity of a local Christian tradition may have played a part. Anglo-Saxon archaeology shows that Roman trinkets were valued by their finders and wonder at the works of the Roman past is evidently attested in such place-names as Fawler, of which there are two in the county, derived from *fagan floran*, 'variegated floor', recording the discovery of a villa with mosaics. Roman roads were more than curiosities and continued to provide routes for communication; Akeman Street continued to be used and one explanation for the first part of the name is that it means the road to Bath, where a charter of 973 refers to *Acemannes ceaster*. Bath itself was the probable setting for the dramatic eighth-century poem *The Ruin*, describing the 'work of giants' falling into decay, but there were no doubt ruins more locally which excited wonder, those of villas and perhaps even buildings in the small towns such as the putative bath-house at Castle Hill, Alchester.[1]

Even if such survivals tended to be fancifully interpreted they provided a basis for speculation about the past. However, during the late Middle Ages and in the sixteenth century this was overlaid by romance, in large part connected with the need felt by scholars to establish the antiquity of the University of Oxford, sometimes in active rivalry with Cambridge. Here not only Romans, but Greeks and even contemporaries of the Hebrew prophets were invoked. Prior to the establishment of schools at Oxford, it was affirmed that there were Greek scholars at Cricklade (glossed as Greek-lade) and Latin scholars at Lechlade (Latin-lade). Bryan Twyne early in the seventeenth century cites a note supposed to be by John Leland to the effect that these schools were transferred to Cal[l]eva, by which Oxford was meant. However, the name, in fact that of Silchester, is a sign of new antiquarian learning being brought to bear on local history including not only documentary sources such as the Antonine Itinerary but numismatics. Leland in his *Itinerary* of the 1540s, indeed, included an archaeological observation with regard to Dorchester: 'In the closis and feeldes that lye southly on the toun that now standith be founde *numismata Romanorum* of gold, silver, and brasse.' Gold coins are not common site finds so is the statement indicative of a hoard or hoards? A more useful comment concerns Iron Age and Roman finds at Little Wittenham (Sinodun Hill):

> This place is wonderful dikid about and stondith on a hille in Barkshir, hanging over the Tamise. It is yn by estimation halfe a mile. And withyn it hath beene sum toune, or, as the commune voice sayith, a castelle in the Britannes tyme, defacid by lykelihod by the Danes.
>
> At this tyme it berith very plentifullye both barley and whete, and *numismata Romanorum* be ther found yn ploughyng.[2]

The new learning became especially linked with the name of William Camden (1551–1623). His *Britannia*, first published in 1586 with a further five editions in his lifetime, was subtitled in its English translation (1610), *a chorographical description of Great Britain and Ireland*. Camden introduced his work with a period-by-period historical introduction, including a section on Roman Britain. The gazetteer which follows is arranged county by county, each with its ancient equivalent. Berkshire is rightly given to the Atrebates; Oxfordshire (like Gloucestershire) to the Dobunni. The author recorded the vestiges of antiquity he found, though in the case of Oxfordshire these were not many and they tend to be quite terse. Writing about Alchester he notes 'some few remaines of a decaied and forlorne ancient station'. He notes the finding of Roman coins at Banbury and Dorchester, regarded as especially significant in the case of Dorchester with its ancient, British name: 'That this towne was in old time inhabited by Romanes, their coined peeces of money oftentimes turned up doe imply.'[3]

However, in the Berkshire section he wrongly places Calleva Atrebatum, 'the chiefe citie in times past of the Attrebatians' at Wallingford and, in the Oxfordshire chapter, describes the road leading from it and then on to Banbury as Akeman Street. Camden had no reliable means of positively rejecting what he found in the Chronicles, much as he would have liked to, and so the old legends like that of the Greek scholars translated to Oxford from Cricklade remain as the heritage of 'sage antiquity', as they would with increasing scepticism until the eighteenth century.[4]

Later editors of *Britannia*, Edmund Gibson (1669–1748) and Richard Gough (1735–1809), enormously expanded Camden's work but they had the advantage of a growing appreciation of the remains of Roman Britain as a whole based on local discoveries by antiquaries. As far as Oxfordshire is concerned the most important of these were surely Robert Plot (1640–96) and Thomas Hearne (1678–1735). As its title implies Plot's *Natural History of Oxfordshire* (1677, with a second edition in 1705) is mainly devoted to natural phenomena though the ninth chapter deals with the arts [of man] and the tenth with antiquities. Plot is at his best where he relies on his own observations. The weight of tradition was still too much to question the great antiquity, Greek as well as Roman, of Oxford itself; the presence of a (minor) Roman road merely added confirmation. False etymology gave credence to Alchester being derived from *Alecti Castrum* and Elsfield to *Alectus-field*, as also to Henley, 'from the British Hen, which signifies old, and Lley a place'.[5]

He begins with British Antiquities, by which he means those of the period prior to the coming of the Romans as revealed by such authorities as Caesar and Tacitus. He describes and illustrates a gold coin of Cunobelin (Fig. 8.1), 'a King here in Britan at the time of the Birth of our Saviour CHRIST; it shewing a Horse, and his Inscription on one side, and an Ear of Corn and CAMU on the Reverse; intimating the place of its Coinage to be Camulodunum, the Royal City and Seat of Cunobelin'. In this he was following Camden, one of whose achievements was to recognise coins of this type for what they were. What is of especial interest to us is the information that: 'This was dug up at Wood-Eaton in the Year 1676'. Another small gold coin, recognised as of the same date, was found at the same time and place. We can now see these as important evidence for a pre-Roman shrine on the site of the Roman temple at Woodeaton whose discovery lay far in the future. A third gold coin is illustrated, dug up at Little Milton, which we can recognise as Catuvellaunian, of Whaddon Chase type, but which Plot sees as a coin of Prasutagus, King of the Iceni. This conjecture is based on wrong but ingenious reasoning. The reverse type is very similar to coins of Boudicca 'where her name is stamped on them'. We now know that the name on those issues is that of Bodvoc(us) of the Dobunni.[6]

It may seem odd to the modern reader that Plot does not at this point attempt to identify British sites, but proceeds directly to the Romans. This becomes less strange when it is realised that he had no way of distinguishing prehistoric monuments from Roman or even those of Anglo-Saxon date. True, he speculates that the two massive banks of Dike Hills south-west of Dorchester might have been 'the Outworks of the Fortifications on Long-Witenham Hill on the other side of the Water, which perhaps was the Sinnodunum of the ancient Britans', but he prefers to see it as a Roman fortification 'such as P. Ostorius Propraetor here in Britan under Claudius, is said by Tacitus to have made on the Rivers *Antona* and *Sabrina*'. He describes the South Oxfordshire Grim's Ditch with its double bank as a Roman road from Wallingford (which, following Camden, he misidentifies as *Calleva*) to Nuffield, Henley and on to Colebrook (*Pontes*); in other words as part of *iter vii* of the Antonine Itinerary. Aves Ditch is identified as a branch from Akeman Street but in this case its Iron Age date was not established until a year or two ago.[7]

He is on firmer ground with the Roman period. He describes a Roman road, often called Akeman-street, across Otmoor but then establishes the route of 'the true Akeman-Street, from Black-thorn on the Buckinghamshire border to Alc[h]ester, crossing the Cherwell near Tackley through Woodstock Park, to Stunsfield, Wilcot, Ramsden and Astall and out into Gloucestershire'. He illustrates part of a Roman mosaic 'plowed up somewhere about Great Tew', and mentions another at Steeple Aston; although taken to be the floors of generals' tents and so no later than Agricola, we can attribute them to Roman villas and assign them to the fourth century. With regard to the Great Tew mosaic his description reveals the careful observation of a trained naturalist: It consisted 'of a Matter much softer than Marble, cut into Squares somewhat bigger than Dice, and of four different Colours, viz. Blue, White, Yellow, and Red, all Polished, and orderly disposed into Works'.[8]

Of other finds the most noteworthy were burials. He illustrates (in engravings by Michael Burghers) a glass jar and a pottery urn (evidently one of twelve) 'found in a place called Bushy-Leas, betwixt Brightwell and Chal-grave'. He speculates as to the use of the glass jar, whether it contained a lamp or was a lachrymatory (which he rejects) or more probably 'one of those Vessels containing some Aromatical Liquor'. It is in fact most likely that it contained a cremation but that the owner, John Stone of Brightwell (who gave the finds to Plot), or perhaps the original finder, had cleared the contents out. However, at Alchester Plot was shown 'a Glass Bottle . . . containing nothing but somewhat like Ashes' set within 'a great square Stone' – undoubtedly a cremation.[9]

It is rather disappointing that he has so little to add to Camden with regard to Dorchester, where he reiterates the finding of Roman coins which shows it was known to the Romans even if 'it never came to its height till Birinus, An.614'. Nor does he have anything new to say about Alchester, the burial excepted.[10]

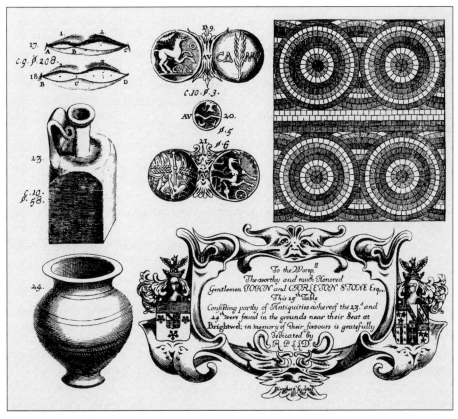

8.1   Plate by Michael Burghers from Plot, *Natural History of Oxfordshire*, showing Celtic coins, mosaic from Great Tew and pottery urn and glass jar from a burial between Brightwell and Chalgrove.

Here another late seventeenth-century scholar, White Kennett, who produced a *Parochial History* centring on this region, has more to add. He prefaced his work with historical chapters, four of which deal with the Romans. Writing of the Roman invasion, he notes after mentioning Corinium, 'the Metropolis or Chief City of the Dobunni', as the site of one Roman fort: 'But the presumption is very fair, that another of these garisons of Plautius was at Alcester, adjoining to Ambrosden, lying as the frontier of the Boduni and Catuellani, and from whence the army of Plautius might agreeably pursue the Britains to Buckingham, or the adjacent banks of the Ouse.' Recent survey and excavation has confirmed Alchester's importance as the site of an invasion period fort or fortress.[11]

Kennett repeats the stories about Allectus but also adds some archaeological observations:

> This area or site of Allchester has been for many ages an arable part of the common field of Wendlebury: so as the teeth of time and of the plough may be thought to have consum'd all the Roman reliques: yet by walking o're the ground, I find it eassie to collect many fragments of brick, tile, urns, vessels, and other materials, all of Roman make, and enough to distinguish this from any adjacent soil. Great variety and plenty of Roman mony, of such especially as is dated from the decline of the Empire, has been within few years gathered and dispers'd . . . And within a few years wherein I have apply'd my self to some enquiry, I have bought up more than one hundred several pieces, most of which have been found by the children of Wendlebury in following the plough, or by turning the clods of earth. They call them Allcester-coin, and are proud of receiving more passable mony for them.[12]

His interest in Roman antiquities is demonstrated by his publication of four pots from a cremation burial at Aston Rowant, one of them a samian platter. Meric Casaubon had already illustrated Roman pottery from a cemetery at Newington as early as 1634 while Sir Thomas Browne's longer description of the Roman cremations at Brampton, Norfolk, in 1667 has something of the same quality. Kennett's account is worth reproducing, together with the fine engraving by Burghers (Fig. 8.2), not only as being the most objective example of archaeological reporting published on Roman Oxfordshire to date, but also as showing a strong desire to preserve Roman finds for posterity.

> Before I pass from the Romans in these parts, I would farther inform the World, that in the beginning of March 1692/3, in Kingston field within the parish of Aston-Rowant, at the bottom of a small stream call'd Colebrook, about a furlong from the lower branch of the Ikenild-street way, was taken up a large earthen pot in which were contained 1. a Roman urn that would hold the quantity of two quarts, narrow at the mouth, which was stopt with lead, and fill'd with pieces of bones, entire at the taking up, and broke in vain hopes of treasure in it: represented by the Figure A. 2. A smaller urn or lacrymatorie unstopt and empty, as Figur'd B. 3. A little pot or vessel of finer earth, containing about one quarter of a pint, which seems to have been fill'd with aromatic liquor, of which a strong

8.2   Plate by Michael Burghers from White Kennett, *Parochial History*, showing burial group from Aston Rowant.

scent does still remain, as in the Figure C. 4. A patine of curious red-earth about six inches Diameter, with this inscription cross the centre, SEXTVS FE. the Potters' name, represented D, the three last of which are now in my custody.[13]

The conditions which antiquaries encountered in the field early in the following century is illustrated by the account of Dr William Stukeley (1687–1765) of his visit to Alchester on his journey through Oxfordshire in 1710. He identified the site, which continued to be as productive as it was in Kennett's time:

by the prodigious blackness and richness of the earth, as they were ploughing; and this shows it to have been once in a very flourishing condition and populous; for the fund of nitrous particles and animal salts lodged in this earth are inexhaustible. The site of this city is a common, belonging to the inhabitants of

Wandlebury, and every one has a certain little portion of it to plough up, whence we may well imagine the land is racked to the last extremity, and no great care taken in the management of it: yet it bears very good crops of wheat.

He continues with the sort of description which still pains the modern archaeologist, faced with damage from agriculture and unrecorded collecting:

As I traversed the spot, at every step I saw pieces of pots and vessels of all sorts of coloured earth, red, green, and some perfectly of blue clay, that came from Aynhoe: I picked up several parcels, thinking to have carried them away, till I perceived them strown very thick over the whole field, together with bits of brick of all sorts: the husbandman told me they frequently break their ploughs

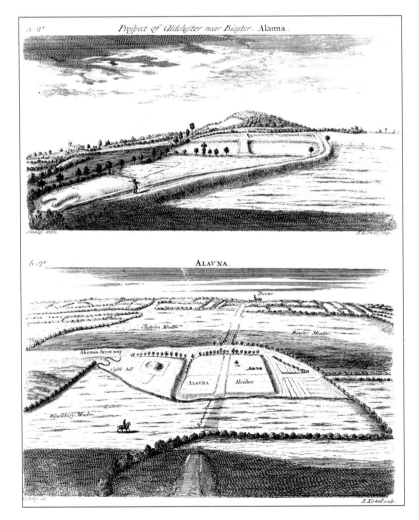

8.3 Two views of Alchester, from *Itinerarium Curiosum* by William Stukeley.

against foundations of hewn stone and brick; and we saw upon the spot many paving stones with a smooth face, and laid in a very good bed of gravel, till they draw them all up by degrees, when the plough chances to go a little deeper than ordinary. Infinite numbers of coins have been found, and dispersed over the adjacent villages without any regard; and after a shower of rain now, they say, sometimes they find them: I got two or three of Tetricus jun. &c.[14]

He mentions the glass urn in a stone, revealing the sad fate of many such antiquities. The former had been broken and lost while the latter was being used as a pig trough. He 'heard likewise, by enquiry, that they have found brass images, lares, and all sorts of antiquities, which I encouraged them to preserve for the future'.

At any rate he was able to give a general description of Alchester with its bank and ditch and provides us with two useful 'prospects' of the site (Fig. 8.3). He firmly scotches the theory that the site had anything to do with Allectus and proposes intelligently (and perhaps rightly), that it was the *Alauna* of the Ravenna Cosmography. Equally judiciously, he derives the name Akeman Street from 'stony agger, or ridge'.[15] In the neighbourhood of the park at Woodstock he takes Dr Plot to task for 'not sufficiently distinguishing [Grims Ditch] from a Roman road' and also meets Akeman-street again.[16] The most notable antiquity he mentions was discovered at Stonesfield, but it was only found in January 1712, a couple of years after his visit. The description he gives of the Stonesfield mosaic is succinct though not lengthy; it did not need to be, for far from being simply of local significance this 'most curious tesselated pavement, for bulk and beauty the most considerable one we know of' was famous in antiquarian circles in Britain and beyond. Stukeley followed the general view of its figured centre as showing 'Bacchus represented in stones properly coloured, with a tiger, a *thyrsus* in his hand enwrapped with vine leaves'.[17]

An illustration was made on site in 1712 by Michael Burghers, engraver to the University of Oxford and as we have seen a skilled artist. A London printmaker called Edward Loving engraved it in the same year and John Pointer of Merton depicted it in his pamphlet on the pavement in 1713. All confirm its identification as Bacchus. Of these only the Burghers engraving from which those of Vertue, Lewington and Fowler were derived has any real claim to accuracy. Pointer's is merely a sketch while the London print shows a seated Bacchus. Hearne describes how it came to be commissioned thus: 'The London Draught is all Fiction. The Engraver was told 'twas a Bacchus & a Tyger, and accordingly he put a jolly big Fellow upon a Tyger, without seeing, or examining, the Pavement: and all People that saw his Draught run away with the Notion, and depended upon his Print as exact.'

The Loving version, however, had the widest circulation, being reproduced in Samuel Pitiscus's *Lexicon Antiquitatum* (1713) and thence into de Montfaucon's *Supplement to Antiquities explained* (1725). By far its most interesting manifestation is the near-contemporary embroidery, now one of the treasures of Oxfordshire Museums, whose provenance was Sutton Court, Somerset, the home of the Strachey family. John Strachey was an antiquary and in 1730 he met Thomas Hearne (1678–1735) who had been deeply involved in, indeed obsessed by, the Stonesfield mosaic, but research has failed to substantiate a Strachey connection. In 1735 the antiquary William Brome mentioned in a letter how a lady friend embroidered a nine-foot carpet with all the colours of the original. This may be the surviving embroidery and the lady was perhaps a member of the Herefordshire Walwyn family. Such a form of reproduction was not unique as the famous Orpheus mosaic found at Littlecote in 1727 was not only engraved by George Vertue but also drawn by William George, and subsequently made the subject of an embroidery by his widow.[18]

Thomas Hearne returns to the Stonesfield pavement again and again in his private diaries in entries which provide a fascinating insight into contemporary archaeological method, thinking out the significance of such a floor in its setting and establishing its subject matter and iconography. Neither was at once straightforward. He paid the first of many visits to the mosaic on 2 February 1712, walking the 8 miles to Stonesfield where he 'had a full view of the Pavemt for several hours, but cannot find yt 'tis Roman, but rather modern, perhaps abt time of Edw. I or later . . .'. He thought it might portray St Michael slaying the dragon and be the floor of a manor house. However, by 4 February he was persuaded that it was Roman: 'The Barbarous Form of the Figures upon the Pavemt at Stunsfield plainly shew yt 'tis not of the more early Roman times.' He was later more precise, dating the pavement to the year AD 369 and ascribing it to one of the generals of Count Theodosius sent to Britain by Valentinian. A later archaeologist would have been more impressed by the coins which Hearne records, several of which were of the House of Constantine and much nearer what we would conceive to be the true date of the mosaic. Like Plot, Hearne finds it hard to get away from the belief that mosaics were the floor coverings of generals' tents, though he notes perceptively on one occasion that Galen mentions 'this sort of Pavement with the Forms or Representations of the Gods' and writes 'In all Probability therefore our Stunsfield Pavement was such a Pavement of a Dining Room, done by some curious and rich Gentleman, and not (as I had once conjectur'd) a Roman General's tent'.[19]

It is not easy to understand at first how so observant a scholar took the subject to be Apollo slaying the Python and maintained this view against most other Oxford opinion which rightly accepted it to be Bacchus holding a thyrsus and standing by (or riding) a feline. In part (as the illustrations confirm) it was because the figure was rather schematised. Hearne writes that 'the figure of Apollo Sagittarius & a monstrous Animal is on the Pavement, but Apollo is not sitting upon the Animal but standing or walking slowly'. What he holds is not a thyrsus but 'an Arrow or Dart'. Neither Hearne nor his critics had other mosaics to compare the figure with. But Hearne knew that Apollo was an important god in Britain under various names: ''Tis withall highly probable that Cassibelin . . . and Cunobelin, two British Kings that are mention'd in Caesar and Dion receiv'd the latter Part of their Names from their Religious concern for and sincere worship of Apollo, in whom they confided as a certain Defender in times of Danger.' He cites a coin of Cunobelin upon which 'is the Figure of Apollo . . . playing upon an Harp'. Before we are too critical of Hearne it is worth pointing out that until very recently most modern commentators misidentified the figure on the coin who is undoubtedly Apollo.[20]

The problem of following this line of argument was to explain why a Roman general should have been drawn to show a British god armed with a weapon which alludes to 'the Darts made use of by the Britains'. Hearne suggests that the object in his other hand might be 'A Harp on purpose to please the Britains, and keep off their malicious Designs against his and his Souldiers Lives'. Apart from any other consideration the three centuries or more from the age of Cunobelin to that of Count Theodosius is too long for such speculation to have any force and Hearne's very considerable learning in numismatics should have told him as much. In this light his diatribe against 'that most silly, ridiculous, injudicious, rhapsodical and illiterate Tract about the Stunsfield Pavement, which bears the Name of that Natural Fool . . . John Poynter of Merton' seems rather misplaced. Pointer had placed the mosaic in the reign of Allectus (showing the continued currency of the Alchester/Allectus-chester story) and was more impressed by the quality of the pavement (as I would be, though seeing it as an important example of a provincial school) but using classical sources he was able to prove the identity of the central figure as Bacchus, quite conclusively.[21]

Nevertheless Hearne through his enthusiastic correspondence helped to galvanise interest in mosaics and other such remains and conducted a wide correspondence on the subject as indeed on coins and other antiquities which he recorded in his *Collections*. One discovery which gave particular delight late in his life was the finding of an inscribed altar at Dorchester in 1731 (Fig. 2.3). Something of the same over-enthusiasm and wish to make such discoveries central to history can still be seen in his comments:

> I take Dorchester in Oxfordshire to have been the chief city of the Dobuni, which contained Oxfordshire and Gloucestershire. It was, therefore, the most proper place to have an Altar erected to Jupiter and the Emperors then reigning. Accordingly, I take the Altar lately found there, to be erected at that place, as the most considerable City of that province, the people of wch therefore used to do their sacrifice there, where was likewise, as I believe, a Temple, of wch the Cancelli are mentioned in the Inscription on the said Altar, and here also games were celebrated in honour of the Emperors.[22]

As we have seen the essentially urban infrastructure of Hearne's imagination belongs more properly to the cantonal capitals such as Cirencester, certainly the capital of the Dobunni and the source of a fine statuette of Cupid which Hearne examined when it was brought to Oxford for sale.[23] We would probably place Dorchester on the borders of the Atrebates and the Catuvellauni, perhaps within the territory of the latter, as would seem to be confirmed by the north-eastern reach of its diocese established in mid-Saxon times, but perhaps influenced by Roman documents still extant in Rome.

Antiquarian study in the eighteenth century, especially from around 1730, took two rather different directions, though these were not mutually exclusive. As travel became easier for the rich, the Grand Tour led to first hand examination of the ancient sites of Italy where archaeological excavation as we would understand the term began at Pompeii and Herculaneum. Reflections of the new polite archaeology are beginning to be apparent in Britain especially from the later responses to the Stonesfield pavement. George Vertue's careful scaled engraving of the Stonesfield pavement (1754) (Fig. 8.4) bears the following legends: above, in Latin: '*Pavimentum hoc Tessellatum Elegantiss Stunsfeldiae prope Woodstochiam in Agro Oxoniensi repertum est,*' addressing thus the scholarly world in general, and below:

This Tessellated Pavement, discover'd at STUNSFIELD near Woodstock in Oxfordshire Ano. Dni. MDCCXII. A most Exquisite Work of the Antient Romans, composed with great variety of Small Tesserae of Beautiful Colours & Symmetry. esteem'd to be the most Elegant Piece of Antiquity of the Kind found in Great Britain. When first open'd, it was seen by Multitudes of Curious Persons, and some Learned Antiquaries have employ'd their Skill to trace out its Original Use. Now only remains this Shade, preserv'd by the Care of Tho. Hearne M.A. of Oxford, and lastly by G. Vertue Member of the Society of Antiquaries London.

Any deficiencies here are due merely to loss and when two geometric pavements were uncovered at Stonesfield in 1779–80 they were engraved to a very high standard by a local Woodstock artist, William Lewington, who also copied the Vertue engraving. No doubt they were designed to appeal to educated customers with private libraries.[24]

The same meticulous attention to international standards of scholarship is shown in John Horsley's *Britannia Romana* of 1733. Much of this is concerned with inscriptions, and of course Oxfordshire had only produced a single inscription, though one which very much delighted scholars, just before Horsley went to press. His comments on the

8.4   The Stonesfield Pavement as engraved by George Vertue.

Dorchester altar (Fig. 2.3) are terse and to the point, not dwelling on the speculations of his informant John Ward but printing his letter as we might have done for what it tells us about the findspot. The altar is of the usual type and in most respects bears a standard inscription.

> There is nothing in the inscription, but what I have explained on other occasions, except the last part, *aram cum cancellis de suo posuit*. The *cancelli* seem to have been some sort of lattices or rails, within which this altar was placed by M.Val.Severus, at whose expence the whole was erected.

He confirms that finds such as this show Dorchester to be Roman 'tho' I cannot certainly tell what Roman name to assign it'.[25]

The Dorchester altar soon had a brother. In the garden of the Manor House at Elsfield is a pedestal like an altar bearing the legend: *I · O · M / ET DIS PATRI(i)S / L · SEP · NVGERIN / VS AEL · NVCERIN(i). / B · COS · / V · S · L · M*. The base seems to date from the mid-eighteenth century and the inscription clearly derives from the Dorchester altar. There was no second *Beneficiarius Consularis*, L. Septimius Nugerinus at Elsfield. In fact the Manor belonged to an antiquary, Francis Wise, Radcliffe Librarian 1748–67, who seems to have embellished his garden with copies of antiquities. This imitation at any rate has survived the real Dorchester altar which, having been moved to Broome Park near Canterbury in the early nineteenth century was last recorded in a distant photographic view in *Country Life* on 6 July 1907. Shortly afterwards the house was sold and the altar is assumed to have been given away.[26]

The worlds of classical archaeology and Romano-British archaeology came closest together when Italy was temporarily inaccessible to Grand Tourists during the Napoleonic wars, a conjuncture which resulted in the lavish publication of major villas with high-quality renderings of their mosaics by Samuel Lysons.[27] Unfortunately, although a Gloucestershire man who produced incomparable coloured lithographs of the Woodchester pavements, he did not show any mosaics from Oxfordshire. However, a contemporary, Henry Hakewill, after making a half-hearted attempt to elucidate the Stonesfield remains in 1812, turned his attention to North Leigh where he ascertained the plan and found no fewer than five mosaics. His *Account of the Roman villa discovered at Northleigh Oxfordshire in the years 1813, 1814, 1815, 1816* was written in 1817 though not published until 1823 in Skelton's *Oxfordshire*. The description is fully up to the standard of Lysons although Hakewill was disappointed that he had not had the opportunity to examine 'the west side of the quadrangle, and some parts of the adjoining ground, to which, there is reason to believe, the Villa had extended'. Nevertheless in 1826 Hakewill reissued the text adding illustrations which, although in monochrome, are useful and accurate, covering mosaics (Fig. 8.5), the excavated hypocaust and a detailed representation of a column base.[28]

Two other rich villas were examined in the early nineteenth century but nowhere near as well recorded. Alfred Beesley in his *History of Banbury* published in 1841 gives a rather confused account from the local minister, Revd Mr Nash, of a villa and burials uncovered at Beaconsfield Farm, Great Tew, in 1810. A small part of the mosaic was saved and preserved by a Mr M. Bolton at Great Tew, allowing it to be

8.5   Three mosaics from North Leigh from Hakewill 1826.

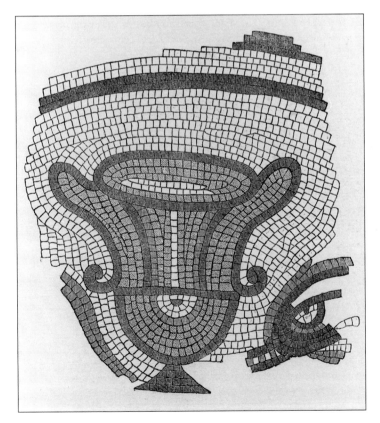

8.6   Mosaic from the villa at Beaconsfield
Farm, Great Tew (with cantharus and
dolphins), from Beesley 1841.

illustrated in Beesley's book (Fig. 8.6). Another villa was excavated somewhat more systematically by Joseph Skelton and Revd C. Winstanley in 1824 at Wigginton, a plan was made and an apsidal mosaic engraved and again published in the *History of Banbury* (Fig. 8.7). Some idea of the date is provided by the coins cited which are mainly of the fourth century.[29]

The other tradition in British archaeology, centred on topography and not necessarily backed by classical learning, continued throughout. On the whole Beesley's account of the Romans around Banbury falls into this tradition whether discussing contemporary inferences about settlement on the site of Banbury and its region (some of it fanciful like the supposed amphitheatre at Banbury) or in reproducing rather older evidence such as a letter from Revd Francis Wise to Roger Gale about Swalcliffe:

> In Swallcliff parish, but nearer Tadmarton is a Roman town which seems to have extended itself round the foot of a hill [Madmarston]. At the bottom, to the west, is a field, part of which is called Money Acre, for a pot of money found there about 100 years since, and which by these pieces of Roman pottery and the richness of the soil was certainly part of the old town.[30]

Classical learning, even if more widespread then than now, was not available to everyone and, in any case, there are limits to what even detailed knowledge of Roman authors or even the remains of foreign sites such as Tivoli or Herculaneum will tell one, in establishing settlement patterns as they once existed in the local countryside.

ROMAN PAVEMENT AT WIGGINTON.

8.7   Mosaic at Wigginton, from Beesley 1841.

Above all the classical tradition does not help in trying to assess such intriguing and anomalous antiquities as the Uffington White Horse (Fig. 1.8) which excited fierce controversy. Admittedly it was not believed to be Roman, but as some thought (correctly in the opinion of this writer) that it is Iron Age, it deserves a place in our story.

In the late seventeenth and eighteenth centuries the horse was usually attributed to the Anglo-Saxons. John Aubrey recorded that 'some will have it to be made by Hengist or Horsa', though in writing of 'Cunobelin's Court at Kimble in Buckinghamshire' he notes that it is 'not many miles from the White Horse which is as rude as that in his coins'. Francis Wise, the antiquary, then Keeper of the University Archives, published a pamphlet in 1738 assigning it to King Alfred after the Battle of Ashdown. This received a vigorous riposte from the Revd William Asplin, Vicar of Banbury, who again championed a British origin comparing it to 'the British coins in Speed'. Stukeley's daughter Anna visited the horse in 1758 and wrote to her father, again making this numismatic comparison. However, the Anglo-Saxon dating was still holding sway in the mid-nineteenth century when in 1846 William Toms again published it as an early Saxon totem though an appendix by J.Y. Akerman again reiterates that 'the figure of the White Horse at Uffington appears to be one of the rudest of its kind, and so strongly resembles those on the more barbarous British coins, that I do not hesitate to class it with the same period'. Although the matter was not resolved, at least with regard to whether it was prehistoric or later, the balance of opinion took a decisive turn.[31]

The early Victorian era was a key period for antiquarian discovery throughout Britain. In part this was due to the increased rate of construction, especially of railways and in part to the growth of learned societies both national and local, of which the Oxfordshire Archaeological and Historical Society was a prime example. The two factors were not unconnected because railways facilitated travel especially among the new middle class.[32]

With regard to the early *Proceedings* of the Society, attention paid to the Roman period is scanty. In part, no doubt, this is because Roman remains are less obvious in this part of England than in many other places, but it is also true that in Oxford (even more than elsewhere, considering the high concentration of clerics in the University) fervour for medieval (Gothic) architecture lay nearer to the members' concerns. What interest there was in the Roman period, to judge from reports on lectures, was not local at all but was centred on Italy.[33]

Nevertheless the topographical tradition was not totally dormant and there are some useful contributions associated in particular with John Henry Parker who much later summarised his thoughts on the subject in chapter three of his book *The Early History of Oxford* published in 1885, which ranges quite widely. He was a reasonably careful observer with a wide knowledge of classical sources. It was natural for him, following Hakewill, to make a comparison between North Leigh villa and Pliny's description of his own villa. In 1862 he gives quite an informative account of a villa at Beckley illustrated with a bird's-eye view of the remains. It seems to have had patterned floors though from the sketch they would seem to have been coarsely tessellated rather than mosaic. It does not help us to read in the report on his paper to the Society that 'the tesserae were of the usual size and character'.[34]

Nevertheless, deficiencies in recording should not really be laid to his charge. There was a desperate 'rescue' situation with nobody to take responsibility for the recording of such monuments discovered by chance:

> The remains sketched in the diagram were no longer so perfect as they appeared when they were drawn some week or so ago; each day made a difference: in a fortnight's time, when he understood the farmer was about to use the stone of which the buildings were composed, there would not be a trace left. Thus it was that yearly before our very eyes the historical monuments of our county were fading away. He would not ask the Society to attempt to preserve the remains in this instance, but he laid great stress upon accurate drawings, plans and measurements being obtained, and that the Society should have a proper receptacle for such, where they would be carefully preserved.[35]

It is not surprising for an historian that it came most naturally to marry topography and ancient history. For example at Dorchester he concentrates on the town's possible role in the Roman invasion of AD 43, for although material finds were listed there were too few of them to make an exciting narrative. Nevertheless there are insights in Parker's account: we would now see Dyke Hills not as a Roman camp but as the oppidum preceding the later town but like him we are conscious of the relationship. His final comment further emphasises the possibility of continuity here, with great perception: 'in reviewing the history of Dorchester as a whole, there seems to be a link between the circumstance of this being chosen as the seat of the episcopal jurisdiction over the south-midland part of the kingdom, and the importance which the place had held as a Roman city'.[36]

More important than these as far as future research was concerned was the beginning of systematic excavation at the other Roman town in Oxfordshire, Alchester, by Hussey and Brown in the middle of the century as a result of railway works and the discovery of pottery kilns at Littlemore in 1879.[37]

Many of the nineteenth-century discoveries were sporadic, including a stone relief of Vulcan from Duns Tew (Fig. 5.16) found in 1861 and now in the Ashmolean Museum, two lead coffins with associated fourth-century coins at Frilford and a complete pottery vessel from the foundations of Mansfield College. Parker, commenting on the Duns Tew relief, believed 'the owner [Sir Henry Dashwood] would present them to Oxford if such a museum could be found as the Society contemplates', and the relief was, indeed, given to the Ashmolean. Other items went elsewhere, among them a small cache of five late Roman silver spoons found in gravel digging south-east of Dorchester, presumably Treasure Trove, and a group of bronzes in the Franks Collection said to have been 'found near Oxford' (Fig. 5.8) and generally attributed on grounds of plausibility to Woodeaton, which are in the British Museum.[38]

The *Victoria County History* gives many instances of the casual discovery of coins, pottery and other items in the late nineteenth and early twentieth-centuries but a more professional and systematic approach is to be seen in Charles Oman's 1895 paper in *Archaeologia Oxoniensis* where he maps the prehistoric and especially Roman finds from Oxford (Fig. 8.8). This approach, commonplace today in every Sites and

Monuments Record in the country, was new then. It reveals the surprising density of settlement along the gravel terrace with particular concentrations, for instance around the University Museum and in the Polstead Road area, which may indicate hamlets. Although more discoveries have been made since, including a small inhumation cemetery in front of the University Museum in 1970–1, Oman's map is still of great use and may be the basis of the half-joking inclusion of North Oxford among the rank of Roman small towns by the Ordnance Survey.[39]

Further advance had to await the development of scientific archaeology following the First World War. This is manifested in a more serious approach to excavation by national societies such as the Society of Antiquaries which reported on excavations in Alchester in early issues when the young Christopher Hawkes elucidated the defences and excavated some internal buildings in the 1920s, followed by local societies. In this instance the leading organisation was the Oxfordshire Archaeological and Historical Society which carried a report on the Roman villa in Ditchley Park by Raleigh Radford in the first issue of *Oxoniensia*. Aided by air photography and a growing appreciation of landscape, this was an early attempt to understand a villa in its setting. Important reports on work at Dorchester by members of the Oxford University Archaeological Society and at Frilford followed in other early volumes.[40]

In 1939 M.V. Taylor with Donald Harden and C.H.V. Sutherland published a superb account of what was known at the time about Romano-British remains in Oxfordshire in the first volume of the Oxfordshire *Victoria County History*, which also stands as a monument to the involvement of staff of the Ashmolean Museum in the Roman archaeology of the region at that time. The account follows the general arrangements used in the *VCH*, surveying roads, town, other settlements and villas, a gazetteer of coins and another of finds in general. At first glance the coverage is remarkable, but a closer reading confirms how very ill-known many places of Roman interest were; many still are. The need for a new survey comes about precisely because of increases in both the amount of evidence and its quality.[41]

Archaeology was beginning to become a fashionable pursuit for the active young at about this time, just before the Second World War; combining as it did social intercourse between the sexes, physical activity and intellectual challenge archaeology was seen as an enjoyable activity. Although, unlike Cambridge, Oxford University did not have an Archaeology faculty until recently, a combination of courses in cognate disciplines such as Classics (Greats) or History with extra-curricular excavations and field surveys has ensured adequate training for professional archaeologists many of whom started off in the Oxford region. These include scholars such as Christopher Hawkes and J.H. Iliffe whose work at Alchester has been mentioned, A.H.A. Hogg and C.E. Stevens at Dorchester, Richard Goodchild at Woodeaton and Frilford and, in more recent times, Dennis Harding at Frilford, Christopher Young at the Churchill Hospital site and Eberhard Sauer on Aves Ditch and at Alchester again. The labour force for many of these excavations consisted of members of the University Archaeological Society, which made a very significant contribution to the archaeology of the Oxford region in this period.[42]

While some of these excavations were stimulated by pure research, in others, especially in more recent decades, there was a rescue need. The archaeological implications of the specific threat of gravel quarrying had indeed been well understood

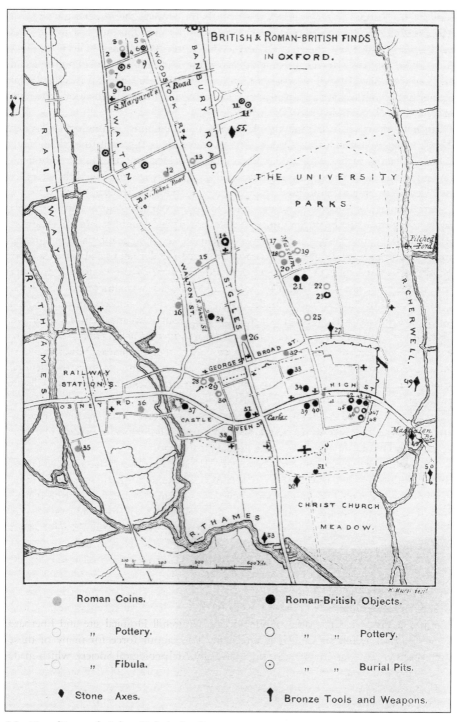

8.8 Map of Roman finds from Oxford, after Oman.

before the Second World War. Even at that time the resources were inadequate to deal with the rate of destruction of sites of all periods. As both the rate and scale of this destruction increased in the post-war period, the increased involvement of professional field archaeologists, who were neither University nor Museum based, became inevitable. At first the Oxfordshire (now Oxford) Archaeological Unit, founded in 1973, was an arm of local government largely limited to working within the county. Now it is one of a number of commercial organisations working in the region within the framework of the planning process.[43] The growth of developer-funded archaeology since legislation changes in 1990 has undoubtedly led to an increase in the volume of work being carried out in the region, with benefit to the database for the Roman as well as other periods.

The increasing scale of many excavation projects has vastly expanded the quantity, quality and range of types of evidence to be analysed and reported upon. This volume of material creates its own problems, but also provides opportunities for new avenues of enquiry and the development of more wide-ranging and sophisticated explanations of past activity. Most of the major developments in understanding of the Roman period in the region in recent times have sprung from large-scale projects, many of which are concerned with landscape as well as individual site-based issues, and all of which routinely involve examination of environmental remains as well as more traditional types of data. In some of these projects, such as Barton Court Farm, examination of the Roman activity has been the primary focus. In many others, like Abingdon, Yarnton or Gravelly Guy, Roman archaeology has formed part of a programme of work covering many different periods, with consequent increased understanding of landscape and settlement pattern developments over the long term. In some projects, the Roman component can seem very minor, but it can nevertheless provide important information about the use of whole landscapes at this time. All our discoveries have to be placed into context, local, national and even international: observations made for example about the economy of Roman Oxfordshire may have relevance to the history of the Roman Empire as a whole.

The important work of the University Archaeology Society has already been mentioned. Its essentially amateur tradition is still maintained in fieldwork. That

8.9 Fragment of second-century monumental inscription on Purbeck Marble, from the northern extramural settlement at Alchester. Width 125mm.

tradition is also exemplified by Dr Anthony Hands, whose work with A.C.C. Broddrib and D.R. Walker at Shakenoak provided one of only two recently excavated villa plans for the county, the publication of which led to the establishment of *British Archaeological Reports* (BAR), revolutionising archaeological publishing in Britain More recently his continuing work at Wilcote provides points of comparison both with Shakenoak and with the nearby Akeman Street settlement at Asthall. Local History and Archaeological Societies at Abingdon, Banbury, South Oxfordshire, Wallingford and The Wychwoods are all contributing to our understanding of the county.[44]

Dr Plot and Dr Stukeley would have been amazed by the range of techniques now employed, such as air photography which improves on Stukeley's 'bird's-eye' views or radiocarbon and remote sensing. They would no doubt have accepted the much more mature approach to art-history and iconography, inherited from the world of the *dilettanti*. No doubt Plot would have adjusted his beliefs in finding that Aves Ditch was pre-Roman, that Woodeaton was a temple and that Roman mosaics came from wealthy fourth-century great houses, probably owned by members of the local gentry. Stukeley would have been delighted that the White Horse belongs to Druidical times, but would have been distressed at continuing damage to sites such as Alchester by ploughing and unrecorded looting by plunderers armed with metal detectors – though he would have welcomed the responsible use of these machines by those who employ them for research.

Plot and Stukeley might well have been surprised, however, by the broad level of interest in the Roman past. Although in public perception 'the Romans' may conjure up images of legionary soldiers, as exemplified by display groups such as the Ermine Street Guard, the impression being built up by analysis of archaeological remains from the civilian parts of the province reveals more and more that 'the Romans' were for the most part the local inhabitants in Roman dress; in Roman dress because they wished to be thought of as Romans. The new Roman Britain is a far more complex entity. In order to understand the Roman Empire or Roman Britain we have to begin by looking at what happened in specific areas of the province. Oxfordshire, fortunately, provides more of interest than has generally been realised. It is opportune that the Oxfordshire County Museum Service is, at the same time, redesigning the Roman display at Woodstock in line with the approach taken in this book, thus providing a visual and material complement to our account.

NOTES

1. Parker 1868, 98–9 (on Birinus); Gelling 1953, 421, Ekwall 1960, 176 and Blair 1994, xxv (Fawler, *fagan floran*);Gelling 1953, 1 and Ekwall 1960, 4 (Akeman Street); Cunliffe 1983 (for The Ruin).
2. Cf. Parker 1885, 5–62; Smith 1964, 118 and 120 (Leland, f. 11 and 13).
3. Camden 1610, 377 (Alchester), 376 (Banbury), 384 (Dorchester).
4. Camden 1610, 281 (Wallingford); 377 (Akeman street); 377 (Oxford legend).
5. Plot 1705, 340 (Alchester); 341 (Elsfield), 339 (Henley); 338–9 (antiquity of Oxford University).

6. Plot 1705, 315–19, tab. xv, nos 19–21.

7. Plot 1705, 329 (Dyke Hills); 329 (Wallingford as Calleva); 324 (Pontes); 327–8 (Aves Ditch).

8. Plot 1705, 326–7 see Gibson 1695, 271; 334–5, tab. xv, no. 22. See Gibson 1695, 269.

9. Plot 1705, 335–7, tab. xv, nos 23 and 24.

10. Plot 1705, 355.

11. Kennett 1695, 7.

12. Kennett 1695, 11 and especially 13.

13. Munby 1977, 418–19 (Casaubon). Browne's *Concerning some urnes found in Brampton-Field, in Norfolk. Anno:1667* is freely available; Kennett 1695, 22–3, tab. 1. See *VCH*, 331.

14. Stukeley 1776, 41–2.

15. Stukeley 1776, 42 and 43. See Munby 1977, 428.

16. Stukeley 1776, 47.

17. Ibid.

18. Taylor 1941; Levine 1978/1987 and for a brief summary Munby 1977, 423–4 (modern sources). Burghers' original watercolour is in the Bodleian Library, Gough Gen. Top. 61, opp. p. 288. Hearne's Discourse is printed in Hearne 1712, pp.vii–xxxv; Pointer 1713. See Salter 1915, 254 (visit of John Strachey to Hearne). Mention of embroidery, Bodleian MS. Ballard 19ff, 61–2, cited in Levine 1987, 118 n. 50. Important new research has been undertaken by Tom Freshwater, Oxfordshire Museums. The Littlecote embroidery is reproduced on the back cover of the guidebook by P.A. Spreadbury (1979).

19. Doble 1889, 297 (Feb. 2; 4); 471–2 (Oct. 15); see p. 396 (general's tent); p. 309 ('curious gentleman').

20. Doble 1889, 400; ibid. 307–8. For the coin see Henig 1972, 210–11, pl. xiA citing Evans & Allen misidentifying coin as Mercury.

21. Doble 1889, 308; Rannie 1898, 254 cf Pointer 1713.

22. Salter 1915, 440

23. Salter 1921, 41; cf. Henig 1993, no. 180.

24. Taylor 1921, 6–7, pls i, ii.

25. Horsley 1733, 339, and see pp. 352–3. RIB 235 and *VCH*, 295–6, for full bibliography.

26. See RIB 2336 for the Elsfield base.

27. Lysons 1797 and 1813–17.

28. Hakewill 1826, pls 1–5.

29. Beesley 1841, 39–41, pl. x, fig. 1 (Beaconsfield Farm, Great Tew); 41–2, pl. xi (Wigginton).

30. Beesley 1841, 17 (Swalcliff); 23–4 (supposed amphitheatre at Banbury).

31. For the White Horse see Piggott 1989, 136–9. See Thoms 1846 and Akerman 1846. For recent work, Cromarty et al. forthcoming b.

32. Wetherall 1998.

33. Ibid., especially 28–32.

34. Parker 1862, 187.

35. Parker 1862, 189.

36. Parker 1868, 98–9.

37. Syer Cumming 1856 (Alchester), cf. Hussey 1841; *Proc. OAHS* N.S. iii (1879), 354 (Littlemore).

38. *Proc. OAHS* N.S.i (1861), 80; PSA 2nd ser. ii (1862), 85 (Duns Tew); Prof Rolleston, *Proc OAHS* N.S. ii (1867), 64 (Frilford); J.L. Myres, *Archaeologia Oxoniensis* (1895), 109–10 (Mansfield College pot); *Proc. Soc. Antiqs* 2nd ser. v (1872), 321 (Dorchester spoons); Henig & Munby 1973 (figurines).

39. [C. Oman], *Archaeologia Oxoniensis* (1895), with map. For rescue work on the Science Area in 1970–1, see Hassall 1972; especially useful is the inventory of sites, Munby 1972. For the most recent work see Booth 1999.

40. Radford 1936; Hogg & Stevens 1937; Bradford & Goodchild 1939.

41. M.V. Taylor, D.B. Harden & C.H.V. Sutherland, *VCH* I (1939), 267–345.

42. Hawkes 1927; Iliffe 1929; 1932; Hogg & Stevens 1937; Bradford & Goodchild 1939; Goodchild & Kirk 1954; Harding 1987; Young 1977; Sauer 1998a and b.

43. Miles 1998.

44. Brodribb et al. 1968–78; Hands 1993; 1998; for Abingdon see for example the multi-period reports of the Abingdon Excavation Committee in *Oxoniensia* 40 (1975), 1–121; Colin Clarke has issued an excellent interim report on the Crowmarsh cemetery (Wallingford Museum 1998).

BIBLIOGRAPHY

Ainslie 1988. R. Ainslie, 'Bladon Round Castle 1987', *South Midlands Archaeol.* 18, 94.

Ainslie 1992. R. Ainslie, 'Excavations at Thrupp near Radley, Oxon.', *South Midlands Archaeol.* 22, 63–5.

Akerman 1860. J.G. Akerman, 'Report on researches in an Anglo-Saxon cemetery at Long Wittenham', *Archaeologia* 38, 327–52.

Akerman 1865. J.G. Akerman, note in *Proc. Soc. Antiqs.* 3, 202–3.

Allen 1981. T. Allen, 'Hardwick with Yelford: Smith's Field', *Counc. Brit. Archaeol. Group 9 Newsletter* 11, 124–7.

Allen 1988. T.G. Allen, 'Excavations at Bury Close, Fawler, Oxon', *Oxoniensia* 53, 293–315.

Allen 1990a. T.G. Allen, *An Iron Age and Romano-British enclosed settlement at Watkins Farm, Northmoor, Oxon*, Thames Valley Landscapes, The Windrush Valley, Vol. 1, Oxford Univ. Committee for Archaeol., Oxford.

Allen 1990b. T. Allen, 'Abingdon Vineyard redevelopment', *South Midlands Archaeol.* 20, 73–8

Allen 1991. T.G. Allen, 'An 'oppidum' at Abingdon, Oxfordshire', *South Midlands Archaeol.* 21, 97–9.

Allen 1993. T.G. Allen, 'Abingdon, Abingdon Vineyard 1992: Areas 2 and 3, the Early Defences', *South Midlands Archaeol.* 23, 64–6.

Allen 1994. T.G. Allen, 'Abingdon, The Vineyard, Area 3', *South Midlands Archaeol.* 24, 32–3.

Allen 1995a. T. Allen, *Lithics and landscape: archaeological discoveries on the Thames Water pipeline at Gatehampton Farm, Goring, Oxfordshire 1985–92*, Thames Valley Landscapes Monograph No. 7, Oxford Archaeol. Unit.

Allen 1995b. T.G. Allen, 'Abingdon, The Vineyard: Area 2 watching brief', *South Midlands Archaeol.* 25, 49.

Allen 1997. T.G. Allen, 'Abingdon: West Central Redevelopment Area', *South Midlands Archaeol.* 27, 47–54.

Allen 1998. T.G. Allen, *Abingdon Abbey Gardens and Abbey Meadows, Historical Restoration Management Plan. Appendix 1: Archaeological background to the Study Area*, Oxford Archaeol. Unit unpublished report.

Allen et al. 1984. T. Allen, D. Miles & S. Palmer, 'Iron Age buildings in the Upper Thames region', in B. Cunliffe & D. Miles (eds), *Aspects of the Iron Age in Central Southern Britain*, Univ. Oxford Committee for Archaeol. Monograph 2, 89–101.

Allen et al. 1993. T.G. Allen, T.C. Darvill, L.S. Green & M.U. Jones, *Excavations at Roughground Farm, Lechlade, Gloucestershire: a prehistoric and Roman landscape*, Thames Valley Landscapes: the Cotswold Water Park Vol. 1, Oxford Univ. Committee Archaeol. (Oxford).

Allen et al. 1997. T. Allen, G. Hey & D. Miles, 'A line of time: approaches to archaeology in the Upper and Middle Thames Valley, England', in J. Graham-Campbell (ed.), 'Riverine Archaeology', *World Archaeology* 29:1, 114–29.

Allen & Moore 1987. T.G. Allen & J. Moore, 'Standlake: Eagle Farm', *South Midlands Archaeol.* 17, 96–7.

Allen & Robinson 1993. T.G. Allen & M.A. Robinson, *The prehistoric landscape and Iron Age enclosed settlement at Mingies Ditch, Hardwick-with-Yelford, Oxon.*, Thames Valley Landscapes: the Windrush Valley Vol. 2.

Aston 1974a. M. Aston, *Stonesfield slate*, Oxfordshire County Council Dept of Museum Services Publication No. 5.

Aston 1974b. M. Aston, 'The Roman defences at Dorchester, Oxon. – an interim assessment', *Counc. Brit. Archaeol. Group 9 Newsletter* 4, 3–4.

Atkinson 1916. D. Atkinson, *The Romano-British site on Lowbury Hill in Berkshire*, Reading.

Atkinson 1942. R.J.C. Atkinson, 'Archaeological sites on Port Meadow, Oxford,' *Oxoniensia* 7, 24–35.

Atkinson 1952–3. R.J.C. Atkinson, 'Excavations in Barrow Hills Field, Radley, Berks, 1944–5', *Oxoniensia* 17–18, 14–35.

Avery et al. 1967. D.M.E. Avery, J.E.G. Sutton & J.W. Banks, 'Rainsborough, Northants, England: Excavations 1961–5', *Proc. Prehist. Soc.* 33, 207–306.

Bagnall Smith 1995. J. Bagnall Smith, 'Interim report on the votive material from Romano-Celtic temple sites in Oxfordshire', *Oxoniensia* 60, 177–203.

Bagnall Smith 1998. J. Bagnall Smith, 'More votive finds from Woodeaton, Oxfordshire', *Oxoniensia* 63, 147–85.

Barber & Walker 1999. A. Barber & G. Walker, 'Wantage, land off Stockholm Way/ Denchworth Road', *South Midlands Archaeol.* 29, 43.

Barclay & Halpin 1999. A. Barclay & C. Halpin, *Excavations at Barrow Hills, Radley, Oxfordshire, Volume I. The Neolithic and Bronze Age monument complex*, Oxford Archaeol. Unit Thames Valley Landscapes Monograph No. 11.

Barclay et al. 1995. A. Barclay, M. Gray & G. Lambrick, *Excavations at the Devil's Quoits, Stanton Harcourt, Oxfordshire 1972–3 and 1988*, Thames Valley Landscapes: The Windrush Valley, Vol. 3, Oxford Archaeol. Unit.

Barnes et al. 1997. I. Barnes, C.A. Butterworth, J.W. Hawkes & L. Smith, *Excavations at Thames Valley Park, Reading, 1986–8*, Wessex Archaeol. Report No. 14, Nottingham.

Barrett 1991. A.A. Barrett, 'Claudius' British victory arch in Rome', *Britannia* 22, 1–19.

Bassett et al. 1992. S. Bassett, C. Dyer & R. Holt, 'Introduction', in S. Bassett (ed.), *Death in towns: urban responses to the dying and the dead, 100–1600*, Leicester, 1–7.

Beesley 1841. A. Beesley, *The history of Banbury*.

Bell & Hey 1996. C. Bell & G. Hey, 'Yarnton Cresswell Field', *South Midlands Archaeol.* 26, 63 and 65.

Benson & Brown 1969. D. Benson & P.D.C. Brown, 'Roman burials from Ardley, Oxon.', *Oxoniensia* 34, 107–11.

Benson & Miles 1974. D. Benson & D. Miles, *The Upper Thames Valley: An Archaeological Survey of the River Gravels*, Oxford.

Bird & Young 1981. J. Bird & C. Young, 'Migrant potters – the Oxford connection', in A.C. & A.S. Anderson (eds), *Roman pottery research in Britain and north-west Europe*, Brit. Archaeol. Rep. (Int. Ser.) 123, Oxford, 295–312.

Birley 1979. A. Birley, *The people of Roman Britain*, London.

Black 1995. E.W. Black, *Cursus Publicus, the infrastructure of government in Roman Britain*, Brit. Archaeol. Rep. (Brit. Ser.) 241, Oxford.

Blair 1994. J. Blair, *Anglo-Saxon Oxfordshire*, Stroud.

Bland & Johns 1993. R. Bland & C. Johns, *The Hoxne treasure. An illustrated introduction*, London, British Museum.

Bland & Orna-Ornstein 1997. R. Bland & J. Orna-Ornstein, 'Didcot, Oxfordshire', in R. Bland & J. Orna-Ornstein (eds), *Coin Hoards from Roman Britain Volume X*, 91–100, British Museum.

Böhme 1986. H.W. Böhme, 'Das Ende der Römerherrschaft in Britannien und die Angelsächsische Besiedlung Englands im 5. Jahrhundert', *Jahrbuch des Römisch-Germanischen Zentralmuseums Mainz* 33, 469–574.

Boon 1958. G.C. Boon, 'A Roman pastrycook's mould from Silchester', *Antiqs J.* 38, 237–40.

Boon 1994. G.C. Boon, 'The coins', in M.J. Fulford & S. Rippon, 'Lowbury Hill, Oxon: a Re-Assessment of the Probable Romano-Celtic Temple and the Anglo-Saxon Barrow', *Archaeol. J.* 151, 173–7.

Booth 1990. P. Booth, 'Ducklington: Gill Mill', *Oxford Archaeol. Unit Newsletter* 18 No. 3, 19–23.

Booth 1996. P. Booth, *Orchard House, Asthall, Oxfordshire, SP 2885 1109, Archaeological Watching Brief Report*, Oxford Archaeol. Unit unpublished report.

Booth 1997. P.M. Booth, *Asthall, Oxfordshire, excavations in a Roman 'small town', 1992*, Thames Valley Landscapes Monograph 9, Oxford Archaeol. Unit.

Booth 1998. P. Booth, 'The regional archaeological setting of the Roman roadside settlement at Wilcote – a summary', in A.R. Hands, *The Romano-British roadside settlement at Wilcote, Oxfordshire II. Excavations 1993–96*, Brit. Archaeol. Rep.(Brit. Ser.) 265, Oxford, 9–20.

Booth 1999. P. Booth, 'Oxford, Mansfield College, proposed Institute for American Studies', *South Midlands Archaeol.* 29, 79.

Booth forthcoming a. P. Booth, 'Quantifying status: some pottery data from the Upper Thames Valley', *J. Roman Pottery Stud.*

Booth forthcoming b. P. Booth, 'Ralegh Radford and the Roman villa at Ditchley: a review', *Oxoniensia*.

Booth & Green 1989. P. Booth & S. Green, 'The nature and distribution of certain pink, grog tempered vessels', *J. Roman Pottery Stud.* 2, 77–84.

Booth & Hardy 1993. P. Booth & A. Hardy, *Appleford Sidings, near Didcot, Oxfordshire: Archaeological Evaluation*, Oxford Archaeol. Unit unpublished report.

Booth et al. 1993. P. Booth, A. Boyle & G.D. Keevill, 'A Romano-British kiln site at Lower Farm, Nuneham Courtenay, and other sites on the Didcot to Oxford and Wootton to Abingdon water mains, Oxfordshire', *Oxoniensia* 58, 87–217.

Booth et al. forthcoming. P. Booth, J. Hiller & J. Evans, *Excavations in the Extramural Settlement of Roman Alchester, 1991*, Oxford Archaeol. Unit Thames Valley Landscapes Monograph.

Bowden et al. 1991–3. M. Bowden, S. Ford & G. Mees, 'The date of the ancient fields on the Berkshire Downs, *Berkshire Archaeol. J.* 74, 109–33.

Bowman 1986. A.K. Bowman, *Egypt after the Pharaohs 332 BC–AD642*, London.

Boyle et al. 1995. A. Boyle, A. Dodd, D. Miles & A. Mudd, *Two Oxfordshire Anglo-Saxon cemeteries: Berinsfield and Didcot*, Thames Valley Landscapes Monograph No. 8, Oxford Archaeol. Unit.

Boyle & Chambers in prep. A. Boyle & R.A. Chambers, 'The Romano-British cemetery', in R.A. Chambers & E. Macadam, *Excavations at Barrow Hills, Radley, Oxfordshire. Volume II: the Romano-British cemetery and Anglo-Saxon settlement*, Oxford Archaeol. Unit Thames Valley Landscapes Monograph.

Bradford & Goodchild 1939. J.S.P. Bradford & R.G. Goodchild, 'Excavations at Frilford, Berks., 1937–8', *Oxoniensia* 4, 1–70.

Bradley 1978. R. Bradley, 'Rescue excavation in Dorchester-on-Thames 1972', *Oxoniensia* 43, 17–39.

Bradley & Ellison 1975. R. Bradley & A. Ellison, *Rams Hill: A Bronze Age Defended Enclosure and its Landscape*, Brit. Archaeol. Rep. (Brit. Ser.) 19, Oxford.

Branigan 1989. K. Branigan, 'Specialisation in villa economies', in K. Branigan & D. Miles (eds), *The economies of Romano-British villas*, Sheffield, 42–50.

Brodribb et al. 1968. A.C.C. Brodribb, A.R. Hands & D.R. Walker, *Excavations at Shakenoak Farm, near Wilcote, Oxfordshire, Part I: sites A and D*, Oxford.

Brodribb et al. 1971. A.C.C. Brodribb, A.R. Hands & D.R. Walker, *Excavations at Shakenoak Farm, near Wilcote, Oxfordshire, Part II: Sites B and H*, Oxford.

Brodribb et al. 1972. A.C.C. Brodribb, A.R. Hands & D.R. Walker, *Excavations at Shakenoak Farm, near Wilcote, Oxfordshire, Part III: Site F*, Oxford.

Brodribb et al. 1973. A.C.C. Brodribb, A.R. Hands & D.R. Walker, *Excavations at Shakenoak Farm, near Wilcote, Oxfordshire, Part IV: Site C*, Oxford.

Brodribb et al. 1978. A.C.C. Brodribb, A.R. Hands & D.R. Walker, *Excavations at Shakenoak Farm, near Wilcote, Oxfordshire, Part V: Sites K and E*, Oxford.

Brown 1973. P.D.C. Brown, 'A Roman pewter hoard from Appleford, Berks', *Oxoniensia* 38, 184–206.

Brown 1994. A. Brown, 'A Romano-British shell-gritted pottery and tile manufacturing site at Harrold, Beds', *Bedfordshire Archaeol.* 21, 19–107.

Bulleid & Gray 1917. A. Bulleid & H.St.G. Gray, *The Glastonbury Lake village, a full description of the excavations and the relics discovered, 1892–1907*, Vol. 2, Glastonbury.

Burnham & Wacher 1990. B.C. Burnham & J.S. Wacher, *The 'small towns' of Roman Britain*, London.

Buschhausen 1971. H. Buschhausen, *Die Spätröischen metallscrinia und Frühchristlichen Reliquiare*, Vienna.

Buxton 1921. L.H.D. Buxton, 'Excavations at Frilford', *Antiqs. J.* 1, 87–97.

Camden 1610. W. Camden, *A chorographical description of Great Britain and Ireland*, 1st English edn.

Campbell 1994. G. Campbell, *Tower Hill, Ashbury, Oxon: Post-excavation assessment and research design*, Oxford Archaeol. Unit unpublished report for English Heritage.

Case 1958. H. Case, 'A late Belgic burial at Watlington, Oxon', *Oxoniensia* 23, 139–42.

Case 1982. H.J. Case, 'Cassington, 1950–2: late Neolithic pits and the Big Enclosure', in H.J. Case & A.W.R. Whittle (eds), *Settlement patterns in the Oxford Region: excavations at the Abingdon causewayed enclosure and other sites*, Counc. Brit. Archaeol. Res. Rep. 44, London, 118–51.

Case et al. 1964. H. Case, N. Bayne, S. Steele, G. Avery & H. Sutermeister, 'Excavations at City Farm, Hanborough', *Oxoniensia* 29/30, 1–98.

Chambers 1976. R.A. Chambers, 'A Roman settlement at Curbridge', *Oxoniensia* 41, 38–55.

Chambers 1978. R.A. Chambers, 'The archaeology of the Charlbury to Arncott gas pipeline, Oxon, 1972', *Oxoniensia* 43, 40–7.

Chambers 1981. R. Chambers, 'Asthall', *Counc. Brit. Archaeol. Group 9 Newsletter* 11, 114.

Chambers 1986. R.A. Chambers, 'A Roman timber bridge at Ivy Farm, Fencott with Murcott, Oxon.', *Oxoniensia* 51, 31–6.

Chambers 1987. R.A. Chambers, 'The Late- and Sub-Roman Cemetery at Queenford Farm, Dorchester-on-Thames, Oxon.', *Oxoniensia* 52, 35–69.

Chambers 1988. R.A. Chambers, 'Stanford-in-the-Vale: Bowling Green Farm', *South Midlands Archaeol.* 18, 87.

Chambers 1989a. R.A. Chambers, 'Bicester: South Farm Development, *South Midlands Archaeol.* 19, 49–50.

Chambers 1989b. R.A. Chambers, 'Stanford in the Vale: Bowling Green Farm', *South Midlands Archaeol.* 19, 54–5.

Chambers 1990. R.A. Chambers, 'Stanford in the Vale, Bowling Green Farm sand quarry', *South Midlands Archaeol.* 20, 82.

Cheetham 1995. C.J. Cheetham, 'Some Roman and Pre-Roman Settlements and Roads by the Confluence of the Cherwell and the Ray near Otmoor', *Oxoniensia* 60, 419–26.

Clare 1993. H. Clare, 'Roman panpipes found in London', *London Archaeologist* 7, no. 4, 87–92.

Clarke & Fulford 1998. A. Clarke & M. Fulford, *Silchester Roman town. The Insula IX 'Town Life' project*.

Clarke 1996. C.M. Clarke, 'Excavations at Cold Harbour Farm, Crowmarsh', *South Midlands Archaeol.* 26, 71–6.

Clarke 1997. C.M. Clarke, *Excavations of a Roman-British cemetery – Cold Harbour Farm – Crowmarsh – Wallingford – Oxfordshire*, Wallingford Hist. and Archaeol. Soc. report (unpublished).

Clifford 1961. E.M. Clifford, *Bagendon: a Belgic Oppidum*, Cambridge.

Collis 1984. J.R. Collis, *Oppida: earliest towns north of the Alps*, Sheffield.

Cook 1955. P.M.M. Cook, 'A Roman site at Asthall, Oxfordshire', *Oxoniensia* 20, 29–39.

Cool & Price 1995. H.E.M. Cool & J. Price, *Roman glass from excavations at Colchester, 1971–85*, Colchester Archaeol. Rep. 8.

Corney & Griffiths forthcoming. M. Corney & N. Griffiths, *A reappraisal of late Roman belt fittings in Britain*.

Crawford 1930. O.G.S. Crawford, 'Grim's Ditch in Wychwood, Oxon.', *Antiquity* 4, 303–15.

Crawford 1983. G. Crawford, 'Excavations at Wasperton: 3rd interim report', *West Midlands Archaeol.* 26, 15–27.

Cromarty et al. forthcoming a. A.M. Cromarty, S. Foreman & P. Murray, 'The excavation of a late Iron Age enclosed site at Bicester Fields Farm, Bicester, Oxfordshire, 1998', *Oxoniensia*.

Cromarty et al. forthcoming b. A.M. Cromarty, C. Gosden, G. Lock, D. Miles & S. Palmer, *Investigations at White Horse Hill, Uffington and Tower Hill, Ashbury: the development of ancestral landscapes*, Thames Valley Landscapes Monograph, Oxford Archaeol. Unit.

Cromarty et al. forthcoming c. A.M. Cromarty, A. Barclay & G. Lambrick, *Settlement and landscape: the archaeology of the Wallingford Bypass*, Thames Valley Landscapes Monograph, Oxford Archaeol. Unit.

Cropper & Hardy 1997. C. Cropper & A. Hardy, 'The excavation of Iron Age and medieval features at Glympton Park, Oxfordshire', *Oxoniensia* 62, 101–7.

Cunliffe 1983. B. Cunliffe, 'Earth's grip holds them', in B. Hartley & J. Wacher (eds), *Roman and her northern provinces*, Gloucester, 67–83.

Cunliffe 1991a. B. Cunliffe, *Iron Age communities in Britain*, 3rd edn, London.

Cunliffe 1991b. B. Cunliffe, 'Fishbourne revisited: the site in its context', *J. Roman Archaeol.* 4, 160–9.

Dark 1994. K.R. Dark, *Civitas to Kingdom. British political continuity 300–800*, Leicester.

Dark 1996. K.R. Dark, 'Pottery and local production at the end of Roman Britain', in K.R. Dark (ed.), *External contacts and the economy of late Roman and post-Roman Britain*, Woodbridge, 53–65.

Darvill & Holbrook 1994. T. Darvill & N. Holbrook, 'The Cirencester area in the prehistoric and early Roman periods', in T. Darvill & C. Gerrard, *Cirencester: town and landscape, an urban archaeological assessment*, Cirencester, 47–56.

Davey & Ling 1981. N. Davey & R. Ling, *Wall-painting in Roman Britain*, Britannia Monograph No. 3.

Day 1991. S.P. Day, 'Post-glacial vegetational history of the Oxford region', *New Phytologist* 119, 445–70.

Dickinson 1976. T.M. Dickinson, *The Anglo-Saxon burial sites of the Upper Thames Region and their bearing on the history of Wessex, circa AD 400–700*, Oxford D. Phil. thesis (unpublished).

Dimes 1980. F.G. Dimes, 'Petrological report', in C. Hill, M. Millett & T. Blagg, *The Roman riverside wall and monumental arch in London*, London and Middlesex Archaeol. Soc. Special Paper 3, 198–200.

Doble 1889. C.E. Doble, *Remarks and collections of Thomas Hearne, Vol. iii 1710–1712*, Oxford Historical Society.

Dodwell 1982. C.R. Dodwell, *Anglo-Saxon art. A new perspective*, Manchester.

Dunning 1976. G.C. Dunning, 'Salmondsbury, Bourton-on-the-Water, Gloucestershire', in D.W. Harding (ed.), *Hillforts. Later Prehistoric Earthworks in Britain and Ireland*, London, 76–118.

Durham & Rowley 1972. B. Durham & T. Rowley, 'A Cemetery Site at Queensford Mill, Dorchester', *Oxoniensia* 37, 32–7.

Eames 1998. B.W. Eames, *The archaeology of Swalcliffe Lea*, OUDCE Diploma in Applied Archaeology dissertation (unpublished).

Eddershaw 1972. D.G.T. Eddershaw, 'Roman finds at Glyme Farm, Chipping Norton', *Oxoniensia* 37, 242.

Ekwall 1960. E. Ekwall, *The concise Oxford dictionary of place-names*, 4th edn.

Ellis 1986. S.E. Ellis, 'Report on the stones from the Temple of Mithras' in J.M.C. Toynbee, *The Roman art treasures from the Temple of Mithras*, London and Middlesex Archaeol. Soc. Special Paper 7, 64–5.

Ellis 1999. P. Ellis, 'North Leigh Roman villa, Oxfordshire: a report on excavation and recording in the 1970s', *Britannia* 30, 199–245.

Esmonde Cleary 1989. A.S. Esmonde Cleary, *The ending of Roman Britain*, London.

Esmonde Cleary 1999. S. Esmonde Cleary, 'The Roman coins and counterfeiter's hoard', in P. Ellis, 'North Leigh Roman villa, Oxfordshire: a report on excavation and recording in the 1970s', *Britannia* 30, 217–25.

Everett & Eeles forthcoming. R.N. Everett & B.M.G. Eeles, 'Investigations at Thrupp House Farm, Radley', *Oxoniensia*

Evison 1965. V.I. Evison, *The fifth-century invasions south of the Thames*, London.

Farwell & Molleson 1993. D.E. Farwell & T.I. Molleson, *Poundbury. 2 The cemeteries*, Dorset Nat. Hist. Archaeol. Soc. Monograph 11.

Fitzpatrick 1984. A.P. Fitzpatrick, 'The deposition of La Tène Iron Age metalwork in watery contexts in Southern England', in B. Cunliffe & D. Miles (eds), *Aspects of the Iron Age in Central Southern Britain*, Oxford Univ. Committee for Archaeol. Monograph 2, 178–90.

Ford 1982a. S. Ford, 'Fieldwork and excavation on the Berkshire Grims Ditch', *Oxoniensia* 47, 13–36.

Ford 1982b. S. Ford, 'Linear earthworks on the Berkshire Downs', *Berks Archaeol. J.* 71, 1–20.

Ford et al. 1988. S. Ford, M. Bowden, G. Mees & V. Gaffney, 'The date of the 'Celtic' Field-Systems on the Berkshire Downs', *Britannia* 19, 401–4.

Ford 1996. W.J. Ford, 'Anglo-Saxon cemeteries along the Avon Valley', *Trans. Birmingham Warwickshire Archaeol. Soc.* 100, 59–98.

Foreman & Rahtz 1984. M. Foreman & S. Rahtz, 'Excavations at Faccenda Chicken Farm, near Alchester, 1983', *Oxoniensia* 49, 23–46.

Foster 1989. A.M. Foster, 'Alchester, Oxon.: a brief review and new aerial evidence', *Britannia* 20, 141–7.

Fowler 1960. P.J. Fowler, 'Excavations at Madmarston Camp, Swalcliffe, 1957–8', *Oxoniensia* 25, 3–48.

Fowler 1978. P.J. Fowler, 'The Abingdon ard-share', in M. Parrington *The excavation of an Iron Age settlement, Bronze Age ring-ditches and Roman features at Ashville Trading Estate, Abingdon (Oxfordshire) 1974–76*, Counc. Brit. Archaeol. Res. Rep. 28, 83–8.

Fowler 1983. P.J. Fowler, *The Farming of Prehistoric Britain*, Cambridge.

Frederiksen 1976. M.W. Frederiksen, 'Changes in the patterns of settlement', in P. Zanker, *Hellenismus in Mittelitalien*, 341–55.

Frend 1992. W.H.C. Frend, 'Pagans, christians and "the barbarian conspiracy" of A.D. 367 in Roman Britain', *Britannia* 23, 121–31.

Frere 1962. S.S. Frere, 'Excavations at Dorchester-on-Thames 1962', *Archaeol. J.* 119, 114–49.

Frere 1983. S. Frere, *Verulamium excavations II* Soc. Antiqs. London Res. Rep. 41.

Frere 1984. S.S. Frere, 'Excavations at Dorchester-on-Thames, 1963', *Archaeol. J.* 141, 91–174.

Frere 1987. S. Frere, *Britannia, A History of Roman Britain*, 3rd edn, London.

Frere & St Joseph 1983. S.S. Frere & J.K.S. St Joseph, *Roman Britain from the air*, Cambridge.

Fuentes 1983. N. Fuentes, 'Boudicca re-visited', *London Archaeologist* 4, 311–17.

Fulford & Hodder 1974. M.G. Fulford & I. Hodder, 'A regression analysis of some later Romano-British pottery: a case study' *Oxoniensia* 39, 26–33.

Fulford & Rippon 1994. M.J. Fulford & S. Rippon, 'Lowbury Hill, Oxon: a Re-Assessment of the Probable Romano-Celtic Temple and the Anglo-Saxon Barrow', *Archaeol. J.* 151, 158–211.

Funari 1996. P.P.A. Funari, *Dressel 20 inscriptions from Britain and the consumption of Spanish olive oil*, Brit. Archaeol. Rep. (Brit. Ser.) 250, Oxford.

Gaffney & Tingle 1989. V. Gaffney & M. Tingle, *The Maddle Farm Project: an integrated survey of Prehistoric and Roman landscapes on the Berkshire Downs*, Brit. Archaeol. Rep. (Brit. Ser.) 200, Oxford.

Gelling 1953. M. Gelling, *The place-names of Oxfordshire, parts i and ii*.

Gelling 1974. M. Gelling, *The place-names of Berkshire, part ii*.

Gent 1983. H. Gent, 'Centralised storage in later Prehistoric Britain', *Proc. Prehist. Soc.* 49, 243–67.

Gibson 1695. E. Gibson, *Camden's Britannia, newly translated into English with large additions and improvements*.

Gingell 1981. C. Gingell, 'Excavation of an Iron Age enclosure at Groundwell Farm, Blunsdon St. Andrew, 1976–7', *Wilts Archaeol. Magazine* 76, 33–75.

Giorgi & Robinson 1984. J.A. Giorgi & M.A. Robinson, 'The environment', in M. Foreman & S. Rahtz, 'Excavations at Faccenda Chicken Farm, near Alchester, 1983', *Oxoniensia* 49, 38–45.

Goodburn & Henig 1998. R. Goodburn & M. Henig, 'A Roman intaglio from Frilford', *Oxoniensia* 63, 239–40.

Goodchild & Kirk 1954. R. Goodchild & J.R. Kirk, 'The Roman temple at Woodeaton', *Oxoniensia* 19, 15–37.

Gosden & Lock 1999. C. Gosden & G. Lock, 'The hillforts of the Ridgeway Project: excavations at Alfred's Castle 1998', *South Midlands Archaeol.* 29, 44–53.

Gray 1973. M. Gray, 'A Romano-British Site at Camp Corner, Milton Common', *Oxoniensia* 38, 6–22.

Gray 1977. M. Gray, 'Northfield Farm, Long Wittenham' *Oxoniensia* 42, 1–29.

Green 1989. M. Green, *Symbol and image in Celtic religious art*, London.

Green 1983. S. Green, 'The Roman pottery manufacturing site at Between Towns Road, Cowley, Oxford', *Oxoniensia* 48, 1–12.

Grimes 1943. W.F. Grimes, 'Excavations at Stanton Harcourt, Oxon., 1940,' *Oxoniensia* 8–9, 19–63.

Grundon 1999. I. Grundon, 'Finmere, Gravel Farm and Foxley Fields Farm', *South Midlands Archaeol.* 29, 31–5.

Hakewill 1826. H. Hakewill, *An account of the Roman villa discovered at Northleigh Oxfordshire in the years 1813, 1814, 1815, 1816*.

Hamerow 1993. H. Hamerow, 'Anglo-Saxon cemetery at West Hendred', *Anglo Saxon Studies in Archaeol. and History* 6.

Hamerow 1994. H. Hamerow, 'Migration theory and the migration period', in B. Vyner (ed.), *Building on the past: papers celebrating 150 years of the Royal Archaeological Institute*, London, 164–77.

Hamlin 1963. A. Hamlin, 'Excavation of ring-ditches and other sites at Stanton Harcourt', *Oxoniensia* 28, 1–9.

Hamlin 1966. A. Hamlin, 'Early Iron Age sites at Stanton Harcourt', *Oxoniensia* 31, 1–27.

Hands 1993. A.R. Hands, *The Romano-British roadside settlement at Wilcote, Oxfordshire I. Excavations 1990–92*, Brit. Archaeol. Rep. (Brit. Ser.) 232, Oxford.

Hands 1998. A.R. Hands, *The Romano-British roadside settlement at Wilcote, Oxfordshire II. Excavations 1993–96*, Brit. Archaeol. Rep. (Brit. Ser.) 265, Oxford.

Harden 1937a. D.B. Harden, 'Excavations at Chesterton Lane, Alchester, 1937', *Oxfordshire Archaeol. Soc. Report* 83, 23–39.

Harden 1937b. D.B. Harden, 'Excavations on Grim's Dyke, North Oxfordshire', *Oxoniensia* 2, 74–92.

Harding 1972. D.W. Harding, *The Iron Age in the Upper Thames Basin*, Oxford.

Harding 1987. D.W. Harding, *Excavations in Oxfordshire, 1964–66*, Univ. of Edinburgh Dept. of Archaeol. Occ. Paper No. 15.

Harman et al. 1978. M. Harman, G. Lambrick, D. Miles & T. Rowley, 'Roman Burials around Dorchester-on-Thames,' *Oxoniensia* 43, 1–16.

Harris & Young 1974. E. Harris & C.J. Young, 'The "Overdale" kiln site at Boar's Hill, near Oxford,' *Oxoniensia* 39, 12–25.

Haselgrove 1987. C.C. Haselgrove, *Iron Age Coinage in South-East England: the archaeological context*, Brit. Archaeol. Rep. (Brit. Ser.) 174, Oxford.

Hassall 1952/3. M. Hassall, 'A pottery mould from Horsepath, Oxon', *Oxoniensia* 17/18, 231–4.

Hassall & Tomlin 1989. M.W.C. Hassall & R.S.O. Tomlin, 'Roman Britain in 1988. Inscriptions', *Britannia* 20, 327–45.

Hassall & Tomlin 1993. M.W.C. Hassall & R.S.O. Tomlin, 'Roman Britain in 1992. Inscriptions', *Britannia* 24, 310–22.

Hassall & Tomlin 1996. M.W.C. Hassall & R.S.O. Tomlin, 'Roman Britain in 1995. Inscriptions', *Britannia* 27, 439–57.

Hassall 1972. T.G. Hassall, 'Roman Finds from the Radcliffe Science Library Extension, Oxford, 1970–71', *Oxoniensia* 37, 38–50.

Hassan 1981. F.A. Hassan, *Demographic Archaeology*, London.

Hattatt 1987. R. Hattatt, *Brooches of antiquity*, Oxford.

Hawkes 1927. C. Hawkes, 'Excavations at Alchester, 1926' *Antiqs. J.* 7, 155–84.

Hawkes 1986. S.C. Hawkes, 'The Early Saxon Period', in G. Briggs, J. Cook & T. Rowley (eds), *The Archaeology of the Oxford Region*, Oxford University Department of External Studies, 64–108.

Hawkes & Dunning 1961. S.C. Hawkes & G.C. Dunning, 'Soldiers and settlers in Britain, fourth to fifth century, with a catalogue of animal-ornamented buckles and related belt-fittings', *Medieval Archaeol.* 5, 1–70.

Henig 1970a. M. Henig, 'Woodeaton intaglios', *Oxoniensia* 35, 105–6.

Henig 1970b. M. Henig, 'Zoomorphic supports of cast bronze from Roman sites in Britain', *Archaeol. J.* 127, 182–97.

Henig 1971. M. Henig, 'A bronze figurine possibly from Woodeaton in the Guildhall Museum, London', *Oxoniensia* 36, 106–7.

Henig 1972. M. Henig, 'The origin of some Ancient British coin types', *Britannia* 3, 209–23.

Henig 1974. M. Henig, 'A gold ring found near Oxford', *Oxoniensia* 39, 97–8.

Henig 1975. M. Henig, 'A signet-ring from Roman Alchester', *Oxoniensia* 40, 325–6.

Henig 1976. M. Henig, 'A Roman tripod-mount from the G.P.O. site, London', *Antiqs. J.* 56, 248–9.

Henig 1977. M. Henig, 'A glass ring from Shakenoak', *Oxoniensia* 42, 260–1.

Henig 1978. M. Henig, *A corpus of Roman engraved gemstones from British sites*, Brit. Archaeol. Rep. (Brit. Ser.) 8, 2nd edn, Oxford.

Henig 1984. M. Henig, *Religion in Roman Britain*, London.

Henig 1990. M. Henig, 'A silver ring from the Wendlebury area', *Oxoniensia* 55, 167–8.

Henig 1993. M. Henig, *Roman sculpture from the Cotswold Region with Devon and Cornwall*, Corpus Signorum Imperii Romani, Great Britain, Vol. 1, Fascicule 7, Oxford.

Henig 1995. M. Henig, *The art of Roman Britain*, London.

Henig 1999a. M. Henig, 'A jeweller's die from Alchester, Oxfordshire', *Antiqs. J.* 79.

Henig 1999b. M. Henig, 'A silver ring-bezel from Gastard, Corsham', *Wilts. Archaeol. Mag.* 92, 125–6.

Henig 1999c. M. Henig, 'A new star shining over Bath', *Oxford J. Archaeol.* 18, 419–25.

Henig 2000. M. Henig, 'From Classical Greece to Roman Britain: some Hellenic themes in provincial art and glyptics', in G.R. Tsetskhladze, A.M. Snodgrass & A.J.N.W. Prag, *Periplous: to Sir John Boardman from his pupils and friends*, London, 124–35.

Henig & Cannon forthcoming. M. Henig & P. Cannon, 'A sceptre-head for the Matres-cult and other objects from West Berkshire', *Britannia* 31.

Henig & Chambers 1984. M. Henig & R.A. Chambers, 'Two bronze birds from Oxfordshire', *Oxoniensia* 49, 19–21.

Henig & Hornby 1991. M. Henig & S. Hornby, 'A cornelian intaglio from Blackthorn Hill, near Bicester', *Oxoniensia* 56, 169–71.

Henig & Munby 1973. M. Henig & J. Munby, 'Three bronze figurines', *Oxoniensia* 38, 386–7.

Henig & Soffe 1993. M. Henig & G. Soffe, 'The Thruxton Roman villa and its mosaic pavement', *J. Brit. Archaeol. Assoc.* 146, 1–28.

Henig & Wilkins 1982. M. Henig & R. Wilkins, 'A Roman intaglio showing the genius of comedy' *Antiqs. J.* 62, 280–1.

Heurgon 1958. J. Heurgon, *Le trésor de Ténès*, Paris.

Hey 1991. G. Hey, 'Yarnton Worton Rectory Farm' *South Midlands Archaeol.* 21, 86–92.

Hey 1995. G. Hey, 'Iron Age and Roman Settlement at Old Shifford Farm, Standlake', *Oxoniensia* 60, 93–175.

Hey 1996. G. Hey, 'Yarnton floodplain', *South Midlands Archaeol.* 26, 63–7.

Hey forthcoming. G. Hey, *Yarnton: Saxon and medieval settlement and landscape*, Thames Valley Landscapes Monograph, Oxford Archaeol. Unit.

Hey et al. 1999. G. Hey, A. Bayliss & A. Boyle, 'Iron Age inhumation burials at Yarnton, Oxfordshire', *Antiquity* 73 no. 281, 551–62.

Hinchliffe & Thomas 1980. J. Hinchliffe & R. Thomas, 'Archaeological investigations at Appleford', *Oxoniensia* 45, 9–111.

Hingley 1982. R. Hingley, 'Recent discoveries of the Roman period at the Noah's Ark Inn, Frilford, South Oxfordshire', *Britannia* 13, 305–9.

Hingley 1983a. R. Hingley, *Iron Age and Romano-British Society in the Upper Thames Valley: an Analysis in terms of Modes of Production*, University of Southampton Ph. D. thesis (unpublished).

Hingley 1983b. R. Hingley, 'Excavations by R.A. Rutland on an Iron Age site at Wittenham Clumps', *Berkshire Archaeol. J.* 70, 21–55.

Hingley 1984. R. Hingley, 'Towards social analysis in archaeology: Celtic society in the Iron Age of the Upper Thames Valley (400–0 BC)', in B. Cunliffe & D. Miles (eds), *Aspects of the*

Iron Age in Central Southern Britain, Univ. Oxford Committee for Archaeol. Monograph 2, 72–88.

Hingley 1985. R. Hingley, 'Location, function and status: a Romano-British 'religious complex' at the Noah's Ark Inn, Frilford (Oxfordshire)', *Oxford J. Archaeol.* 4, 201–14.

Hingley 1988. R. Hingley, 'The influence of Rome on indigenous social groups in the Upper Thames Valley', in R.F.J. Jones, J.H.F. Bloemers, S.L. Dyson & M. Biddle (eds), *First millennium papers: Western Europe in the first millennium AD*, Brit. Archaeol. Rep. (Int. Ser.) 401, Oxford, 73–98.

Hingley 1989. R. Hingley, *Rural Settlement in Roman Britain*, London.

Hingley & Miles 1984. R. Hingley & D. Miles, 'Aspects of Iron Age settlement in the Upper Thames Valley', in B. Cunliffe & D. Miles (eds), *Aspects of the Iron Age in Central Southern Britain*, Oxford University Committee for Archaeology Monograph 2, 52–71.

Hogg & Stevens 1937. A.H.A. Hogg & C.E. Stevens, 'The defences of Roman Dorchester', *Oxoniensia* 2, 41–73.

Holbrook 1998. N. Holbrook (ed.), *Cirencester. The Roman town defences, public buildings and shops*, Cirencester Excavations V.

Holbrook & Thomas 1996. N. Holbrook & A. Thomas, 'The Roman and Early Anglo-Saxon Settlement at Wantage, Oxfordshire, Excavations at Mill Street, 1993–4', *Oxoniensia* 61, 109–79.

Hood & Walton 1948. S. Hood & H. Walton, 'Excavations at Roden Down', *Trans. Newbury and District Field Club* 9 (1), 11–62.

Howlett 1994. D.R. Howlett, *The Book of Letters of Saint Patrick the Bishop*, Dublin.

Howlett 1995. D.R. Howlett, *The Celtic Latin Tradition of Biblical Style*, Dublin.

Howlett 1997. D.R. Howlett, *British Books in Biblical Style*, Dublin.

Howlett 1998. D.R. Howlett, *Cambro-Latin Compositions: their Competence and Craftsmanship*, Dublin.

Hughes & Jones 1997. G. Hughes & L. Jones, *Archaeological excavations at Slade Farm, Bicester, Oxfordshire 1996*, unpublished post-excavation assessment and research design, Birmingham University Field Archaeol. Unit.

Hussey 1841. R. Hussey, *An account of the Roman road from Alchester to Dorchester*, Ashmolean Society.

Iliffe 1929. J.H. Iliffe, 'Excavations at Alchester, 1927', *Antiqs. J.* 9, 106–36.

Iliffe 1932. J.H. Iliffe, 'Excavations at Alchester, 1928', *Antiqs. J.* 12, 35–67.

Janes 1996. D. Janes, 'The golden clasp of the late Roman state', *Early Medieval Europe* 5, no. 2, 127–53.

Jewitt 1851. L. Jewitt, 'On Roman remains, recently discovered at Headington, near Oxford', *J. Brit. Archaeol. Assoc.* 6, 52–67.

Jones 1986. M. Jones, 'Towards a model of the villa estate', in D. Miles (ed.), *Archaeology at Barton Court Farm, Abingdon, Oxon: an investigation of late Neolithic, Iron Age, Romano-British and Saxon settlements*, Counc. Brit. Archaeol. Res. Rep. 50, 38–42.

Jones 1996. M.E. Jones, *The End of Roman Britain*, Cornell.

Keevill & Booth 1997. G. Keevill & P. Booth, 'Settlement, sequence and structure: Romano-British stone-built roundhouses at Redlands Farm, Stanwick (Northants) and Alchester (Oxon)', in R.M. & D.E. Friendship-Taylor (eds), *From round house to villa*, Upper Nene Archaeol. Soc., 19–45.

Kendal 1993. R.J. Kendal, *Romano-British settlement in the north eastern Berkshire Downs: a programme of fieldwork*, University of Reading unpublished M.A. dissertation.

Kennett 1695. W. Kennett, *Parochial Antiquities attempted in the history of Ambrosden, Burcester, and other adjacent villages in the counties of Oxford and Bucks*.

Kent 1994. J.P.C. Kent, *The Roman Imperial Coinage Volume X*, London.

Keppie 1998. L.J.F. Keppie, 'Roman Britain in 1997. Scotland', *Britannia* 29, 376–80.

King 1983. A.C. King, 'The Roman church at Silchester reconsidered', *Oxford J. Archaeol.* 2, 225–37.

King 1989. A. King, 'Villas and animal bones', in K. Branigan & D. Miles (eds), *The economies of Romano-British villas*, Sheffield, 51–9.

King 1997. C. King, 'Crowmarsh, Oxfordshire', in R. Bland & J. Orna-Ornstein (eds), *Coin Hoards from Roman Britain Volume X*, British Museum, 91–100.

Kirk 1949. J.R. Kirk, 'Bronzes from Woodeaton, Oxon', *Oxoniensia* 14, 1–45.

Kirk & Leeds 1952–3. J.R. Kirk & E.T. Leeds, 'Three early Saxon graves from Dorchester, Oxon.', *Oxoniensia* 17/18, 63–76.

Knight 1938. W.F.J. Knight, 'A Romano-British site at Bloxham, Oxon.', *Oxoniensia* 3, 41–56.

Lambrick 1969. G. Lambrick, 'Some old roads of North Berkshire', *Oxoniensia* 34, 78–93.

Lambrick 1979. G. Lambrick, 'Berinsfield, Mount Farm', *Counc. Brit. Archaeol. Group 9 Newsletter* 9, 113–15.

Lambrick 1984a. G. Lambrick, 'Pitfalls and possibilities in Iron Age pottery studies – experiences in the Upper Thames Valley', in B. Cunliffe & D. Miles (eds), *Aspects of the Iron Age in Central Southern Britain*, Oxford Univ. Committee for Archaeol. Monograph 2, 162–77.

Lambrick 1984b. G. Lambrick, 'Clanfield: Burroway', *South Midlands Archaeol.* 14, 104–5.

Lambrick 1988. G. Lambrick, *The Rollright Stones: megaliths, monuments, and settlement in the prehistoric landscape*, English Heritage Archaeol. Rep. No. 6.

Lambrick 1992a. G. Lambrick, 'The development of prehistoric and Roman farming on the Thames gravels', in M. Fulford & E. Nichols (eds), *Developing Landscapes of Lowland Britain. The Archaeology of the British Gravels: A Review*, Soc. Antiqs. London Occ. Papers 14, 78–105.

Lambrick 1992b. G. Lambrick, 'Alluvial archaeology of the Holocene in the Upper Thames basin 1971–1991: a review', in S. Needham & M.G. Macklin (eds), *Alluvial archaeology in Britain*, Oxbow Monograph 27, Oxford, 209–26.

Lambrick 1996. G. Lambrick, 'Ducklington, Gill Mill', *South Midlands Archaeol.* 26, 56.

Lambrick & McDonald 1985. G. Lambrick & A. McDonald, 'The archaeology and ecology of Port Meadow and Wolvercote Common, Oxford', in G. Lambrick (ed.), *Archaeology and Nature Conservation*, Oxford, 95–109.

Lambrick & Robinson 1979. G. Lambrick & M. Robinson, *Iron Age and Roman riverside settlements at Farmoor, Oxfordshire*, Counc. Brit. Archaeol. Res. Rep. 32.

Lambrick & Robinson 1988. G. Lambrick & M. Robinson, 'The development of Floodplain Grassland in the Upper Thames Valley', in M. Jones (ed.), *Archaeology and the Flora of the British Isles*, Oxford Univ. Committee for Archaeol. Monograph, 55–75.

Lambrick & Wallis 1988. G. Lambrick & J. Wallis, *Ducklington Gill Mill, Oxon: archaeological assessment 1988*, Oxford Archaeol. Unit unpublished report.

Lambrick et al. forthcoming. G. Lambrick, T. Allen & F. Healey, *Gravelly Guy, Stanton Harcourt: the development of a prehistoric and Romano-British landscape*, Oxford Archaeol. Unit Thames Valley Landscapes Monograph.

Letts 1995. J. Letts, 'Charred plant remains', in T. Allen, *Lithics and landscape: archaeological discoveries on the Thames Water pipeline at Gatehampton Farm, Goring, Oxfordshire 1985–92*, Oxford Archaeol. Unit Thames Valley Landscapes Monograph No. 7, 107–8.

Letts & Robinson 1993. J. Letts & M. Robinson, 'Charred plant and molluscan remains' in T.G. Allen, T.C. Darvill, L.S. Green & M.U. Jones, *Excavations at Roughground Farm, Lechlade, Gloucestershire: a prehistoric and Roman landscape*, Oxford Archaeol. Unit, 175–6.

Malpas 1987. F.J. Malpas, 'Roman roads south and east of Dorchester-on-Thames', *Oxoniensia* 52, 23–33.

Manning 1984. W.H. Manning, 'Objects of iron', in S.S. Frere, Excavations at Dorchester-on-Thames, 1963, *Archaeol. J.* 141, 139–52.

Margary 1973. I.D. Margary, *Roman roads in Britain* (3rd edn), London.

Marsden 1997. A.B. Marsden, 'Between Principate and Dominate: Imperial styles under the Severan dynasty', *J. Brit. Archaeol. Assoc.* 40, 1–16.

Mattingly 1997. D. Mattingly (ed.), *Dialogues in Roman imperialism*, J. Roman Archaeol. Supplementary Ser. No. 23.

Mawer 1995. C.F. Mawer, *Evidence for Christianity in Roman Britain. The small-finds*, Brit. Archaeol. Rep. (Brit. Ser.) 243.

May 1922. T. May, 'On the pottery from the Waste Heaps of the Roman Potters' Kilns discovered at Sandford, near Littlemore, Oxon., in 1879', *Archaeologia* 72, 225–42.

May 1977. J. May, 'Romano-British and Saxon Sites near Dorchester-on-Thames, Oxfordshire', *Oxoniensia* 42, 42–79.

Mays 1992. M. Mays, 'Inscriptions on British Celtic coins', *Numismatic Chronicle* 152, 57–82.

McGavin 1980. N. McGavin, 'A Roman cemetery and trackway at Stanton Harcourt', *Oxoniensia* 45, 112–23.

Miles 1976. D. Miles, 'Two bronze bowls from Sutton Courtenay', *Oxoniensia* 41, 70–6.

Miles 1977. D. Miles, 'Cropmarks around Northfield Farm', in M. Gray, 'Northfield Farm, Long Wittenham', *Oxoniensia* 42, 25–9.

Miles 1982. D. Miles, 'Confusion in the countryside: some comments from the Upper Thames region', in D. Miles (ed.), *The Romano-British countryside: studies in rural settlement and economy*, Brit. Archaeol. Rep. (Brit. Ser.) 103, Oxford, 53–79.

Miles 1984. D. Miles, 'Romano-British settlement in the Gloucestershire Thames Valley', in A. Saville (ed.), *Archaeology in Gloucestershire*, Cheltenham, 191–211.

Miles 1986. D. Miles (ed.), *Archaeology at Barton Court Farm, Abingdon, Oxon: an investigation of late Neolithic, Iron Age, Romano-British and Saxon settlements*, Counc. Brit. Archaeol. Res. Rep. 50.

Miles 1989. D. Miles, 'Villas and variety: aspects of economy and society in the Upper Thames landscape', in K. Branigan & D. Miles (eds), *The economies of Romano-British villas*, Sheffield, 60–72.

Miles 1998. D. Miles, 'Oxford Archaeological Unit: the first twenty-five years', *Oxoniensia* 63, 1–9.

Miles & Palmer 1995. D. Miles & S. Palmer, 'White Horse Hill', *Current Archaeol.* 142, 372–8.

Miles & Wait 1987. D. Miles & G.A. Wait, *Frilford Noah's Ark Inn Archaeological Assessment 1987*, Oxford Archaeol. Unit unpublished report.

Millett 1990. M. Millett, *The Romanization of Britain*, Cambridge.

Millett 1995. M. Millett, 'Strategies for Roman small towns', in A.E. Brown (ed.), *Roman Small Towns in Eastern England and Beyond*, Oxbow Monograph 52, Oxford, 29–37.

Moloney 1997. C. Moloney, 'Excavations and building survey at Bell Street, Henley-on-Thames 1993–1994, *Oxoniensia* 62, 109–33.

Morris 1955. M.O. Morris, 'Notes on decorative and building stone from the temple site, Colchester', in M.R. Hull 'The south wing of the Roman 'Forum' at Colchester: recent discoveries', *Trans. Essex Archaeol. Soc.* 25, 47–50.

Mould 1996. C. Mould, 'An archaeological excavation at Oxford Road, Bicester, Oxfordshire', *Oxoniensia* 61, 65–108.

Mudd 1993. A. Mudd, 'Stanford in the Vale, Bowling Green Farm', *South Midlands Archaeol.* 23, 79–80.

Mudd 1995. A. Mudd, 'The excavation of a late Bronze Age/Early Iron Age site at Eight Acre Field, Radley', *Oxoniensia* 60, 21–65.

Muir & Roberts forthcoming. J. Muir & M.R. Roberts, *Excavations at Wyndyke Furlong, Abingdon, Oxfordshire, 1994*, Oxford Archaeol. Unit Occasional Paper.

Munby 1972. J. Munby, 'An inventory of sites and finds from the Science Area, Oxford', *Oxoniensia* 37, 48–50.

Munby 1975. J. Munby, 'Some moulded face-flagons from the Oxford kilns', *Britannia* 6, 182–8.

Munby 1977. J. Munby, 'Art, archaeology and antiquaries', in J. Munby & M. Henig (eds), *Roman Life and Art in Britain*, Brit Archaeol. Rep. (Brit. Ser.) 41, 415–36.

Myres 1931. J.N.L. Myres, 'A prehistoric settlement on Hinksey Hill, near Oxford', *J. Brit. Archaeol. Assoc.* 36, 360–90.

Mytum 1986. H.C. Mytum, 'An Early Iron Age site at Wytham Hill, near Cumnor, Oxford', *Oxoniensia* 51, 15–24.

Mytum & Taylor 1981. H. Mytum & J.W. Taylor, 'Linch Hill Corner', *Counc. Brit. Archaeol. Group 9 Newsletter* 11, 139.

Neal 1981. D.S. Neal, *Roman mosaics in Britain*, Britannia Monograph No. 1.

Neal et al. 1990. D.S. Neal, A. Wardle & J. Hunn, *Excavation of the Iron Age, Roman and medieval settlement at Gorhambury, St. Albans*, English Heritage Archaeol. Rep. No. 14, London.

Needham & Ambers 1994. S. Needham & J. Ambers, 'Redating Rams Hill and reconsidering Bronze Age enclosure', *Proc. Prehist. Soc.* 60, 225–43.

Niblett 1999. R. Niblett, *Excavation of a ceremonial site at Folly Lane, Verulamium*, Britannia Monograph No. 14.

OCD. Oxford Classical Dictionary.

Onians 1999. J. Onians, *Classical Art and the cultures of Greece and Rome*, New Haven and London.

Parrington 1975. M. Parrington, 'Excavations at the Old Gaol, Abingdon', *Oxoniensia* 40, 59–78.

Parrington 1979. M. Parrington, *The excavation of an Iron Age settlement, Bronze Age ring-ditches and Roman features at Ashville Trading Estate, Abingdon (Oxfordshire) 1974–76*, Counc. Brit. Archaeol. Res. Rep. 28.

Parsons & Booth 1996. M. Parsons & P. Booth, *Sansomes Farm, Woodstock, Oxfordshire, archaeological evaluation report*, Oxford Archaeol. Unit unpublished report.

Philpott 1991. R. Philpott, *Burial practices in Roman Britain*, Brit. Archaeol. Rep. (Brit. Ser.) 219, Oxford.

Plot 1705. R. Plot, *The Natural History of Oxfordshire*, 2nd edn (1st edn 1677).

Radford 1936. C.A.R. Radford, 'The Roman villa at Ditchley, Oxon.', *Oxoniensia* 1, 24–69.

Rahtz & Rowley 1984. S. Rahtz & T. Rowley, *Middleton Stoney, excavation and survey in a North Oxfordshire parish 1970–1982*, Oxford.

Rannie 1898. D.W. Rannie, *Remarks and Collections of Thomas Hearne, vol. iv. 1712–1714*, Oxford Historical Society.

RCHME 1976. *The County of Gloucester: Volume one, Iron Age and Romano-British monuments in the Gloucestershire Cotswolds*, Royal Commission on Historical Monuments (England), London.

RCHME 1995. Royal Commission on Historical Monuments of England, Thames Valley aerial photograph transcriptions.

Reece 1980. R. Reece, 'Town and country: the end of Roman Britain', *World Archaeol.* 12 No. 1, 7–92.

Rees 1979. S. Rees, 'The Roman scythe blade', in G. Lambrick & M. Robinson, *Iron Age and Roman riverside settlements at Farmoor, Oxfordshire*, Counc. Brit. Archaeol. Res. Rep. 32, 61–4.

Reynolds 1979. P.J. Reynolds, *Iron Age Farm: The Butser Experiment*, British Museum Publications, London.

Rhodes 1950. P.P. Rhodes, 'The Celtic Field-Systems on the Berkshire Downs', *Oxoniensia* 15, 1–28.

RIB. The Roman inscriptions of Britain.

RIB I. R.G. Collingwood and R.P. Wright, *The Roman inscriptions of Britain, Volume I, Inscriptions on stone*, Oxford (1965).

Rivers-Moore 1951. C.N. Rivers-Moore, 'Further Excavations in the Roman House at Harpsden Wood, Henley-on-Thames', *Oxoniensia* 16, 23–7.

Rivet & Smith 1979. A.L.F. Rivet & C. Smith, *The Place-Names of Roman Britain*, London.

Robinson 1975. M.A. Robinson, 'The environment of the Roman defences at Alchester and its implications', in C.J. Young, 'The defences of Roman Alchester', *Oxoniensia* 40, 161–70.

Robinson 1981. M. Robinson, 'The Iron Age to Early Saxon Environment of the Upper Thames terraces', in M. Jones & G. Dimbleby (eds), *The Environment of Man: the Iron Age to the Saxon period*, Brit. Archaeol. Rep. (Brit. Ser.) 87, Oxford, 251–86.

Robinson 1992a. M. Robinson, 'Environmental archaeology of the river gravels: past achievements and future directions', in M. Fulford & E. Nichols (eds), *Developing Landscapes of Lowland Britain. The Archaeology of the British Gravels: A Review*, Soc. Antiqs. London Occ. Papers 14, 47–62.

Robinson 1992b. M. Robinson, 'Environment, Archaeology and Alluvium on the River Gravels of the South Midlands', in S. Needham & M.G. Macklin (eds), *Alluvial Archaeology in Britain*, Oxbow Monograph 47, Oxford, 197–208.

Robinson & Lambrick 1984. M.A. Robinson & G.H. Lambrick, 'Holocene Alluviation and Hydrology in the Upper Thames Basin', *Nature* 308, 809–14.

Robinson & Wilson 1987. M. Robinson & B. Wilson, 'A survey of environmental archaeology in the South Midlands', in H.C.M. Keeley (ed.), *Environmental Archaeology: a regional review Vol. II*, Hist. Buildings and Monuments Commission for England Occ. Paper No. 1, 16–100.

Rolleston 1869. G. Rolleston, 'Researches and excavations carried on in an ancient cemetery at Frilford, near Abingdon, Berks, in the years 1867–1868', *Archaeologia* 42, 417–85.

Rolleston 1880. G. Rolleston, 'Further researches in an Anglo-Saxon cemetery at Frilford, with remarks on the northern limit of Anglo-Saxon cremation in England', *Archaeologia* 45, 405–10.

Rowley 1975. T. Rowley, 'The Roman towns of Oxfordshire', in W. Rodwell & T. Rowley (eds), *Small towns of Roman Britain*, Brit. Archaeol. Rep. (Brit. Ser.) 15, Oxford, 115–24.

Rowley 1985. T. Rowley, 'Roman Dorchester', in J. Cook & T. Rowley (eds), *Dorchester through the ages*, Oxford Univ. Dept. for External Studies, 21–8.

Rowley & Brown 1981. T. Rowley & L. Brown, 'Excavations at Beech House Hotel, Dorchester-on-Thames 1972', *Oxoniensia* 46, 1–55.

Rudling 1998. D. Rudling, 'The development of Roman villas in Sussex', *Sussex Archaeol. Coll.* 136, 41–65.

Salter 1997. C. Salter, 'Metallurgical debris', in P.M. Booth, *Asthall, Oxfordshire, excavations in a Roman 'small town', 1992*, Thames Valley Landscapes Monograph 9 Oxford Archaeol. Unit, 89–99.

Salter 1915. H.E. Salter, *Remarks and Collections of Thomas Hearne, vol. x 1728–1731*.

Salter 1921. H.E. Salter, *Remarks and Collections of Thomas Hearne, vol. xi 1731–1735*.

Salway 1981. P. Salway, *Roman Britain*, Oxford.

Salway forthcoming. P. Salway, 'Roman Oxfordshire', *Oxoniensia*.

Sauer 1998a. E. Sauer, 'Merton/Wendlebury, The Roman military base at Alchester', *South Midlands Archaeol.* 28, 70–3.

Sauer 1998b. E. Sauer, 'Middleton Stoney/Upper Heyford, Aves Ditch, an Iron Age linear earthwork', *South Midlands Archaeol.* 28, 73–5.

Sauer 1999a. E. Sauer, 'The military origins of the Roman town of Alchester, Oxfordshire', *Britannia* 30, 289–97.

Sauer 1999b. E. Sauer, 'Middleton Stoney/Upper Heyford, Aves Ditch, earthwork and tribal boundary of the Iron Age', *South Midlands Archaeol.* 29, 65–9.

Sauer & Crutchley 1998. E. Sauer & S. Crutchley, 'Alchester: A Roman fort and parade ground?' *Current Archaeol.* 157, 34–7.

Saunders & Weaver 1999. M.J. Saunders & S. Weaver, *Coxwell Road, Faringdon, Oxfordshire, an assessment of the archaeological excavations*, Thames Valley Archaeol. Services unpublished report.

Scott 1993. E. Scott, *A Gazetteer of Roman Villas in Britain*, Leicester Archaeol. Monographs No. 1, Leicester.

Sellwood 1989. B.W. Sellwood, 'The Rock-Types Represented in the Arena Wall', in M. Fulford, *The Silchester Amphitheatre: Excavations of 1979–85*, Britannia Monograph Ser. No. 10, 139–42.

Sellwood 1984. L. Sellwood, 'Tribal Boundaries viewed from the perspective of Numismatic evidence', in B. Cunliffe & D. Miles (eds), *Aspects of the Iron Age in Central Southern Britain*, Oxford Univ. Committee for Archaeol. Monograph 2, 191–204.

Shawyer 1998. E. Shawyer, 'Swalcliffe Lower Lea Roman village', *South Midlands Archaeol.* 28, 66–9.

Shawyer 1999. E. Shawyer, 'North Oxon Field Archaeology Group report for 1997–8', *South Midlands Archaeol.* 29, 53–61.

Smith 1984. D.J. Smith, 'Roman mosaics in Britain: a synthesis', in R. Farioli Campanati, *III colloquio internazionale sul mosaico antico, Ravenna*, 357–80.

Smith 1964. L.T. Smith, *The Itinerary of John Leland in or about the years 1535–1543, parts i to iii*, I.

Smith 1987. R.F. Smith, *Roadside Settlements in Lowland Roman Britain*, Brit. Archaeol. Rep. (Brit. Ser.) 157.

Steane 1996. J. Steane, *Oxfordshire*, Pimlico County History Guide.

Stevens 1933. C.E. Stevens, *Sidonius Apollinaris and his age*, Oxford.

Sturdy & Young 1976. D. Sturdy & C.J. Young, 'Two early Roman kilns at Tuckwell's Pit, Hanborough, Oxon', *Oxoniensia* 41, 56–64.

Sutherland 1936. C.H.V. Sutherland, 'A late Roman coin hoard from Kiddington, Oxon.', *Oxoniensia* 1, 70–80.

Sutherland 1940. C.H.V. Sutherland, 'A Theodosian silver hoard from Rams Hill', *Antiqs. J.* 20, 481–5.

Sutton 1966. J.E.G. Sutton, 'Iron Age Hillforts and some other Earthworks in Oxfordshire', *Oxoniensia* 31, 28–42.

Taylor 1941. M.V. Taylor, 'The Roman tessellated pavement at Stonesfield, Oxon', *Oxoniensia* 6, 1–8.

Taylor & Collingwood 1921. M.V. Taylor & R.G. Collingwood, 'Roman Britain in 1921 and 1922', *J. Roman Stud.* 11, 200–44.

Thomas 1981. C. Thomas, *Christianity in Roman Britain to A.D. 500*, London.

Thomas 1998. C. Thomas, *Christian Celts. Messages and Images*, Stroud.

Thomas 1980. R. Thomas, 'A Bronze Age field system at Northfield Farm', *Oxoniensia* 45, 310–11.

Thomas et al. 1986. R. Thomas, M. Robinson, J. Barrett & R. Wilson, 'A late Bronze Age riverside settlement at Wallingford, Oxfordshire', *Archaeol. J.* 143, 174–200.

Thurnam & Davies 1865. J. Thurnam & J.B. Davies, 'Ancient Roman Skull. From a tumular cemetery, on White Horse Hill, Berkshire', *Crania Britannica II*, 51, 1–6.

Timby 1998. J.R. Timby, *Excavations at Kingscote and Wycomb, Gloucestershire: A Roman Estate Centre and Small Town in the Gloucestershire Cotswolds with Notes on Related Settlements*, Cirencester.

Timby et al. 1997. J.R. Timby, P. Booth & T.G. Allen, *A new Early Roman fineware industry in the Upper Thames Valley*, Oxford Archaeol. Unit unpublished report.

Tingle 1991. M. Tingle, *The Vale of the White Horse survey*, Brit. Archaeol. Rep. (Brit. Ser.) 218, Oxford.

Tomlin 1996. R.S.O. Tomlin, 'A five-acre wood in Roman Kent', in J. Bird, M. Hassall & H. Sheldon (eds), *Interpreting Roman London*, Oxford, 209–15.

Tomlin & Hassall 1999. R.S.O. Tomlin & M.W.C. Hassall, 'Roman Britain in 1998. Inscriptions', *Britannia* 30, 375–86.

Van Arsdell & de Jersey 1994. R.D. Van Arsdell & P. de Jersey, *The coinage of the Dobunni: money supply and coin circulation in Dobunnic territory, with a gazetteer of findspots*, Oxford Univ. Committee for Archaeol. Monograph 38.

van der Veen 1989. M. van der Veen, 'Charred grain assemblages from Roman-period corn driers in Britain', *Archaeol. J.* 146, 302–19.

VCH. D.B. Harden & M.V. Taylor, 'Roman-British remains', *Victoria County History of Oxfordshire I* (1939), 267–245.

VCH Berks I. P.H. Ditchfield & C.M. Calthrop, 'Romano-British Berkshire', *Victoria County History of Berkshire I* (1906), 197–227.

Wacher 1995. J. Wacher, *The towns of Roman Britain*, 2nd edn, London.

Walker 1995. G.T. Walker, 'A Middle Iron Age settlement at Deer Park Road, Witney: excavations in 1992', *Oxoniensia* 60, 67–92.

Walters 1984. B. Walters, 'The "Orpheus" mosaic in Littlecote Park, England', in R. Farioli Campanati, *III colloquio internazionale sul mosaico antico, Ravenna*, 433–42.

Ware & Ware 1993. M. Ware & F. Ware, 'Fieldwalking a Romano-British site above Shipston', *Wychwoods History* 8, 50–65.

Watts 1998. D. Watts, *Religion in late Roman Britain. Forces of Change*, London.

Webster 1975. G. Webster, 'Small towns without defences', in W. Rodwell & T. Rowley (eds), *Small towns of Roman Britain*, Brit. Archaeol. Rep. (Brit. Ser.) 15, Oxford, 53–66.

Webster 1993. G. Webster, *The Roman invasion of Britain*, revised edn, London.

Webster & Cooper 1996. J. Webster & N. Cooper (eds), *Roman imperialism: post-colonial perspectives*, Leicester Archaeol. Monographs No. 3.

Wightman 1970. E.M. Wightman, *Roman Trier and the Treveri*, London.

Willett 1948. F. Willett, 'A Romano-British pottery kiln on Foxcombe Hill, Berks.', *Oxoniensia* 13, 32–8.

Williams 1951. A. Williams, 'Excavations at Beard Mill, Stanton Harcourt, Oxon., 1944', *Oxoniensia* 16, 5–23.

Williams 1971. J.H. Williams, 'Roman Building-materials in South-East England', *Britannia* 2, 166–95.

Williams & Zeepvat 1994. R.J. Williams & R.J. Zeepvat, *Bancroft: The late Bronze Age and Iron Age Settlements and Roman Temple-Mausoleum and the Roman Villa*, Buckinghamshire Archaeol. Soc. Monograph Ser. No. 7.

Wilson & Wallis 1991. B. Wilson & G. Wallis, 'Prehistoric activity, early Roman building, tenement yards and gardens behind Twickenham House, Abingdon', *Oxoniensia* 56, 1–15.

Wilson 1992. D. Wilson, *Anglo-Saxon paganism*, London.

Wilson & Sherlock 1980. D.R. Wilson & D. Sherlock, *North Leigh Roman villa*, English Heritage.

Woltering 1999. P.J. Woltering, 'Roman panpipes from Uitgeest, the Netherlands', in H. Sarfatij, W.J.H. Verwers & P.J. Woltering, *In Discussion with the Past. Archaeological studies presented to W.A. van Es*, 173–85.

Woodfield 1995. C. Woodfield, 'New thoughts on town defences in the western territory of

Catuvellauni', in A.E. Brown (ed.), *Roman Small Towns in Eastern England and Beyond*, Oxbow Monograph 52, Oxford, 129–46.

Woodward & Leach 1993. A. Woodward & P. Leach, *The Uley Shrines*, English Heritage Archaeol. Rep. 17.

Woolf 1998. G. Woolf, *Becoming Roman: the origins of provincial civilisation in Gaul*, Cambridge.

Yates 1999. D.T. Yates, 'Bronze Age Field Systems in the Thames Valley', *Oxford J. Archaeol.* 18, 157–70.

Young 1975. C.J. Young, 'The defences of Roman Alchester', *Oxoniensia* 40, 136–70.

Young 1977. C.J. Young, *Oxfordshire Roman Pottery*, Brit. Archaeol. Rep. (Brit. Ser.) 43, Oxford.

Young 1986. C. Young, 'The Upper Thames Valley in the Roman Period', in G. Briggs, J. Cook & T. Rowley (eds), *The Archaeology of the Oxford Region*, Oxford, 58–63.

Zanker 1988. P. Zanker, *The power of images in the age of Augustus*, Ann Arbor.

INDEX

Note: entries in *italics* indicate illustrations.